Nathaniel Hawthorne
and European Literary Tradition

Nathaniel Hawthorne and European Literary Tradition

By

JANE LUNDBLAD

NEW YORK

RUSSELL & RUSSELL · INC

1965

FIRST PUBLISHED IN 1947
REISSUED, 1965, BY RUSSELL & RUSSELL, INC.
BY ARRANGEMENT WITH JANE LUNDBLAD
L. C. CATALOG CARD NO: 65—13950

LIBRARY

SEP 10 1968

UNIVERSITY OF THE PACIFIC

187553

PRINTED IN THE UNITED STATES OF AMERICA

To my Father

CONTENTS

FOREWORD

Nathaniel Hawthorne has traditionally been regarded as the paramount interpreter of the New England mind, and he has been interpreted, edited, and commented upon chiefly by New Englanders. Mr. Edmund Wilson, in his anthology, "The Shock of Recognition," illustrates what T. S. Eliot has termed the Hawthorne aspect, i.e. the line of development that, from obscure beginnings, leads up to Henry James and Eliot himself, and Mr. F. O. Matthiessen, in his work on the "American Renaissance" stresses the same point of view.

This view of Hawthorne being, of course, incontestable, a European reader experiences, nevertheless, also other "shocks of recognition" in reading Nathaniel Hawthorne's work. At the same time that it reveals, first and foremost, a national character, a moral personality, and a historical period, it also contains details, types, and ideas that seem familiar as having appeared, previously or simultaneously, in Europe.

The object of this thesis is to follow up a few of these parallels or lines of influence, some of which have been mentioned or suggested by earlier commentators, but that have seemed to merit a closer study. Though the conclusions reached here are based to some extent on inferences and hypotheses yet to be confirmed, I venture to believe that the result is sufficiently positive to be of interest to future research. Opinions such as those vindicated here may strip Hawthorne of some of his former reputation as an original, native genius, isolated from outside influence. This study stresses that he was eminently an offshoot from that plant of thinking and writing that had its roots in the old European centres of culture, and whose fruits had much of the same flavour when gathered on American as on European soil.

My thanks are due, in the first place, to my teacher, Professor S. B. Liljegren of Upsala, who, in founding the Center of American Studies in the University of Upsala, has created possibilities for the study of American literature and culture in the Department of English. His sound counsel, his helpful, sometimes provocative, criticism, and kind interest have stimulated me to undertake and complete my task.

It is a pleasant duty to acknowledge the help given me by the Rockefeller Foundation in endowing me with a grant-in-aid for the continuation of my studies in the United States, as well as the support lent me by Columbia University by granting me a Killough scholarship and according me the privilege of using the Columbia University Library. My very sincere thanks are due to the American Scandinavian Foundation and Dr Henry Goddard Leach, its former president, for helpful advice, and for facilitating my contacts with American universities and libraries. To the custodians of the collection of Hawthorne letters and manuscripts deposited at the Yale University Library — and especially to Mr. Norman Holmes Pearson, whose counsel and helpfulness have been indefatigable — I am deeply indebted for the permission to use and to quote from their valuable material, as also to the Huntington Library and its staff for their help and hospitality, and for permission to quote from Hawthorne manuscripts and rare books. The Pierpont Morgan Library has given me access to their manuscripts of Hawthorne's notebooks, and the Public Library of New York has kindly allowed me to study the Hawthorne material in the Berg Collection. To the staffs of Upsala University Library, the Royal Library of Stockholm, and, especially, the Nobel Library in Stockholm, I extend sincere thanks for helpful cooperation.

I am faced by the impossibility of acknowledging specifically my indebtedness to the many authors and sources referred to or used in my work. The references to Hawthorne's writings are to the Riverside edition, by kind permission of the Houghton Mifflin Company. Lastly, I warmly thank Mrs. Stina Melander and Mrs. Anna Greta Wideland whose friendship I have abused in the proof-reading process, and Mrs. Erica Odelberg, of the British Council in Stockholm, who has kindly undertaken to scrutinize my manuscript with a view to the language.

Upsala, in August, 1947.

Jane Lundblad.

We find thoughts in all great writers (and even in small ones) that strike their roots far beneath the surface, and intertwine themselves with the roots of other writers' thoughts; so that when we pull up one, we stir the whole, and yet those writers have had no conscious society with one another.

NATHANIEL HAWTHORNE

in a letter to Delia Bacon

INTRODUCTION:
THE CULTURAL AND LITERARY NEW ENGLAND
BACKGROUND BEFORE 1820

The Pilgrim Fathers who landed on Plymouth Rock did not possess many wordly goods. Their mental equipment consisted of their ingrained love of freedom, their vigorous individualism, and their confidence in God. They also brought with them the seed of a democratic society, but little cultural tradition. Spiritually, the English dissenters were descendants of John Wyclif and the Lollards, earnest, hard-working people with few possessions. They believed that God would crown a strenuous life in His service with eternal bliss. They feared a life of idleness and leisure, and the social and cultural pleasures belonging to it — and to the privileged class against whom they were half unconsciously warring — as the snares of the Devil. Ever since the times of Chaucer and Shakespeare, these English dissenters had felt a deep-rooted antagonism to the art and literature cherished by the well-to-do classes which they hated. In this respect, they differed from those Protestants of the European Continent who harboured artists such as Cranach and Holbein, writers like Melanchton and Erasmus, and composers like Bach.

Dissent — sometimes inaccurately termed Puritanism — thus constituted the spiritual background of the development in New England. For generations it placed its stamp on the outlook on life, especially among the population of rural communities. Material progress, commerce, and the gradual growth of cities, however, in course of time brought about the formation of a new, leisured class with cultural and literary interests. The intellectual life of this New England aristocracy flourished in the cities, and its capital was Boston. Other important centres were New Haven, Hartford, and Salem. In colonial times, American intellectual life was — for obvious reasons — mainly influenced by England, and even after the Revolution this influence continued, owing to the common language, heredity and other affinities. The English classics were also the fathers of American literature; they were read in the schools, and familiarity with these classics was essential for the education of a gentleman — an ideal type that was as firmly rooted in American as in English social and cultural consciousness. To that education also belonged familiarity with the Roman and Greek classics read in all colleges. The American situation in the 18th century in this respect was defined in 1818 by W. C. Bryant in an article in *The North American Review*:

"We were content with considering ourselves as participating in the literary fame of that nation, of which we were a part, and of which many of us were natives, and aspired to no separate distinction."[1]

We can, however, also trace a considerable French element in the culture of 18th century New England. H. Mumford Jones, who has studied the French influence on American culture[2], shows how the knowledge of French increased, especially between 1670 and 1700[3]. Cotton Mather, according to the same author, was sufficiently versed in the French language to write one of his tracts in it, and to quote both Ronsard and Rabelais in his *Magnalia*. This increasing interest in French was due partly to the religious policy of Louis XIV. and to the amount of Calvinist literature written in the French language, partly to the fact that French was at that time the language of merchants as well as of diplomats. A knowledge of French thinking was necessary for any deeper insight into English philosophy or literature. In this way, late 17th century Americans of the leisured classes — not only "Cavalier" Virginians, but also "Puritan" New Englanders — were often men more or less well versed in the belles lettres of England and France. It was, however, only natural that in their libraries preference was given to works of practical use, and it is true that theological treatises and sermons were more plentiful on the bookshelves of New Englanders, but at the same time it

---

[1] *Brown's Essay on American Poetry*, The North American Review, 1818.

[2] Howard Mumford Jones, *American and French Culture*, University of North Carolina Press, 1927.

[3] Cp. the similar situation of that time in England itself, as a consequence of the religious unrest under Louis XIV and the Edict of Nantes.

should be noted — as Wright[1] points out — that the religious
literature of those times often evinced more true literary art than
the romances and ballads. This religious literature was written by
men with a university training, in a forceful and well-balanced
language modelled on classical patterns. Moreover, the library
lists of 17th century America contain titles belonging to world
literature common both to Northern and Southern colonists.
Encyclopedias and historical works lined their shelves along with
Roman and Greek authors in the original or in translation, neither
were the masterpieces of great thinkers of all nationalities missing,
such as Erasmus, Montaigne, Sir Thomas More, Bacon, Macchia-
velli, Hobbes, Descartes, Locke, Grotius, and Butler.

In the latter part of the 18th century, French had acquired the
position of the leading language of polite society. It became the
vehicle of the memoir-writers, the novelists, the people who fre-
quented the literary and political *salons*, of which the influence
was felt even in the distant New World. A French scholar, Bernard
Faÿ, has, by a careful study[2] of the books imported into America
between 1770 and 1800, arrived at the conclusion that an eighth of
all foreign books were French. In New York, the figure is even
given as a fourth — a fact probably due to the settling of Huguenot
refugees in that part of the country. A definite increase in the
interest in French can be observed about 1770. The political
alliance with France contributed to the vogue of everything French,
and the French language soon became a subject of regular instruction at the universities. Harvard appointed a professor of French
in 1780, and even permitted students to substitute that language
for Hebrew. In 1792, J. G. de Nancrède published in Boston a
French paper called *l'Abeille*, which had a small circulation but a
very distinguished body of readers. In it were published, for
example, the *Lettres à M. Malesherbes* by Rousseau, and many
quotations from Helvetius and Gessner. Moreover, Mr. Nancrède
announced translations of the principal works of Bernardin de

---

[1] Louis B. Wright, *The Purposeful Reading of our Colonial Ancestors. ELH,
A Journal of English Literary History*, Vol. 4, Johns Hopkins Press, Baltimore,
June, 1937.

[2] Bernard Faÿ, *Bibliographie critique des ouvrages français relatifs aux Etats-
Unis* (1770—1880), Paris, 1925.

Saint-Pierre, Condorcet, Necker, and others.[1] After the execution of Louis XIV. in 1792, the enthusiasm for French philosophy and culture in general decreased among the conservative strata of American society, and the teaching of French at Harvard was dropped at the beginning of the 19th century. Its influence continued, however, to make itself felt — the political and literary leaders of the first half of the 19th century were all more or less familiar with French cultural tradition, and it was partly through a French author, Mme de Staël, that the knowledge of the revolutionary and Romantic currents in German literature first reached America. A translation of Mme de Staël's *De l'Allemagne* appeared in New York in 1814.

Not only literature, but the theatre, music, painting, and architecture as well aroused an increasing interest in the growing cities of the New World. It is true that Benjamin Franklin had declared that "nothing is good or beautiful but in the measure that it is useful," and that Mark Twain's Connecticut Yankee, somewhat later, showed a distinct lack of appreciation of the works of art of the Classic or Renaissance periods, but these spokesmen rather expressed the view of rural America, of the strict descendants of English dissenters or of poor immigrants from continental Europe. Parallel with this opinion, supported by superior numbers, went the development in the urbanized areas, where the inhabitants vied with their European counterparts in cultural and literary interests.

The culture of New England differed, for historical and religious reasons, in some respects from that of the other provinces. While the South eagerly accepted the French ideas that paved the way for the revolution, the doctrinarian religious leaders of New England resisted what they considered to be dangerous French atheism. The tenets of equality and liberty arrived in New England by a back door, Unitarianism, which appeared a generation after Jefferson and Franklin and their acceptance of the philosophy of Enlightenment. Another distinguishing feature of the cultural life of Boston — as opposed to the more aristocratic South — was its middle class spirit, a characteristic it shared with the general attitude of Romanticism. Boston and Harvard, the centres of the *bourgeois*,

[1] Bernard Faÿ, *La langue française à Harvard 1636—1936. Harvard et la France*, Paris, 1936.

academic culture of New England, were two strongholds of conservatism. When Romanticism finally invaded them, there resulted from the forceful impact of new and old, the characteristic flowering of general, philosophical, and literary culture that has been called the New England Renaissance.

If Boston was the literary metropolis of New England, Salem might be chosen to illustrate the high standard of the fine arts. In the late 17th century, Salem had been one of the early settlements of the dissenters, and one of the communities noted for severity to nonconformists. Dark tales of intransigency and cruelty, of witch-trials, of persecutions of the Quakers, were handed down to later generations by historians such as Increase and Cotton Mather, or in chronicles such as *The Annals of Salem*. But — in course of time — Salem had developed a different attitude. By the middle of the 18th century, it was one of the American cities that possessed a face of its own. Trade had furnished wealth, and hand in hand with the shipbuilding and carving of fine figureheads went a strong interest in the fine arts: painting, decoration and — above all — architecture:

"Salem men had long shown a liking for fine houses: many of the early dwellings with gambred roofs, spacious rooms, airy interiors still remained standing at the time of the Revolution, and a succession of others had been built ... These houses were furnished with rich rugs, brasses, porcelains, exotic carvings, and sometimes strange gods from the Far East. Portraits by Smibert, Greenwood, Blackburn, Copley hung on Salem walls as did the work of many admirable journeymen painters; nor were the subjects of such portraits drawn only from families who had acquired great fortunes. Mates, masters, and lesser men were also delineated — highly individualized characters who still look out firmly from old canvasses."[1]

In the late decades of the century, a social library of books imported from London was established, and the Philosophical Society of Salem was the second foundation of its kind in the United States — the first having been founded by Benjamin Franklin at Philadelphia. The taste for literature remained, nevertheless,

---

[1] Constance Rourke, *The Roots of American Culture*, New York, 1942, pp. 36—37.

austere in this community with its inheritance from Puritan forefathers. Fielding, Smollett, and Richardson were read, but their
popularity could never compete with that of scientific or philosophical authors. Salem kept its brooding atmosphere, and this characteristic feature lingered on, as the importance of shipping decreased owing to the development of the port of Boston. Salem
never turned its face wholly toward the future, like the rest of
America. It kept looking back — to old tales, old traditions of
religious and social orders, guarding its treasures of architectural
and poetic beauty.

*

The American revolution, with its great national awakening,
infused a new element into the cultural setting, an element which
strangely anticipated Romanticism. The newborn country had to
assert itself — politically, economically, and culturally. This last
was to gain more and more importance, but it was, nevertheless,
firmly linked to the other two, and to what F. V. Calverton[1] calls
the colonial complex: the sense of inferiority of political and economic origin, inevitable in the class of poor dissenters who had from
the beginning constituted the population in the former British
colonies. The self-assertion of the new community in the economic
field went hand in hand with a series of declarations of literary
independence. In a review of the novel *Redwood*, in *The North
American Review* of 1825, W. C. Bryant asserted that only an
American writer must and could do justice to the American national
character:

"It is he that must show how infinite diversities of human character are yet further varied by causes that exist in our own country,
exhibit our peculiar modes of thinking and action, and mark
the effect of these upon individual fortunes and happiness. A
foreigner is manifestly incompetent to the task."[2]

Charles Brockden Brown wrote in the preface to his novel *Edgar
Huntly* that it was the duty of an author to delineate

"the field of investigation opened up to us by our own country.
The sources of amusement to the fancy and instruction to the heart

---

[1] V. F. Calverton, *The Liberation of American Culture*, New York, 1932.
[2] *Redwood, The North American Review*, April, 1825.

that are peculiar to ourselves are equally numerous and inexhaustible."[1]

The classic expression of these endeavours came with Emerson's address, in 1837, on *The American Scholar*:

"Our day of dependence, our long apprenticeship to the learning of other lands, draws to a close. The millions that around us are rushing into life cannot always be fed on the mere remains of foreign harvests . . ."[2]

When these words were uttered, Romanticism had achieved its New England flowering: the speaker was the foremost figure of its national expression — transcendentalism. He and his contemporaries had, in their artistic endeavours, to fight two attitudes that were peculiar to their native environment: what has here been termed the colonial complex, and the old contempt for art as belonging to another and more aristocratic class of society than that of the original dissenters. The meaning and form of Romanticism on American soil is markedly determined by these facts: the heightening of Romantic nationalism by the colonial complex, and the strong influence of still-surviving dissenting tradition both as to religion and as to the disparagement of art.

F. V. Parrington[3] distinguishes between what he calls three major strands in the influences that, in the first decades of the 19th century, invaded the new continent from Europe: the social utopianism from revolutionary France, the idealistic metaphysics from revolutionary Germany, and the new cultural and literary Romanticism. The same author also recalls the fact that the three elements are constantly intertwining and are hence difficult to separate.

It is a commonplace to state that Transcendentalism drew its origin from German metaphysics as accepted by German Romanticism and interpreted by English thinkers — in the first place Coleridge. German neoplatonism had, in its religious and mystic implications, some features in common with the ingrained religiosity of the population of New England, and the idealistic and pantheistic teachings of Emerson, with their truly American stamp

---

[1] C. B. Brown, *Edgar Huntly*, New York, 1801.

[2] R. W. Emerson, *Complete Works*, Vol. I, p. 83.

[3] F. V. Parrington, *Main Currents in American Thought*, Vol. 2, Part II, p. 319.

of practicability in everyday life and their Romantic individualistic appeal, constituted a happy infusion of Old World conceptions into New World ideas.

Emerson never learnt German. He was acquainted with the German authors only in translations, and chiefly by means of the interpretations of Coleridge and Wordsworth. But in America, contact with German culture had been kept up by colonists ever since the 17th century, and in the post-revolutionary era, this interest developed more and more. In this connection, it deserves to be mentioned that the Reverend William Bentley of Salem, in 1800—1819, compiled his *Impartial Register*, summarizing the German advances in the fields of science, art, and literature. The acquaintance with the new Germany was widely furthered by Mme de Staël's *De l'Allemagne* (1810). Next followed the English interpretations of the philosophers, and finally came the personal contacts. In 1816, a young Boston student, George Ticknor, and somewhat later his friend Edward Everett, went on a European tour. When they came home, they introduced the new German and Spanish literature. Ticknor acquired a considerable library of foreign works, later bequeathed to Harvard university. In the wake of these two there followed several, equally arduous students: Joseph Green Cogswell, George Bancroft, John Lothrop Motley, and others.

Thus, the new German literary ideas became known in America. The knowledge of the German language increased at the same time but, to a great extent, the acquaintance with the works of the German authors was due to descriptive articles, such as Carlyle's classic *State of the German Literature* (1829) or translations, published either in separate volumes, like the same English author's specimens of *German Romance*, printed in England in 1827, in America in 1841, or the collection of *Tales from the German* that appeared in 1829. · *Blackwood's Magazine*, *The Edinburgh Review*, *The Westminster Review*, and the rest of the contemporary British magazines were eagerly read in America, and on native soil such distinguished counterparts as *The North American Review*, *The American Quarterly Review*, *The Democratic Review*, and *The National Magazine* were published.

With the Romantic literary currents also came political and social ideas. Liberalism and humanitarianism entered the United States

by way of British books and magazines. The interest for France
and its culture became, in the early decades of the 19th century,
more of an intellectual luxury, and persisted along two different
lines. The image of French culture and French arts was not very
exact, but enticing, "à la fois romantique, désuète et audacieuse"[1],
and constituted a great attraction for intellectual and artistic circles.
The other current from France was of a social kind; it inherited
the goodwill earned by Marquis de Lafayette, who once personified
French liberalism in America. French teachings of social theory,
and preeminently the ideas of community living advanced by
Francois Charles Marie Fourier, were warmly welcomed in the
New World.

European Romanticism, in a word, filled the air of New England
during those early decades of the 19th century. The mutual intellectual exchange with congenial contemporaries in diverse
cultural fields was intense, and the readings of the literary-minded,
extensive. There was — to quote H. M. Belden — "an aura of
second and third hand knowledge around every star in the literary
firmament."[2]

It must be added that English influences had suffered a severe
set-back during the war of 1812, when everything British became
intensely unpopular.[3] The bonds were, however, too strong to be
broken, and the cultural and literary relations were re-established.
The most popular of British authors was Sir Walter Scott, whose
colourful stories appealed strongly to American readers. S. G.
Goodrich, the expert publisher and author, always in close touch
with public opinion, wrote in his *Recollections*:

"The appearance of a new tale from his [Scott's] pen caused a
greater sensation in the United States than did some of the battles
of Napoleon, which decided the fates of thrones and empires. —
Everybody read these works; everybody — the refined and the
simple — shared the delightful trances ... Of course, there were
many editions of these works in the United States."[4]

---

[1] Bernard Faÿ, *La langue française à Harvard 1636—1936, Harvard et la
France*, Paris, 1936, p. 185.

[2] Henry Marvin Belden, *Poe's Criticism of Hawthorne*, Anglia XXIII, 1900.

[3] Cp. J. C. McCloskey, *The Campaign of Periodicals after the War of 1812
for National American Literature*, PMLA, 1935.

[4] S. G. Goodrich, *Recollections of a Lifetime*, New York & Auburn, 1846,
p. 108.

Of special interest to the literary historian is the fact that Scott's novels also made clear to American authors the possibilities of the novel as a vehicle of nationalism. As has been mentioned above, English and Scottish Romantic poets and critics were eagerly read, and English magazines and reviews were widespread. The drop of bitterness in the cup they offered was the critical attitude adopted by the British towards the former colonies after the War of Independence. The criticism may have originated, as C. Rourke has pointed out[1], in the British habit of self-criticism, extended to embrace the daughter nation as well. Nevertheless, it was scathing. One much-quoted expression was the article by Sydney Smith in *The Edinburgh Review* of January, 1820:

"Thus far we are the friends and admirers of Jonathan [viz. the United States]: But he must not grow vain and ambitious; or allow himself to be dazzled by that galaxy of epithets by which his orators and newspaper scribblers endeavour to persuade their supporters that they are the greatest, the most refined, the most enlightened and the most moral people upon earth. The effect of this is unspeakably ludicrous on this side of the Atlantic — and, even on the other, we should imagine, must be rather humiliating to the reasonable part of the population. The Americans are a brave, industrious, and acute people; but they have hitherto given no indication of genius, and made no approaches to the heroic, either in their morality or character. They are but a recent offset indeed from England; and should make it their chief boast, for many generations to come, that they are sprung from the same race with Bacon and Shakespeare and Newton. Considering their numbers, indeed, and the favourable circumstances in wich they have been placed, they have yet done marvellously little to assert the honour of such a descent, or to show that their English blood has been exalted or refined by their republican training and institutions. Their Franklins and Washingtons, and all the other sages and heroes of their revolution, were born and bred subjects of the King of England, — and not among the freest or most valued of his subjects. And, since the period of their separation a far greater proportion of their statesmen and artists and political writers have been foreigners, than ever occurred before in the history of any civilized and educ-

---

[1] Constance Rourke, *American Humor*, New York, 1931, p. 13.

ated people. During the thirty or forty years of their independence, they have done absolutely nothing for the Sciences, for the Arts, for Literature, or even for the statesman-like Studies of Politics or Political Economy ... In the four quarters of the globe, who reads an American book? or goes to an American play? or looks at an American picture or statue? ... Finally, under which of the old, tyrannical governments of Europe is every sixth man a slave, whom his fellowcreatures may buy and sell and torture?"

The British attitude could not fail to inflict a deep wound on the feelings of the population of the United States, and a strong resentment of the British gibes pervades much of the contemporary American literature. The situation, as it appeared from an American point of view, was outlined in a speech by C. J. Ingersoll of 1823, in which he states that

" ... the English language makes English reading American: and a generous, especially a parental nationality, instead of disparaging a supposed deficiency in the creation of literature, should remember and rejoice that the idiom and ideas of England are also of this country and of this continent, destined to be enjoyed and improved by millions of educated and thinking people spreading from the bay of Fundy to the mouth of the Columbia.

"But speaking and writing the language of an ancient and refined people, whose literature preoccupies nearly every department, is, in many respects, an unexampled disadvantage in the comparative estimate. America cannot contribute in any comparative proportion to the great British stock of literature, which almost supercedes the necessity of American subscriptions. Independent of this foreign oppression, the American mind has been called more to political, scientific, and mechanical, than to literary exertion."[1]

The author even asserts that, in America, "every husbandman understands the philosophy of politics better than many princes in Europe." He recalls that

" ... it is not yet half a century since the United States were politically emancipated; it is only since the late war that they have begun to be intellectually independent. Colonial habits and reverence still rebuke and counteract intellectual enterprise ... "

---

[1] C. J. Ingersoll, *A Discourse concerning the Influence of America on the Mind* in the *American Philosophic Society*, October 18th, 1823, Philadelphia, 1823.

and ends by declaring that the American mind will require
time to be "freed from European tutelage." Still

" . . . within the last ten years, especially, the mind of America
has thought for itself, piercing the veil of European beau ideal."

The haughty European attitude could also be countered with
true Yankee humour, as in the passage from *Mrs. Mowett's Fashion*,
quoted by Constance Rourke:

"In a word, madam, said the Count, I have seen enough of
civilized life — wanted to refresh myself by a sight of barbarian
countries and customs — had my choice between the Sandwich
Islands and New York — chose New York."[1]

Nevertheless, many of the British and, indeed, the Old World
authors of the time were indebted to the New World for inspiration
and subjects. The primitivism of the new continent, the noble
savage, the mystery of the wilderness, furnished subjects for Wordsworth, Blake and Coleridge, as well as for Herder, Goethe, and
Chateaubriand. A spokesman for American literary independence,
Thomas C. Upham, proudly stated that

"Europeans may ridicule our name, our country and our prospects, but in the clime so grossly misrepresented and defamed
it is not possible for them to deny, that an ample and most interesting field is open to literary speculations and exertions . . ."

and he pointed out that European poets like Campbell, Southey,
More, and Chateaubriand had "paid the tribute of splendid genius"
to the American scene.[2]

*

The account given here of the literary interests of New England
refers — as has been previously pointed out — to the cultured
society of the merchant centres of the country. The spiritual food
of the broad strata of society was of a somewhat different kind. The
counterpart of the intellectual magazines consisted, for the bulk of
middle class readers, of the successors of the popular almanacks:
the so-called annuals or gift-books. Their era began in the eighteen-
twenties, and the high-watermark of their influence was reached
in the thirties. The standard, however, soon fell, although the

[1] Constance Rourke, *American Humor*, New York, 1931, p. 29.
[2] Thomas G. Upham, *American Sketches*, New York, 1819, p. 15.

quantity of these publications steadily grew well into the forties. A specialist on this subject, Frederick Faxon, has listed nearly two thousand different annuals and giftbooks issued in English during the period, more than half of them in America, and there are, of course, volumes that escaped his notice.[1]

The other great popular branch of literature was the Gothic novel, the "bowl-and dagger-department" of the novel, as Carlyle termed it, and the pet aversion of enlightened magazines like *The Edinburgh Review* that wrote about

" . . . the irruption of these swarms of publications now daily issuing from the banks of the Danube, which like their ravaging predecessors of the darker ages, though with far other and more fatal arms, are overrunning civilized society. Those readers whose purer taste has been formed on the correct models of the old classic school, see with indignation and astonishment the Huns and Vandals once more overpowering the Greeks and Romans. They behold our minds, with a retrograde but rapid motion, hurried back to the reign of Chaos and old Night, by distorted and un-principled compositions, which in spite of strong flashes of genius unite the taste of the Goths with the morals of Bagshot."[2]

This attempt to lay the responsibility for the Gothic romance at the door of the Germans, is, however, not true to fact. As early as 1765, the Gothic craze had begun to develop on English soil. The term Gothic is derived mainly from the Gothic style of architecture which played an eminent rôle in the works of fiction of the school of terror and wonder, on the pattern of Horace Walpole's *Castle of Otranto*. Using Clara Reeve's distinction that "the Novel is a picture of real life and manners and of the time in which it is written. The Romance, in lofty and elevated language, describes what never happened nor is likely to happen,"[3] modern historians have divided 18th and 19th century romance as opposed to the novel into three sections: the historical, exemplified by John Leland's *Longsword*, the Oriental, by William Beckford's *Vathek*,

[1] Frederick W. Faxon, *Boston Book Company's List of American and English Periodicals*, Boston, 1899.

[2] *The Edinburgh Review*, March, 1831.

[3] In *The Progress of Romance*, 1845. Cited from Wilbur Cross, *The Development of the English Novel*, London, 1905, p. XIV.

and the Gothic, by Walpole's *Castle of Otranto*. The distinction cannot be carried too far: the three groups mingle, and there is also considerable trespassing into the domain of the novel.

The predilection for Gothic architecture was very widespread in both Europe and America in the beginning of the 19th century, and on the latter continent that taste has subsisted until quite recently. One of the outstanding specimens from the middle of the 19th century, on American soil, is Washington Irving's summer house, not far from Sleepy Hollow at Tarrytown-on-Hudson, a miniature mediaeval fortress only lacking the moat. The general taste may be sampled by an extract from *The North American Review* of April, 1830:

" . . . the poetry of architecture, the most curious and the most imposing of all styles — the Gothic architecture, which, notwithstanding the fastidiousness of the southern taste, will long continue to command the admiration of the northern nations, with the wild songs and irregular dramas of the romantic school of poetry."

If Walpole's Strawberry Hill was copied in stone and masonry all over two continents, the emulation provoked by his novel was not less widespread. English masters of the Gothic novel came from different social strata. Mrs. Anne Radcliffe's vivid interest in ghosts and general weirdness produced a long line of nervcracking stories from the pen of this middle-class lady, tales such as *The Italian* and *The Mysteries of Udolpho*, translated and read all over the civilized world. More surprising is to find a skilled Gothic romancer in a young English diplomatist like Matthew Gregory Lewis, author of *The Monk*, marking the climax of the craze, or in a British clergyman, the Reverend Mathurin, father of the diabolical and much-travelled *Melmoth*. The range of the disciples of these masters is wide. Godwin, the social reformer, the husband of Mary Wollstonecraft and the father of Mary Shelley — to whom we owe the Gothic novel *Frankenstein* — has inherited many traits from the terror novelists, appearing for example, in his *Caleb Williams*. On the whole, it may be said that most English Romantic poets show traces of acquaintance with Gothic literature.

In Germany, the Gothic novel was also cherished by the Romanticists who, in the beginning of the 19th century, continued on the path paved by the English authors. *Die Elixiere des Teufels* by

E. T. A. Hoffmann shows most of the traditional features of the Gothic romance, though they here attain an artistically higher level than ever before. It was not long before German authors found that subjects of this kind were better suited to short stories, and it was on German soil that the short story of terror first appeared. Except by Hoffmann, it was also cultivated by Tieck, Fouqué, Spiess, and others among the German Romanticists. In French literature, features of Gothic romance are to be found in George Sand, in Nodier, and Balzac — especially in the juvenile productions of the latter. In America, the style was first adopted by Charles Brockden Brown, all of whose work belonged to this domain. The short story of terror and/or wonder preferred by the Germans was introduced into America, about 1820, by Washington Irving. Common to both these American writers is the feature that the weird atmosphere, in itself skilfully wrought up, hides mysteries that generally find a rational, if not a prosaic, explanation. The genre may be illustrated by a quotation from the introductory note to Brockden Brown's *Wieland* (1792):

"His [the writer's] purpose is neither selfish nor temporary, but aims at the illustration of some important branches of the moral constitution of man ... The incidents related are extraordinary and rare. Some of them, perhaps, approach as nearly to the nature of miracles as can be done by that which is not truly miraculous. It is hoped that intelligent readers will not disapprove of the manner in which appearances are solved, but that the solution will be found to correspond with the known principles of human nature. The power which the principal person is said to possess[1] can scarcely be denied to be real. It must be acknowledged to be extremely rare; but no fact, equally uncommon, is supported by the same strength of historical evidence."

Irving, moreover, adds a generous portion of his characteristic humour and common sense. In addition to these authors, who rightly claim to be counted among the representatives of true literary tradition, the genre was nursed by a host of obscure writers of more popular than artistic appeal. Just as the Romantic recurrence to the past was symbolized in architecture by a predilection for Gothic villas, so the love of gardening and of natural scenery was

---

[1] Ventriloquism is the cause of the numerous and intricate entanglements of the story.

certainly to some extent an expression of an unconscious protest against the growing urbanization of the country. And so the terror and/or wonder craze in literature was an outlet for pent-up emotions and a protest against the religious severity that had for centuries ruled the land.

Self-assertion was in the air in the New World. America was waiting for its own national geniuses to emerge in all fields: in the arts, in science, and in literature. They appeared by and by, heralded by romantic visions like that of Nathaniel Hawthorne in his fantastic tale of *A Select Party*:

"But now appeared a stranger, whom the host had no sooner recognized than, with an abundance of courtesy unlavished on any other, he hastened down the whole length of the saloon in order to pay him emphatic honor. Yet he was a young man in poor attire, with no insignia of rank or acknowledged eminence, nor anything to distinguish him among the crowd except a high, white forehead, beneath which a pair of deepest eyes were glowing with warm light. It was such a light as never illuminates the earth save when a great heart burns as the household fire of a grand intellect. And who was he? — who but the Master Genius for whom our country is looking anxiously into the mist of Time, as destined to fulfil the great mission of creating an American literature, hewing it, as it were, out of the unwrought granite of our intellectual quarries? From him, whether moulded in the form of an epic poem or assuming a guise altogether new as the spirit itself may determine, we are to receive our first great original work, which shall do all that remains to be achieved for our glory among the nations."[1]

The European Romanticists sought their subjects in the past, they took them from far-off countries and from strange religions. Their American contemporaries also had access to these sources. They explored them, and at times felt something like jealousy of the older nations who owned a past full of memories and traditions. They turned to the resources of their own country, to their comparatively short history. Some of them held the opinion that the great American romance was the time in which they lived, the awakening and expanding nation full of great expecta-

---

[1] *Works* II, p. 79.

tions and looking forward to a future that seemed to offer unlimited
possibilities. Others tried their hand at old-time legends, and the
dramas of the soul that had been enacted while a new, American
way of life slowly took form in the communities founded by Old
World dissenters on the new continent.

HAWTHORNE: LIFE AND READINGS

A recent biographer of Nathaniel Hawthorne remarks that his death in 1884 "made his life much more of an integrated work of art on the part of Providence than those of Emerson, Longfellow, and Lowell, which overlapped awkwardly the world of Mark Twain, William Dean Howells, and Sidney Lanier".[1] This opinion is not in accordance with Hawthorne's own attitude. Though a lover of allegory and symbols, he never allows any kind of supernatural or allegorical considerations to enter his or his family's everyday life; he has, for example, nowhere left any sign of attaching symbolical importance to the fact that he was born on July 4th, the American Independence Day, in 1804. To his readers of a later period it may indeed seem strangely in keeping with the well-managed allegories of his work that his own lifetime so exactly covered the era of American cultural life that closes with the Civil War in 1861.

If Hawthorne did not allow his imagination to establish any connection between the supernatural world and his own existence, he was the more interested in establishing his relation to the past. He belonged to an old family and, even in early childhood, his imagination had been occupied with his ancestors and their world. It became one of the most important ingredients of his literary work, and the subject involving the late descendant who returns to the home of his ancestors and who slowly and with difficulty traces the history of the family and detects its secrets, recurs in the four fragments that form the literary remains from his last years.

The first American member of the family of the Hawthornes, or Hathornes as their name was spelt before Nathaniel adopted the

---

[1] Lawrence Sargent Hall, *Hawthorne, Critic of Society*, New Haven, 1944, p. 158.

form he made famous, was Mayor William Hathorne, who in 1630 emigrated from Wigcastle in Wiltshire to Dorchester in New England. Although they had sailed from a British emigration port, Nathaniel Hawthorne found reasons to believe that the family was of old French origin. In the colonies, William Hathorne became a fur merchant, but he also took an active part in the fights against the Indians and in the political life of Salem, where he finally settled down, and for nearly a quarter of a century was speaker of the General Court. To the imagination of his descendant, William Hathorne "that first ancestor, invested by family tradition with a dim and dusky grandeur"[1] was alive as far back as he could remember, and life and conditions in the old town of Salem was one of his chief studies as a boy. In the old chronicles of the first settlers, Mayor Hathorne is often mentioned as a man who handled dissenters with special severity; the Quakers especially became objects for his reformatory zeal, a fact which two hundred years later was to torment the conscience of his late-born descendant seriously, and was to be dealt with over and over again in his stories and romances. The same severity characterized the representative of the next generation, John Hathorne, who was also a soldier with a colonel's title, but first and foremost an official and a judge. During his time, the witch persecutions were raging at their worst, and John Hathorne was a dutiful and indefatigable executor of the divine commandment, not to leave any witch alive.

The later generations of the family show fewer outstanding characteristics. Nathaniel Hawthorne's father was a sea-captain, and in outward appearance very much the same type of a man as his son: his was a tall and lithe body carrying a small head, whose fine features were shadowed by a thick cluster of curls. Their inner dispositions also seem to have been similar. They were earnest men with a bent for contemplative and solitary habits.

Nathaniel's mother, the former Elizabeth Clarke Manning, became a recluse from the moment of her husband's death in 1808, adopting habits that were — to use the words of her grandson, Julian Hawthorne — "almost Hindoolike". She moved with her children to the home of her own family, the so-called Manning house in Herbert Street, in Salem, and shut herself up in her room.

---

[1] *Works* V, p. 24.

She seldom went out, and did not even take her meals with the
children. Gradually, they adopted the same mode of life. It was a
dreary environment for a small boy to grow up in, and there is
difficulty in agreeing with the biographer who asserts that "there
seems to have been no attempt to interfere with his natural development", that he led "a strangely secluded life but not stranger than
that of any youth of his temperament born into the dreary waste of
provincial life",[1] and ascribes his later solitary attitude to the
education he received. On the contrary, Hawthorne's education,
as far as school and teaching is concerned, seems to have been of
the average kind received by American boys at the time. The
early habits of seclusion were, however, fortified by his misfortune
of injuring his foot at the age of ten, which made him an invalid
for a considerable time. He spent the better part of his invalidism
in his uncle Manning's home in Maine, where he regained his
health completely, and at the same time acquired a closer contact
with nature. James T. Fields quotes some words uttered by
Hawthorne in a conversation in December, 1883, concerning this
period of his life:

---

[1] Herbert Read, *Hawthorne*, in *The Sense of Glory*, Cambridge (England),
1929, p. 157.

Another recent writer, Mr. Manning Hawthorne, has, in an essay on *Hawthorne's Early Years*, in *The Essex Institute Historical Collections* LXXIV, 1938,
tried to show that Mrs. Hawthorne led a normal, active life and that the relations between her and her children were of a very natural and confidential kind.
These assertions may, however, be regarded as refuted beforehand, not least
by rather bitter comments of Nathaniel Hawthorne himself, viz. this passage
in one of his letters to Sophia: "I have thought much of thy parting injunction
to tell my mother and sisters that thou art her daughter and their sister. I do
not think that thou couldst estimate what a difficult task thou didst propose
to me — not that any awful and tremendous effect would be produced by the
disclosure; but because of the strange reserve, in regard to matters of feeling,
that has always existed among us. We are conscious of one another's feelings,
always; but there seems to be a tacit law, that our deepest heart-concernments
are not to be spoken of. I cannot gush out in their presence — I cannot take
my heart in my hand, and show it to them. There is a feeling within me (Though
I know it is a foolish one) as if it would be indecorous to do so, as to display to
them the naked breast. And they are in the same state as myself. None, I think,
but delicate and sensitive persons could have got into such a position; but doubtless this incapacity of free communion, in the hour of especial need, is meant
by Providence as a retribution for something wrong in our early intercourse
..." (Febr. 27th, 1842. Cited from the manuscript in the Huntington Library.)

"I lived in Maine like a bird of the air, so perfect was the freedom I enjoyed. But it was there I first got my cursed habits of solitude."[1]

The enforced loneliness and lack of exercise during this period encouraged the boy's taste for reading. From his earliest years he had shown a vivid interest in the tales told him by his aunt Manning and other Salem veterans: tales of the past, in which his own ancestors sometimes played a prominent part. They concerned the first immigrants of Salem, generally called Puritans, and their controversies and fights with the Indians, their treaties with old sachems, and their acquaintance with Indian customs and what they considered to be black magic. Other tales were about the persecution of the Quakers, and, later on, the witch proceedings. Some were of a later date and had as their subject the liberation battles against the English that had been fought not far from Salem — at Lexington, Concord, and Boston. Nathaniel and his sisters Elizabeth and Louisa were fascinated by these stories. When Nathaniel learnt to read, at four, one of the first books put into his hands was Bunyan's *Pilgrims Progress*. This happened in 1808, shortly after his father's death, a fact that made the impact of the tale on the four-year-old boy's sensitive mind all the stronger. Another classic that early gained a firm hold on his imagination was Spenser's *Faerie Queene*[2], which is said to have been the first book he bought with money out of his own pocket. On the shelves of the library in Herbert Street he found, in the years which followed, the English classics: Shakespeare, Milton, Pope, and Thomson, especially *The Castle of Indolence*, were read by him as a small boy.

When Nathaniel was prevented, by the injury to his foot, from going to school, a friend of the family, the wellknown lexicographer Dr. Worcester, who was then living in Salem, came daily to see the boy and to instruct him. Hawthorne may have acquired some of his detailed learning from him; he extended it later in life, and always kept a taste for encyclopedias and calendars of diverse kinds, among which a curious preference of his early years was the *Newgate Calendar*, something which, says his early bio-

---

[1] J. T. Fields, *Yesterdays with Authors*, Boston, 1901, p. 113.

[2] Cp. Randall Stewart, *Hawthorne and the Faerie Queene, The Philological Quarterly*, April, 1933.

grapher G. B. Lathrop, "excited a good deal of comment among his family and relatives, but no decisive opposition."[1] A book more appropriate for a boy in his teens is indicated by an entry in Hawthorne's diary of 1818:

"I have read Gulliver's Travels, but do not agree with Captain Britton that it is a witty and uncommonly interesting book; the wit is obscene, and the lies too false."[2]

History was another preference of his during these years in Salem and Maine. One of his most beloved books, both at this early age and later on in life, was Felt's *Annals of Salem*. Julian Hawthorne[3] moreover mentions three books that were regarded as family heirlooms and bore early printing dates, in one case as far back as the 16th century. They were *The Poetical Works* of Du Bartas, in an old English translation, The Countess of Pembroke's *Arcadia*, by Sir Philip Sidney, and another translation, this time from the Italian, with the bloodcurdling title *God's Revenge. Against the Crying and Execrable Sin of Murder*, containing nothing but Italian murder tales. A fourth book which we know that Hawthorne read, is an account of the *Wars with the Indians*, one of the first American books to have been printed on the new continent. The fly-leaf of that book bore the autograph of Mayor William Hathorne and all of his descendants in succession, down to Nathaniel himself. Clarendon's *History of the Rebellion* is also listed among the books read by Hawthorne during these years, as well as a translation of Froissart's *Chronicles*. He also became acquainted at an early age with the works of Rousseau, to which he was later to revert.[4]

In letters written to his mother or sisters from Maine, Hawthorne now and then mentions his reading. There is one passage, quoted in most biographies, where he tells his sister Elizabeth that he has read:

". . . Waverley, The Mysteries of Udolpho, Adventures of Fer-

---

[1] G. P. Lathrop, *A Study of Hawthorne*, Cambridge, 1891, p. 69.

[2] *Hawthorne's First Diary, With an Account of its Discovery and Loss*, by Samuel T. Pickard, Boston, 1897, p. 83.

[3] Julian Hawthorne, *Hawthorne Reading*, The Rowfant Club, Cleveland, 1902, p. 34.

[4] Cp. J. T. Fields, *Yesterdays with Authors*, Boston, 1901, p. 65, also *Works* X, p. 535.

dinand Count Fathom, Roderick Random, and the first volume of the Arabian Nights."[1]

And in another letter he states:

"I have bought the 'Lord of the Isles' and intend either to send or to bring it to you. I like it as well as any of Scott's other poems. I have read Hogg's Tales, Caleb Williams, St. Leon, and Mandeville. I admire Godwin's Novels, and intend to read them all. I shall read the Abbott by the Author of Waverley as soon as I can hire it. I have read all of Scott's novels except that. I wish I had not that I might have the pleasure of reading them again. Next to these I like Caleb Williams."[2]

A little scrap of paper also exists which Hawthorne's daughter, Una, estimated to have been written "when Papa was about fifteen" and which states:

"I have read all most all the Books which have been published for the last hundred years. Among them are, Melmoth by Mathurin, Tom Jones, and Amelia by Fielding, Rousseau's Eloisa which is admirable Memoirs of R. L. Edgeworth The Abbott Romantick Tales by M. G. Lewis I hear" (the rest is illegible) Signed: Nathaniel Hawthorne.[3]

Julian Hawthorne[4] has drawn up a list of some of the books which he remembers from his fathers library of later years, including The English humorists, Fielding, Sterne, Smollett, and *The Spectator*. He also mentions the *Essays* and *Novum Organum* of Bacon.

Another form of literature was also represented in Nathaniel Hawthorne's literary pursuits: the comparatively new trend of journalism. His interest for newspaper reading is evident from a little publication issued in the year 1820 from the Hawthorne schoolroom and having for editor the male member of the family, while his sisters contributed prose and verse. *The Spectator*, which has recently been edited by Elizabeth Lathrop Chandler[5],

---

[1] Dated September 28th, 1819. Cited from a copy in the Yale University Collection.

[2] Dated October 31st, 1820. Cited from a copy in the Yale University Collection.

[3] Cited from the manuscript in the Huntington Library.

[4] J. Hawthorne: *Hawthorne Reading*, pp. 64—65.

[5] *The New England Quarterly*, Vol. 11, June, 1938.

shows clear traces of its author's reading of the Salem press as well as of 18th century literature. Its *Prospectus*, in the first issue, gives the amusingly precocious — but at the same time no doubt seriously intended — ironical tone of the publication:

". . . Although we would not insinuate that in commencing this Publication we are guided solely by disinterested motives, yet the consideration that we may reform the morals and instruct and amuse the minds of our Readers, that we may advance the cause of Religion, and give to truth and justice a wide sway, has been of the greatest weight with us."

Another item, *On Industry*, reads as follows:

"It has been somewhere remarked, that an Author does not write the worse for knowing little or nothing of his Subject. We hope the truth of this saying will be made manifest in the present article.

"With the benefits of Industry, we are not personally acquainted, (it not being one of the attributes of literary men) but we have often seen them conspicuously displayed in others . . . How far preferable is the sweet consciousness that we have diligently performed our Duty, to the self reproaches which continually invade us, when we feel that we have idly neglected what should have been performed . . . To conclude, Industry alone can render the Spectator worthy of its extensive patronage."

From the remark on the "attributes of literary men" we may with some justification draw the inference that the sixteen-year-old editor had already at this time begun to dream of a literary career. That his mind had not turned to prose only is shown by a little poem, dated Salem, February 13th, 1817, entitled *Moderate Views*, and conceived entirely in the moralizing style of the time:

> "With passions unruffled untainted by pride
> By reason my life let me square.
> The wants of my nature are cheaply supplied
> And the rest are but folly and care.
> How vainly through infinite trouble and strife
> The many their labours employ,
> Since all, that is truly delightful in life
> is what all if they please may enjoy."[1]

---

[1] Cited from a copy in the Yale University Collection.

The ironical attitude towards this kind of effusion, however, did not take long to appear. In a letter to his sister Louisa of September 9th, 1819, the young writer, without transition, suddenly bursts into rhyme:

> "Oh, earthly pomp is but a dream
> And like a meteor's short-lived gleam;
> And all the sons of glory soon
> Will rest beneath the mould'ring stone
> And Genius is a star whose light
> Is soon to sink in endless night,
> And heavenly beauty's angel form
> Will bend like flower in winter's storm."

And then he immediately makes these rather critical comments on his effusion:

"Though these are my rhymes, yet they are not exactly my thoughts. I am full of scraps of poetry; can't keep it out of my brain,

> I saw where in a lonely grave
> Departed Genius lay;
> and mournful yew-trees o'er it wave,
> To hide it from the day.

I could vomit up a dozen pages more if I were a mind to turn over."[1]

Evidently, the writer's estimate of his own poetical abilities is not too high. Self-criticism developed early in him, and at times assumed large proportions.

The preceding, necessarily incomplete, survey of Hawthorne's childhood reading affords us a picture that mirrors in an interesting way the general American reading situation of the day as referred to in the first chapter of the present study. This American boy knows the history of his country, with an emphasis on the events of religious strifes[2], and also the history of the world. He is well versed in English literature, from the classics up to the modern authors of his time, and notably those with a Gothic strain

---

[1] Cited from a copy in the Yale University Collection.

[2] Concerning the influence of Cotton and Increase Mather's works on Hawthorne's fiction, especially his witch stories, see H. Arlin Turner, *Hawthorne's Literary Borrowings*, PMLA, June, 1936.

in them. He knows fairy tales, also such as derive from the East, and is acquainted with French literature and ways of thinking, and also with the world of Antiquity. In addition, he writes a prose which is remarkably good for a schoolboy.

In 1820, Hawthorne was for a short time employed as a part-time clerk in the office of his uncle, William Manning. Since, however, another uncle, Robert, offered to pay for a college education, he left the office desk and entered Bowdoin college at Brunswick, in 1821.

Bowdoin college that year registered several young men who later played an important part in American political and cultural life. Henry W. Longfellow was one of them; Franklin Pierce, later President, an other. Horatio Bridge, afterwards Lieutenant in the United States' Navy, became Hawthorne's closest friend. The teaching staff was not to be compared with that of Harvard or Yale, but included some excellent men; President Allen was the author of a biographical dictionary; Parker Cleveland, an outstanding geologist and chemist, belonged to the faculty, and in 1824, Thomas C. Upham, who had published some literary work, was assigned to the chair of philosophy. Life at Bowdoin was simple and rural. Henry James, in his classical and penetrating essay on Hawthorne, which bears so clear an imprint of being written by an American in love with England, and — significantly enough — is written to include Hawthorne as the first American among authors whose biographies appear in the series "English Men of Letters,"[1] quotes Hawthorne's own description of life at Bowdoin, of

"lads ... at a country college — gathering blueberries in study hours under those tall, academic pines ... shooting pigeons and gray squirrels in the woods; or bat-fowling in the summer twilight; or catching trouts in that shadowy little stream ... in short (as we need not fear to acknowledge now), doing a hundred things the faculty had never heard of ..."[2] and calls it "a pretty picture, but a picture of happy urchins at school" as compared with undergraduate life at Oxford or Cambridge. The learning imparted at Bowdoin is by James characterized as "a civilizing influence, working

---

[1] Henry James, *Hawthorne*, English Men of Letters Series, London, 1902, p. 20.

[2] *Works* III, p. 387.

... toward the amenities and humanities and other collegiate graces", which is certainly an unnecessary minimizing of the seat of learning that fostered men such as the above-mentioned. Hawthorne is reported to have been a good, though not a brilliant scholar. His favourite subjects were English and Latin. The English professor later declared that his themes were "written in the sustained, finished style that gives to his mature productions an inimitable charm."[1] Longfellow has praised the elegance of his Latin translations at college[2], and passages in Hawthorne's Italian notebooks as well as his *Wonder-book* and his *Tanglewood Tales* tell us of his familiarity with the world of Antiquity. French was taught at Bowdoin, but there is no evidence of German instruction.

Concerning Hawthorne's reading during these years, the evidence is not abundant, though all sources agree on the fact that he consumed large quantities of literature. The list of books checked out of the library during the time that Hawthorne was a student at Bowdoin, does not include his name. He was, however, a member of the Athenaean Society which had a library of eight hundred volumes. It is probable that, during this period, he acquired his obviously great familiarity with English contemporary literature. In these years, some of Scott's most popular novels appeared[3], and from the passage in Hawthorne's English notebook, when, many years later, he visited Abbotsford, it is clear that his familiarity with Scott's works had been very great in his youth.[4] The same applies to other English authors of both older and later date: at Uttoxeter, he remembers Dr. Johnson[5], at Rydal Lake, Wordsworth[6], at Oxford, Pope[7], between Sheffield and Manchester, the Brontës[8], and so on.

At this time Hawthorne probably read W. Austin's popular

[1] George P. Lathrop, *A Study of Hawthorne*, Boston, 1876, p. 111.
[2] Ibid.
[3] Viz., *The Pirate, Peveril of the Peak*, and *Quentin Durward*.
[4] *Works* VIII, pp. 268—275. Cp. Neal Frank Doubleday, *Hawthorne and Literary Nationalism, American Literature*, Jan., 1941.
[5] *Works* VII, pp. 149—51, 160—61.
[6] *Works* VIII, p. 25.
[7] *Works* VII, p. 219.
[8] *Works* VII, p. 170.

story about *Peter Rugg, the Missing Man*, first published in *The
New England Galaxy* of 1824, and referred to in *The Virtuoso's
Collection*.[1] It is the story of a man travelling with his small boy
between Boston and Providence, and never arriving, although he
began his journey at the time of the Boston Massacre in 1770.
The atmosphere of the story — that has often been compared
to Chamisso's Peter Schlemihl — has not a little in common
with that of Hawthorne's work. Austin has the same faculty of
mystifying himself together with the reader. *Peter Rugg* was,
according to the evidence of the editor of *The New England
Galaxy*, "reprinted in other papers and books, and read more
than any newspaper communication that has fallen within my
knowledge."[2]

In these years Washington Irving's *Bracebridge Hall* and *Tales
of a Traveller*, Cooper's *The Spy*, *The Pioneers*, and *The Pilot* also
appeared. There is no direct evidence — but great probability —
that Hawthorne had read these contemporary American works of
fiction. Julian Hawthorne also speaks of his having acquainted
himself "in one form or another" with the leading Italian poets,
an assertion which is corroborated only by allusions to Boccaccio,
Petrarca, etc. in the *Italian Note-books*, and which seems not to
be too reliable.

As has been mentioned, a young teacher of philosophy with
literary interests, Thomas C. Upham, came to Bowdoin in 1824.
Horatio Bridge, in his recollections, characterizes Mr. Upham as
"young, scholarly, gentle, and kind to the students, by all of whom
he was much beloved."[3] It seems to be reasonable that his pupils
were interested in his productions, and that the spirit that pervades
his little volume *American Sketches*, also found expression in his
classes. The sketches are short poems, all on American subjects,
and preceded by a preface in ardent language, giving vent to the
hopes for an American renaissance in art and literature.[4] Under
the motto

---

[1] *Works* II, p. 556.
[2] W. Austin, *Peter Rugg, the Missing Man*, With an introduction by Thomas
Wentworth Higginson, Boston, 1908, p. 10.
[3] Horatio Bridge, *Personal Recollections of Nathaniel Hawthorne*, New York,
1893, p. 53.
[4] Thomas C. Upham, *American Sketches*, New York, 1819.

"Si neque tibias
Euterpe cohibet, nec Polyhymnia
Lesboum refugit tendere barbitum"

Mr. Upham asserts, with the corroboration of Gibbon, that
"the prominent object of a poet's study is the human heart, and that description of external nature, from the hyssop on the wall to the cedar of Lebanon, from the dew of the flowret to the humid radiance of the evening cloud, are chiefly valuable as interpreters of the passions, and as helps in developing the hidden mysteries, ties and operations of the soul." He continues to depict, how ". . . every country exhibits certain peculiarities of scenery, certain striking features in the character of its inhabitants, and is remarkable for marvellous events in some periods of its history, and for affecting local incidents worthy of the effort of genius, and of being commemorated in song."[1]

The following poems have titles such as *Dark-rolling Connecticut*, *Bunker Hill*, or *The Iroquois*. Some of them are treatments of themes given in an appendix, like that of *Lucinda*,
"the story of Miss Mc Rea, celebrated by Barlow in the 6th book of the Columbiad, under the name of Lucinda, her ardent attachment to Heartly, and the untimely extinction of her hopes."
Untimely is a mild word for what befell Lucinda when looking for her beloved on the shores of the Hudson:

"Two Mohawks heard her tender prayer,
And springing from their nightly rest,
They seized her golden wreaths of hair,
And plunged their hatchets in her breast;
Her snowy arms were red with gore.
Adieu, dear Heartly, then she cried,
In heaven we'll meet to part no more,
And, like a drooping lily, died."

The *Soldier of Hadley*, the widespread tale of the attack by Indians on a worshipping congregation at Hadley, and the appearance of a stranger in uncommon dress, leading the Christians to victory, appears here in a version that might be added to previous research on the subject:

[1] Ibid., p. 10.

"Oh, then from the woods near the battle that towered,
Came a brightly arm'd soldier and sternly he cried,
To the few who were living, though quite overpower'd,
And encouraged when hope from the bravest had died.
A sash rich with gold round his bosom was twining,
A plume dipp'd in blood o'er his brow was reclining,
His robe white as snow far behind him was shining,
And the few who were living were soon at his side."

Even if the acute critical sense that characterized young Hawthorne was roused by the versificatory and other shortcomings of his preceptor, the patriotic pathos expressed by him must have been contagious, and the poem last quoted may have something to do with Hawthorne's tale of *The Gray Champion*.[1] Perhaps we may also assume that the ideas of Mr. Upham had mingled with the aspirations of the editor of the *Spectator*, when Hawthorne in 1826 left Bowdoin, with no definite plans for the future.

In his letters from this period, Hawthorne refers mostly in banter to his literary ambitions.[2] But the urge to become a writer that had appeared in glimpses all through his childhood and adolescence was still there, this much is averred by his friend Bridge, who has described their schoolboy rambles together: "On such occasions I always foretold his success if he should choose literature as a profession. He listened without assenting, but, as he told me long afterwards, he was cheered and strengthened in his subsequent career by my enthusiastic faith in his literary powers."[3]

The prospects for an author were, however, not very enticing in the America of the eighteen-twenties. The only American who

---

[1] G. Harrison Orians: *The Angel of Hadley in Fiction, American Literature IV*, Nov., 1932.

A detailed study of the use of the Hadley theme in American fiction is given by G. Harrison Orians. Mr. Upham's work is, however, not mentioned in this survey that notes twelve instances in English and American literature before Hawthorne.

[2] Letter to his mother, dated March 13th, 1821: "What do you think of my becoming an author, and relying for support on my pen? . . . How proud you would feel to see my works praised by the reviewers, as equal to the proudest productions of the scribbling sons of John Bull." Cited from a copy in the Yale University Collection.

[3] Horatio Bridge, *Personal Recollections of Nathaniel Hawthorne*, New York, 1893, p. 15.

had tried to live by his pen, Charles Brockden Brown, had died in 1810 without having attained prosperity by means of his writings, though widely read and admired. The pirating of English literature was general, and went on unpunished. It bore most of the blame for this state of affairs. Why should a publisher take the risks connected with introducing a new name, and even pay money for it, when the best works of living authors writing in the same language, were to be had for nothing? Even if patriotism was strong, such a practical demonstration of it had a somewhat limited appeal. This Hawthorne knew. Moreover, he was a diffident young man, and even if in his heart of hearts he cherished a very firm conviction of his destination, his alert sense of self-criticism told him that he still had much to learn. He therefore settled in his mother's home in Salem, in the little room that has afterwards become an American literary Mecca, the "lonely chamber under the eaves" of the Herbert Street house.

Hawthorne himself later on viewed his seclusion of these years as a morbid way of life, and as such it has usually been described. The habits of the young hermit of Salem were, however, far from self-torture or excentricities of any physical kind. It is true that he did not like to take his exercise in the daytime. But his nightly walks were regular, and he generally returned home before midnight to get his bowl of bread and chocolate — which was, after all, a great concession to normality on the part of a young writer with aspirations, at a time when the really important part of a poet's life was supposed to be spent under a moonlit, starry sky. The nightly rambles were a Romantic epidemic, and just as much part of a young 19th century Romanticist's equipment as, for example, the waistcoats of Gautier. Judging by the portraits of Hawthorne during these years, he also affected the garb of a Romanticist, modified to suit his environment, a small New England town. He wore his wavy hair rather long, and sported high collars with a broad, dark tie with long, loose ends. No description of the colours of his attire is to be found, although his wife later on tells us of a morning coat of Burgundy red, and also mentions that he intensely disliked to see her dressed in dark colours.

Reading and writing took up the daytime of the nightly roamer. There are no actual records of his reading up to 1828. After that time, we possess one clue: the list of books drawn from the Athenaeum library of Salem, of which Hawthorne became a member in that year.[1] As is always the case when any personal library, or list of books bought by a person is quoted, the evidence of his having actually read the books is, of course, open to doubt. Hawthorne may have borrowed books for the benefit of his sisters or his mother. But with the certain knowledge we possess of his studious habits, it cannot be too bold to assume that most of the volumes borrowed were meant for his own instruction and amusement. A statistical condensation of the entries on the Athenaeum ledger — omitting periodicals and non-literary titles — shows the following items:

American	14	German	3
English	81	Italian	2
French	127	Spanish	2

The fact that Hawthorne also had access to private libraries explains the low proportion of American books. We have already mentioned his great interest in American history and folklore. His knowledge in these fields was deepened and enlarged through a thorough study of works of old native authors such as Cotton and Increase Mather, the *History of the United States* by Bancroft, the *History of Massachusetts* by Hutchinson, and the *Annals of America* by Holmes. The extent of these studies has been expertly and thoroughly explored, and may be considered established beyond doubt.[2] Many of the entries in the Athenaeum list not included in the statistics given above, refer to this field.

That Hawthorne was an assiduous reader of the press of his time is also evident both from the entries in the Athenaeum list, and from frequently recurring references in his diaries and letters, especially in those he wrote to his fiancée and wife in later years. When taking a rest or spending a leisurely hour between professional duties, he usually turned over the leaves of some current publication:

"Next, at about half past nine o'clock, he [thine husband] will

[1] *Books read by Nathaniel Hawthorne 1828—1850, The Essex Institute Historical Collections*, Vol. LXVIII, Salem, Mass., Jan., 1932.

[2] Edward Dawson, *Hawthorne's Knowledge and Use of New England History; A Study of Sources*. A Summary of a Thesis. The Joint University Libraries, Nashville, Tennessee, 1939.

go to the Athenaeum and turn over the Magazines and Reviews till eleven or twelve, when it will be time to return to the Custom-House."[1]

He also obtained a deep knowledge and appreciation of classic and modern English literature during these years. Even if he himself, in a letter to Longfellow about his life in Salem and Boston, writes that:

"I have indeed turned over a good many books, but in so desultory a way that it cannot be called study, nor has it left me the fruits of study",[2]

we still find reminiscences of that turning over of books scattered through his published work. His style, so clear and poised, shows the influence of the Augusteans, of whom he was especially fond — a predilection manifested in Hawthorne's notebooks, when he later on was able to visit the places where they had lived. Swift was one of the authors with whom he was most familiar, and his influence may be traced through the greater part of Hawthorne's production.[3] He knew Pope well, was an admirer of Dr. Johnson's, and had read Goldsmith and Richardson. Among contemporary British authors, he mentions reading Dickens and Thackeray, and had a deep admiration for De Quincey, whose visionary faculty was in a way related to his own, though the temperaments of the two authors were very dissimilar. Julian Hawthorne, writing in later years about the books that his father had read aloud to his children, mentions "almost all of Scott, Wordsworth, De Quincey, Macaulay's Roman Ballads, Mark Anthony's speech over Caesars body — but never a Shakespeare play as a whole."[4] Hawthorne's familiarity with English, and indeed world literature was, some years later, shown off in one of his essays, a sort of quizz-master's *tour de force*, which was, a little self-consciously, called *A Virtuoso's Collection*.[5] This essay, which lacks

---

[1] Letter to Sophia, dated March 11th, 1840. Cited from the manuscript in the Huntington Library.

[2] Letter to Longfellow, June 4th, 1837. Cited from a copy in the Yale University Collection.

[3] Alice Lovelace Cooke, *Some Evidences of Hawthorne's Indebtedness to Swift. University of Texas Publications. Studies in English*, 1938.

[4] Julian Hawthorne, *Nathaniel Hawthorne's Blue Cloak, The Bookman*, Sept., 1932.

[5] *Works* II, p. 537.

the charm of Hawthorne's best writing, is an ingenious cataloguing of literature, and must have been a delight to people who enjoyed examining their own and other people's memory of things read. Among objects listed in the collection are "the milk-white lamb which Una led", Rosinante, Dr. Johnson's cat Hodge, the bull Apis, Prospero's magic wand, the golden case in which the queen of Gustavus Adolphus treasured up that hero's heart; the pen of steel with which Faust signed away his salvation, the original manuscripts of the Koran and the Mormon Bible; Wordsworth's Eglantine, Burns' Mountain Daisy, and a sprig from Southey's Holly tree, together with Peter Schlemihl's missing shadow.

There are not many French names to be found among the treasures of the Virtuoso, which include the sword of the Cid Campeador and the easy-chair of Rabelais. But the frequency of French titles in the lists from the Salem Athenaeum is nevertheless a highly significant fact.[1] Voltaire's name occurs 51 times, and this corresponds well with Julian Hawthorne's[2] later observation of his father's reading a good deal of French literature together with his wife in the Old Manse.

His son also mentions Racine, Molière, and Corneille, an assertion corroborated by the fact that Hawthorne's interest for these authors was, according to the Salem list, alert as early as 1831. Rousseau, an old acquaintance from earlier years, still fascinates him, and is mentioned in 18 entries. Montaigne's name appears five times. Hawthorne's biographer, G. P. Lathrop, who had also consulted the Athenaeum lists, adds that they are by no means complete:

"When Miss Elizabeth Peabody made his acquaintance in 1836—37, he had, for example, read all of Balzac that had then appeared . . ."[3]

Of German authors there are only three entries. Schlegel's

---

[1] Hawthorne's reading acquaintance with French is attested by an entry in his notebook of January 6th, 1858, when he first set his foot on French soil and heard French spoken around him: "If they would speak slowly and distinctly I might understand them well enough, being perfectly familiar with the written language, and knowing the principles of its pronounciation;" *Works* X, p. 12.

[2] Cp. Julian Hawthorne, *Hawthorne Reading*, p. 118.

[3] G. P. Lathrop, *A Study of Hawthorne*, p. 164.

name appears twice in July, 1828, and Schiller's works were borrowed for a week in February, 1835. Hawthorne may have had other means of knowing German literature at this time. At any rate, his borrowing of German books was infrequent, as compared, for example, to his borrowing of Voltaire and Rousseau. The amount of magazines read is considerable — *The Edinburgh Review*, *The Quarterly Review*, *Blackwood's*, *Wilkinson's*, *The Gentleman's*, *The European*, and *The Monthly* magazines all occur frequently in the list, and their main subject of interest outside literature in the English language was, as has been already pointed out, the new Romantic movement in Germany and its protagonists.

There is in these years little that points to an interest in Hawthorne for the modern philosophy of his time. His meditation was far more occupied with the old religious dogmas and moral intransigencies of his ancestors, and with search for truth along personal lines, influenced by his reading of moral philosophers of older times — American, English, and French.

A great part of his reading was of a purely informative kind. Different kinds of encyclopedias, dictionaries, anthologies, and the like constituted all through his life one of his principal sources of knowledge.

A curious predilection of Hawthorne's, persisting from his childhood interest in the *Newgate Calendar*, was recordings of crimes of various kinds, a taste that followed him all through life. One of his son's latest recollections was that of Hawthorne studying an enormous volume of the series "English State Trials". In the Essex Athenaeum lists, this trend is illustrated by five entries of *State Trials* in spring, 1832.

But the young man of the solitary and studious habits also gave much of his time to creative work. If many hours were spent in musing and philosophizing, there were others when he put pen to paper and tried his hand at creating literature. His first productions were all New England stories and — according to his sister Elizabeth who was one of the few ever to read them — of a weird and fantastic kind. Only one of them has survived — *Alice Doane's Appeal*. It was not published in any of his short story collections but is included in his Collected Works.[1] A young

---

[1] *Works* XII, p. 279.

printer in Salem was entrusted with the task of printing the volume, the title of which was to be *Seven Tales of my Native Land*, but, unfortunately, he was rather slow in performing it, and, in the meantime, the author's diffidence asserted itself: the manuscript was withdrawn and burnt. The next venture went a little further. *Fanshawe*, a novel of which the setting was taken from Bowdoin college, was printed in 1828 by March and Capen in Boston. With a view to the uncertainty of the success of a young and unknown author, the firm made him pay $ 100 for the printing — and, unhappily, their fears proved justified. *Fanshawe* had a very poor sale — seven or eight copies — and, despondent and deceived in his aspirations, Hawthorne collected all available copies and destroyed them.

Twenty years more were to pass before Hawthorne once more tried his hand at a novel. He turned to the short story, and to a special sort of essay-writing of a fantastical, whimsical kind, related to that of Charles Lamb.

Publication was still the great problem. In 1830, Hawthorne got into touch with S. G. Goodrich. He was the publisher of one of the first annuals, *The Token*, and the man who first printed the works of American authors in the years before 1820, a period which he later on in his memoirs called the "darkest hour before the dawn" of American literature. Mr. Goodrich first planned to publish a collection of Hawthorne's short stories under the title *Provincial Tales*. The publication was, however, delayed and finally it was agreed that some of the stories were to appear in *The Token*. In that publication appeared *The Gentle Boy* — for which the author received $ 35 — and successively most of the other short stories by Hawthorne, not under his full name, but with signatures, of which the most frequent was "The Author of the Gentle Boy" — the same kind of pen-name as " The Author of Waverley" had cherished.

By Goodrich, Hawthorne was drawn into more active — and also slightly more remunerative — literary work. In March, 1836, he became employed by the Bewick Company in Boston, to edit *The American Magazine of Useful and Entertaining Knowledge*, with a salary of $ 500 a year.

The editorship had, in itself, a charm for Hawthorne, the lover of useful reading and of the periodical press. He was, however, far from given a free hand with the publication. Its general policy was already established when Hawthorne moved to Boston to begin his work, and the pictures, which consisted of engravings and were a very prominent if not the most important feature of the magazine, were to be chosen by the publishers. The editor's task was to provide them with texts, biographical or explanatory articles of a didactic kind, in short, mere hackwork. Hawthorne soon came to detest it. "I am ashamed of the whole concern,"[1] he wrote, on Febr. 5th, to his sister Elizabeth, who was of great help to him as a compiler and writer of articles. Arlin Turner, who has in a detailed study followed Hawthorne's editorship and published parts of his contributions to *The Magazine of Useful and Entertaining Knowledge*, estimates the amount of original writing of Hawthorne's to about one fourth of the contents of each issue.[2] However, everything he touched received something of his stamp, and a perusal of the articles also gives us an idea of the huge amount of reading of the most varied kind to which this work forced him. Turner divides the items into five classes: 1. Biographical sketches; 2. Accounts of history and geography; 3. Information on nature, science, industry and architecture; 4. Literary criticism, and 5. Miscellaneous items of curious, paradoxical, or provocative information.

The biographies and historical surveys include first and foremost great Americans, like Washington, Lincoln, Hamilton, and John Adams, and show the author's wide reading in this field. Geographical articles range widely: they may deal with a *Trip on the Ontario*, and be mainly based on personal experience, but may also treat of *Death of Hindoos on the Ganges*, or of *Laplandish Customs*, and the variation is just as wide in the other groups. Some information as to the works read by Hawthorne may be deduced from these titles. Pepy's *Diary* is mentioned in the article *Kissing A Queen*, and Mrs. Trollope's much-discussed work on contemporary American customs[3] is referred to in an article on *Wild Horsemen*. A French magazine, *Le magasin universel*, to which, says Hawthorne, "we are indebted for much useful and entertaining

---

[1] Cited from a copy in the Yale University Collection.
[2] Arlin Turner, *Hawthorne as Editor*, Louisiana, 1941, p. 8.
[3] Mrs. Trollope, *Domestic Manners of the Americans*, London, 1831.

matter" is mentioned together with Chaucer's *Canterbury Tales*
and Froissart's *Chronicles* in an article on *Fashions of Hats*.

When Hawthorne left the Magazine, in August 1836, he in-
formed his readers of the fact in a short editorial note, where he
also mentioned something about the limits set for his editorship,
whereby his "humble duty" had "consisted merely in preparing
the literary illustrations." He was weary of the work and glad to
leave it, and when offered a similar one later, politely refused it.
He continued his contributions to *The Token*, however, and, in
1837, the stories — chiefly at the instigation of Hawthorne's friend
Horatio Bridge — were collected and published under the title
Twice-told Tales. By this time, the author of *The Gentle Boy* was
known to the public, and his volume was warmly welcomed.

The most enthusiastic review was written by Longfellow, Hawthorne's former college mate, to whom he had sent the volume
with a rather shy note. The poet did not hesitate to characterize
the author of the work as a man of genius, and went on:

"As to the pure mind all things are pure, so to the poetic mind
all things are poetical. To such souls no age and no country can
be utterly dull and prosaic. They make unto themselves their age
and country . . ."[1]

A passage that must have delighted the many who hoped for the
birth of a truly American literary tradition, was this one:

"One of the most prominent characteristics of these tales is that
they are national in their character. The author has wisely chosen
his themes among the traditions of New England: the dusty legends
of 'the good Old Colony Times, when we lived under a king'. This
is the right material for story. It seems as natural to make tales out
of old tumble-down traditions, as canes and snuff-boxes out of
old steeples, or trees planted by great men. The puritanical times
begin to look romantic in the distance."[2]

Bertha Faust, in her work on Hawthorne's contemporaneous
reputation[3], rates this review of Longfellow's as the first effective
one bestowed on Hawthorne. It was followed by several others
in the same appreciative vein. Longfellow, a year later, visited

---

[1] *The North American Review*, July, 1837.
[2] *Ibid.*
[3] Bertha Faust, *Hawthorne's Contemporaneous Reputation*, Philadelphia, 1939.

Salem, and notes in his journal: "After dinner found Hawthorne at the Coffee House. Passed the afternoon with him; discussing literary matters. He is much of a lion here; sought after, fed, and expected to roar. A man of genius and fine imagination. He is destined to soar high."[1]

One of the readers to welcome and enjoy the *Twice-told Tales* and wanting to "lionize" Mr. Hawthorne was Miss Elizabeth Peabody, a friend of Emerson's and William Ellery Channing's. She was the daughter of a Salem doctor, and the family had been neighbours of the Hawthornes, though never suspecting Nathaniel of being a writer. Miss Peabody now succeeded in bringing about social relations between the two families, and it was not long before the young recluse had fallen deeply in love with Miss Elizabeth's younger sister, Sophia Peabody, and she with him.

Sophia Peabody was a semi-invalid, having suffered from severe headaches since childhood. In this way, however, she had time and leisure to cultivate her mind and artistic bents. She was a young lady after the heart of these Romantic times, frail and languid and fond of poetry and philosophy, speaking or reading French, German, Spanish, Latin and Greek, doing drawing, embroidery, and even sculpture. One entry in her diary, dated March 25th, 1838, reads:

"Rain and clouds. I read Degerando, Fénélon, St. Luke and Isaiah, Young, The Spectator, and Shakespeare's Comedy of Error, Taming of A Shrew, All's well that Ends Well, and Love's Labour Lost."[2]

The two were soon secretly engaged, with an understanding that the engagement should not be made public till Miss Sophia had become well enough to marry. The influence of her fiancé had already shown itself to be very beneficial to her health. Meanwhile, her sister Elizabeth had used her acquaintance with leading politicians to secure Hawthorne a post as a weigher and gauger in the Boston Custom House. Realizing the necessity of earning more money than the rather meagre income from his writings, and feeling also a need of contact with reality, Hawthorne moved

---

[1] Cited from the original journal of Henry W. Longfellow, through the courtesy of Mr. Henry Wadsworth Longfellow Dana, of Craigie House.

[2] Cited from Julian Hawthorne, *Nathaniel Hawthorne and His Wife*, Boston, 1886, p. 77.

with alacrity to Boston and began his existence as a government official. His letters to his fiancée from this time afford the picture not only of a singularly beautiful relationship, but also of the man himself and of his intellectual habits and occupations, a picture that had counterparts, during these twenties and thirties of the 19th century, in many lonely garrets where young, aspiring men in loose cravats and rather long hair meditated on life, love and literature. It is true that all of them had not spent twelve years in a loneliness as absolute and determined as the one experienced by the young weigher and gauger of the Boston Custom House. Neither had they imbibed the stern but morally invigorating religious atmosphere of New England. If he was not himself a church-goer, not even a believer in the old dogmas, Hawthorne still retained the moral outlook upon life inherited from his ancestors. A keen intellect and much reading had freed him from their prejudices and disposed him to analyze rather than moralize. He saw himself as their interpreter to the modern world, in America, and perhaps outside that continent. But in so seeing himself, all his scepticism, all his detachment, did not succeed in freeing him from the Romantic germs which filled the air around him. Could any picture of a Romanticist, drawn by himself, be more true to type than the letter he wrote, a couple of years later during a visit to Salem, to Sophia, to depict his own view of himself during this period of his life:

"Dearest, I have been out only once, in the day time, since my arrival. How immediately and irrevocably (if thou didst not keep me out of the abyss) should I relapse into the way of life in which I spent my youth! If it were not for my Dove, this present world would see no more of me forever. The sunshine would never fall on me, no more than on a ghost. Once in a while, people might discern my figure gliding stealthily through the dim evening — that would be all. I should be only a shadow of the night; it is thou that givest me reality, and makest all things real for me."[1]

The wildness and dissipation, dear to so many writers and poets of the Romantic school, is lacking in their New England colleague. As a boy at Bowdoin, Hawthorne had taken part in his comrades' drinking parties, and had even once been punished on that account. Later in life, he liked to take a drink with his friends

[1] Dated Sept. 3rd, 1841. Cited from the manuscript in the Huntington Library.

and even became something of a connoisseur of wines, a fact that often recurs in his notebooks. But he was temperate in that respect; and he indulged in no byronic love-adventures: Sophia could be absolutely certain of being the one woman in his life.

He had, indeed, but one passion more: that of becoming an author. The boyish dream had ripened into an adult's attitude towards life. And — typically enough — he saw his own aspirations as inspired by his beloved. His striving was to be done for her sake:

"Oh, beloved, if we had but a cottage somewhere . . . Then how happy I would be — and how good . . . And you should draw, and paint, and sculpture, and make music, and poetry too, and your husband would admire and criticize, and I, being pervaded with your spirit, would write beautifully and make myself famous for your sake, because perhaps you would like to have the world acknowledge me — but if the whole world glorified me with one voice, it would be a meed of little value in comparison with my wife's smile and kiss."[1]

Two years were spent in Boston. Then the opposite political party, the Whigs, came into power, and, according to American custom, Hawthorne had to leave his post. Casting round for an occupation, he soon chanced on an enticing project.

The Transcendental club, the nucleus of that first American cultural movement, Transcendentalism, had been formed at Boston. Hawthorne was not a member, but the club included several people he knew. The best known of them were Ralph Waldo Emerson; Bronson Alcott, preacher and reformer; the nature-loving poet Thoreau; the temperamental champion for women's rights, Margaret Fuller; Elizabeth Peabody, and George Ripley who was the founder of the phalanstery of Brook Farm.

Brook Farm was a social and literary experiment, chiefly planned after the lines drawn up by the French social philosopher Fourier, but adapted to American standards. The community living on the estate in West Roxbury purchased by Ripley, was to labour for its own bread during a certain part of the day, and use the rest of the time for literary or cultural pursuits. The enterprise was to be an illustration of the Wordsworthian "plain living and high thinking,"

---

[1] Dated Boston, Aug. 21st, 1839. Cited from the manuscript in the Huntington Library.

and though neither Emerson nor Margaret Fuller was a member of the community, its philosophy was closely related to Transcendentalism, and the Transcendentalist leaders often visited the farm. Margaret Fuller, for example, held a couple of her famous "conversations" there. Other evenings were devoted to the reading aloud of literary masterpieces such as the *Divine Comedy*.

Hawthorne had two aims in joining the community. He was eager to try an existence that would combine the open air life he loved so much with mental labours, and also to accomplish something physically useful while he continued with his literary work. His second plan was to acquire, by contributing his share to the common funds, a future home for himself and his bride. Possibly the thought of using this new and interesting subject for literary purposes also entered into his considerations. The first two of his hopes were not fulfilled. Like most of his friends and co-workers, he came to the conclusion that hard manual labour and creative intellectual work cannot be combined for long, and that even the most high-souled and idealistic community is open to frictions of diverse kinds. His reaction is freely expressed in one of his letters from the Farm dated August 12th, 1841:

"And — joyful thought — in a little more than a fortnight, thy husband will be free from his bondage — free to think of his Dove — free to enjoy nature — free to think and feel. I do think that a greater weight will then be removed from me, than when Christian's burden fell off at the foot of the cross. Even my Custom-House experience was not such a thraldom and weariness; my mind and heart were freer. Oh, belovedest, labor is the curse of the world, and nobody can meddle with it, without becoming proportionally brutified. Dost thou think it a praiseworthy matter that I have spent five golden months in providing food for cows and horses? Dearest, it is not so. Thank God, my soul is not utterly buried under a dung-heap. I shall yet retain it, somewhat defiled, to be sure, but not utterly unsusceptible of purification."[1]

Even if the dissociation with the brotherhood of Brook Farm meant an economic loss, Hawthorne was no doubt happy to leave the experience behind him. And so much the happier since he and his betrothed had finally decided to marry and to take the chance

---

[1] Cited from the manuscript in the Huntington Library.

of living by his pen. The marriage took place in July, 1842, and the couple went to live at Concord, in an old parsonage belonging to the Rev. Ezra Ripley and generally called "The Manse."

Concord was at the time a quiet little village, but writers and philosophers had already begun to gather there. Emerson lived there, and Alcott, and their friends from the Transcendentalist circle often visited them. Hawthorne and his wife, however, led a happy life in comparative seclusion, and did not associate overmuch with the Concord intellectuals. A letter written by Hawthorne to Margaret Fuller to ward off a visit of Ellery Channing and his newly-wedded bride arranged by the former energetic lady, is as courteously definite as beautifully turned, and gives an excellent picture of his attitude. One daughter, Una, was born at Concord.

Hawthorne began for the first time to feel established as an author. He kept a regular journal, and also continued to write short stories. Now, they were quickly published and brought in larger sums. He had, however, never been very fertile, and the financial status of the happy couple put an end in 1846 to their prolonged honeymoon at the Old Manse, that had given its name to a collection of stories written there.

The *Mosses from an Old Manse* were, like their predecessors, partly historical or romantic tales, partly essays or meditations. They gained a wide popularity which has lasted until recent times. Hawthorne was now a recognized author, even if not yet of the first rank. One of his critics, and the one whose verdict meant most and was most widely discussed, was Edgar Allan Poe: " . . . no American prose composition can compare with some of the articles, and none of them would do dishonor to the best of the British essayists."[1]

In October 1845, Hawthorne and his wife moved to Salem, to the old family house in Herbert Street, on the strength of the hope of a postmastership in that town. This project failed, but early in 1846, Hawthorne was nominated Surveyor of the Custom house at Salem, a post that enabled him to support his family.

The work was, however, of an exacting kind, and did not leave him much time over for writing. A collection of short stories —

---

[1] *Graham's Magazine*, April, 1842.

of which the chief inspiration was the old town of Salem — appeared in 1848 under the title *The Snow Image and Other Tales*. This was the only literary outcome of four years, apart from the growth in his mind of the central idea of *The Scarlet Letter* and its famous preface. The atmosphere of the little town, with its merchant and middle-class population still imbibed with stern Calvinistic ideas and with little appreciation of literature, was not friendly to the young author. Hawthorne had always been a recluse, and even from his youth he had declined the ouvertures of Salem society, perhaps partly owing to his financial situation. He still kept aloof, and never became a popular man in his native town. A political intrigue in 1849 resulted in ousting him from his position. This extreme action certainly caused the feelings of the little town to change in favour of Hawthorne, but he refused to accept any form of compensation, and withdrew from civil service, after having wholly cleared himself of all accusations as to his manner of discharging his official functions.

This was a crucial moment. But now, when the family appeared to be completely devoid of economic means, Sophia Hawthorne proved to be the ideal and resourceful artist's wife she had aspired to become. She proudly displayed a little fund of savings sufficient for the subsistence of the family that now consisted of four members — a son having been born in 1846 — during the time her husband would need to write the novel which she knew had begun to take form in his mind. In six months Hawthorne completed *The Scarlet Letter*, written first as a short story and later elaborated into a novel, on the advice of Hawthorne's lifelong friend and publisher, James T. Fields.

From the beginning, *The Scarlet Letter* was a great success. Here was at last a novel with an all-American theme, written in a spirit peculiar to one of its most characteristic provinces. New England exulted, and Hawthorne's position as one of its greatest interpreters was secured. Herman Melville wrote in *The Literary World* about "Hawthorne and his Mosses":

"Now I do not say that Nathaniel of Salem is a greater man than William of Avon, or as great. But the difference between the two men is by no means immeasurable. Not a very great deal more, and Nathaniel were verily William."

And about *Twice-Told Tales* and *The Scarlet Letter* the same critic averred that:

"there are things in those two books which, had they been written in England a century ago, Nathaniel Hawthorne had utterly displaced many of the bright names we now revere on authority."[1]

On the other hand, the boldness of the subject caused an ecclesiastical New England reviewer to term *The Scarlet Letter* "this brokerage of lust" and to attribute its "undercurrent of filth" to the influence of French authors like George Sand and Eugène Sue:

"Is the French era actually begun in our literature? And is the flesh, as well as the world and the devil, to be henceforth dished up in fashionable novels, and discussed at parties by spinsters and their beaux, with as unconcealed a relish as they give to the vanilla in their ice-cream?"[2]

On the other side of the Atlantic, H. F. Chorley, writing in *The Athenaeum*, though reacting strongly against what he termed the "painful" quality of Hawthorne's art, placed him with the best authors of America, if not of England:

"We rate him as among the most original and peculiar writers of American fiction. There is in his works a mixture of Puritan reserve and wild imagination, of passion and description, of the allegorical and the real, which some will fail to understand, and which others will positively reject — but which, to ourselves, is fascinating, and which entitles him to be placed on a level with Brockden Brown and the author of 'Rip van Winkle'."[3]

With this success, Hawthorne's way was clear. Four years of intense productivity and increasing reputation followed. In the spring of 1850, he moved with his family to Lenox, where he set to work on his next romance. The life led by the Hawthornes at Lenox, was as always quiet; their occasional guests were relatives or members of their small circle of friends. One new friendship of literary importance was, however, formed by Hawthorne during these years. Herman Melville lived not far from Lenox, and he occasionally came over to have long talks with Hawthorne.

During the first years of his marriage, Hawthorne had tried, aided by his wife, to master the German language, but had ap-

---

[1] *The Literary World*, August 24th, 1850.
[2] A. G. Coxe in *The Church Review*, Jan. 1851.
[3] *The Athenaeum*, June 15th, 1850.

58

parently never progressed very far. Sophia Peabody writes about these attempts in her journal:

"it seems to me he does not want to go on with German"[1],

but evidently he got as far as attempting to translate the pioneer poem of German ghost romance, Bürger's *Lenore*:

"After journalizing yesterday afternoon, I went out and sawed and split wood till teatime, then studied German (translating 'Lenore') with an occasional glance at a beautiful sunset... After lamplight finished 'Lenore'."[2]

Hawthorne's knowledge of German literature and the influence it may have exercised on him has been an object of reiterated discussion.[3] Contemporary criticism mentioned the possibility of such an influence, as for example the author in the *National Magazine* of 1853, who cursorily remarked: "Saving certain shadowy resemblances to some of the Germans ..." in an otherwise benevolent article. More serious was the criticism of *Mosses from an Old Manse* by E. A. Poe, where Hawthorne is deliberately accused of having imitated Tieck. The discussion especially of the resemblances between Hawthorne's *Feathertop*[4] and Tieck's *Die Vogelscheuche* has been vivid and prolonged. But Hawthorne did not learn German till 1843[5], and Tieck's story can hardly have reached foreign readers till 1842. Though the publication date of *Feathertop* is 1848, the first notion of the theme of the story appears in Hawthorne's notebooks as early as 1840.[6] Mr. A. Schönbach after a very thorough investigation, arrives at the conclusion

---

[1] *Sophia Peabody's Journal*, July—September, 1838. Quoted from J. Hawthorne, *Hawthorne and His Wife*, Boston 1886, p. 185.

[2] *The American Note-books*, April 8th, 1843.

[3] E. A. Poe, *Hawthorne's Tales*, Godey's Magazine and Lady's Book XXXV, 1847.

E. D. Forgues, *Nathaniel Hawthorne, La revue des deux mondes*, April 15th, 1852.

A. Schönbach, *Beiträge zur Charakteristik Nathaniel Hawthornes*, Englische Studien, 1884.

H. M. Belden, *Poe's Criticism of Hawthorne, Anglia*, 1900.

Walter Just, *Die romantische Bewegung in der amerikanischen Literatur: Brown, Poe, Hawthorne*, Weimar, 1910.

Randall Stewart, *Hawthorne's American Notebooks*, Yale, 1932.

Wilhelm Veen, *Die Erzählungstechnik in den Kurzerzählungen Nathaniel Hawthornes*, Münster, 1938.

[4] *Works* II, p. 253.

[5] Randall Stewart, *op. cit.*, p. 320.   [6] *Works* IX, p. 211.

"... wie Poe es glaubte, und seither mit Ausdauer nachge-schrieben wird, dass Tieck Hawthornes Muster gewesen und von ihm nachgebildet worden sei, das ist mir schon aus diesen inneren Gründen höchst unwahrscheinlich. In Tiecks Erzählungen sind Dargestelltes und Darsteller von derselben Stimmung erfüllt: wird das Reale an einer Stelle verlassen, dann aber sofort auch an allen und im Ganzen."

The House of the Seven Gables, Hawthorne's second great romance, appeared early in 1851, followed later in the same year by *The Wonderbook for Girls and Boys*, a series of adaptations of classical and historical myths and tales, as well as a new collection of short stories, *The Snow Image and Other Tales*.

The House of the Seven Gables was rated by Hawthorne himself[1] and by many reviewers as a higher accomplishment than *The Scarlet Letter*. Duyckinck wrote in *The Literary World*:

"Verily this Hawthorne retains in him streaks of a Puritan an-cestry. Some grave beater of pulpit cushions must be among his ancestry; for of all laymen he will preach to you the closest sermons, probe deepest into the inestimable corruption, carry his lantern ... into the most secret recesses of the heart."[2]

And when *The Blithedale Romance* followed, in 1852, the eminent critic E. Whipple wrote in *Graham's Magazine*:

"The 'Blithedale Romance' just published, seems to us the most perfect in the execution of any of Hawthorne's works, and as a work apart, hardly equalled by anything else which the country has produced."[3]

The enthusiasm provoked by both romances was due in part to their American character. *The House of the Seven Gables* took its theme from a family life which in its seclusion bears ressem-blance to the existence led by the inmates of the house in Herbert Street at Salem, and a family history that has features in common with that of the Hawthornes. *The Blithedale Romance* brought to mind the literary colony at Brook Farm. But the real merit of these

---

[1] Letter to Pike, July, 1850: "At any rate it has sold finely, and seems to have pleased a good many people better than the other; and I must confess that I myself am among the number ..." Cited from a copy in the Yale Uni-versity Collection.

[2] *The Literary World*, April 26th, 1851.

[3] *Graham's Magazine*, Sept., 1852.

works was not in their depiction of American scenes, though these no doubt endeared them to the hearts of American readers. They bore the same stamp of true art as *The Scarlet Letter*, in composition, in style, and in the original treatment of human psychology. European readers saw the new author in a somewhat different light. In his very appreciative review of *The House of the Seves Gables*, E. D. Forgues mentioned reminiscences from "Walter Scott, Lewis, Mme Radcliffe et Washington Irving, sans parler de Maturin, de Hoffmann et de bien d'autres encore . . ."[1] Another French critic, writing in the same publication, put his finger on the trait that separated Hawthorne from contemporary European writers. Emile Montégut mentions Hawthorne's dependence of his Puritan ancestry:

". . . il n'a plus leur *âme*, mais il a leur *esprit*, il a leur ferme méthode de stricte investigation et d'impitoyable analyse. Un descendant des puritains seul pouvait être capable de se livrer à ce perpétuel examen de conscience que nous trouvons dans les écrits de M. Hawthorne, à cette confession silencieuse et muette des erreurs de l'esprit; lui seul était capable d'entreprendre ces fouillis dans l'âme humaine pour y découvrir non des trésors, mais des sujets d'épouvante, des reptiles engourdis, des témoignages de crimes oubliés . . ."[2]

Before *The Blithedale Romance* was written, the Hawthornes had, in 1851, moved to West Newton, a rather dreary little suburb of Boston. Early in the following year, Hawthorne acquired a house of his own in Concord, "The Wayside," bought from Bronson Alcott. His first work there, undertaken after due reflection, was a biography of his old college friend, Franklin Pierce, who ran as a Democrat for the presidential election of that year. The task lay outside Hawthorne's proper domain, and was of a rather delicate nature, Pierce being a Democrat, and a pro-slavery man. Friendship however prevailed, and the work was accomplished. When Pierce was elected, he had to overcome some reluctance on Hawthorne's part to make him accept the reward customary in American politics of the time. Early in 1853, however, Hawthorne was persuaded to acknowledge his appointment as American Consul in Liverpool; and in July the same year, he sailed for England.

---

[1] *La Revue des deux mondes*, April 15th, 1852.

[2] *Ibid.*, Dec. 1st, 1852.

Hawthorne's years in England are better recorded than any other part of his life in those notebooks which were later published, after slight revision, under the title *Our Old Home*. From this period we also possess information of other kinds. Hawthorne's correspondence with his publisher, George Ticknor, is preserved complete and has been printed. Many Englishmen have given written accounts of their impressions of the literary American consul, and many Americans have witnessed to his zeal and helpfulness as the official representative of his country. Though very conscious of the antagonism existing between the United States and their mother country, Hawthorne had been, from his first childhood, too strongly attached to the "Old Home" by ancestry, and by literary and cultural bonds, not to have a strong feeling for it. As an exponent of the warring sentiments of a cultured American of that day, he is unequalled. The new edition of his English notebooks[1], where the alterations made by himself for the *Our Old Home* issue, and later on by his wife for the first posthumous printing of the notebooks, have been as far as possible restored, is one of the most important and interesting documents of American cultural history. They describe not only the American political and psychological attitude of the period, but also give a picture of England, seen with the eyes of a foreigner with all the advantages of freshness of impressions, as well as of thorough familiarity with the English language, traditions and literature.

English literature was, as we have mentioned, during colonial times and afterwards, regarded as the foundation of American literature, and Hawthorne's familiarity with it added a specific value to his English experiences. His work as a consul did not give him much leisure to read, but his travels evoked echoes of past literary joys. As regards living contemporary authors, Hawthorne was well acquainted with the work of some of them, but his shyness prevented him from trying to get into personal contact with them. Leigh Hunt, whom he greatly admired, he met and liked, but he never became acquainted with Thackeray or Dickens. Although he received an invitation from the daughters of Thomas De Quincey, whose *Opium Eater* belonged to Hawthorne's most cherished reading, he never met the author.

---

[1] *Hawthorne's English Notebooks*. Edited by Randall Stewart, New York, 1941.

An episode during Hawthorne's stay in England which deserves
mentioning was his collaboration with Miss Delia Bacon, the ardent
champion of the theory that Shakespeare's plays should be attributed to Sir Francis Bacon. He helped her to have her work printed
in America, and wrote a biographical sketch of the characterful
lady under the title *Recollections of a Gifted Woman*.[1]

With political changes, Hawthorne's consular appointment
came to an end in 1857, and the year 1858 saw the realization of an
old dream. With his family, Hawthorne undertook a trip across
France, to spend a year or more in Italy.

Italy was known to Hawthorne, theoretically, as the home of
Antiquity, as the scene of the tales told by his beloved classical
Roman authors, but also as the home of Machiavelli, and the
country where the villains of Horace Walpole and Mrs. Radcliffe
were engendered. His approach to the country was one of mingled
admiration and suspicion, and his actual experiences justified his
expectations. He continued to keep his journals. The entries from
the journeys through France and back, with an occasional trip to
Switzerland, give some interesting glimpses of his reactions: comparisons with America, souvenirs from his reading of Rousseau, of
French history. Rome proved a disillusion to him at first, but later
captivated his imagination. An old Italian castle outside Florence
became his home for a couple of months, when he began work on
what was to be his great Italian romance, *The Marble Faun*.

It may with tolerably great certainty be said that Hawthorne
read less and less, as life went on. In Italy, he seems to have made
little effort to acquaint himself with its literary culture, but he
showed all the more interest in its art. His friends were mostly
artists, painters and sculptors. In Florence, he came to know the
Brownings; but in Rome, his most intimate friends were an American sculptor, William Story, and his artist colleagues. Hawthorne's
notebooks are full of observations on art and philosophical remarks
on artists and their work — a sphere of life that had always highly
interested him. However, during several months, his view of life
was darkened through the illness of his daughter Una.

The former young Romantic author who had aspired to become
a painter of American life, was at fifty-five years of age engaged in

[1] *Works* VII, p. 113.

writing an Italian romance. His approach to life had always been pessimistic and sceptical and he felt that he had not succeeded in endowing the American scene with the glowing romance that his European colleagues had given to their works. Underestimating his own contribution — the deep probing of a national character, new to the literature of the world — he attempted a task entirely alien to his own temperament and abilities. And such was still the hold of Romanticism and Gothicism, that he himself believed to have succeeded, when, on his return to England, he finished *The Marble Faun* Its reception in England, where it was first published, was lukewarm. In America, it has been more appreciated, even up to modern times.

In June 1859, Hawthorne had left Italy for England, where he lived for some time at Bath, completing his romance. After its publication, he sailed, in the summer of 1860, for America, and settled at the Wayside in Concord. The remaining years of his life were obscured by the political struggles of his country, and by a growing sense of difficulty in attacking literary work. Hawthorne completed the editing of his English notebooks which appeared in 1863 under the title *Our Old Home,* causing some stir owing to certain criticisms of England and English life. But the fifth great romance that he had planned never received its final form. There are four posthumous fragments of attempts to tell the story of an American descendant of an English family and his return to the old country, all wrapped up in legends of bloody footsteps, of sealed caskets, secret chambers, and elixirs of long life. Physically, Hawthorne became weaker and weaker and, in May 1864, he died while away from home on a tour with his old friend George Ticknor. He was buried in Concord with all the honours due to the first great New England romancer.

HAWTHORNE: THE MAN AND THE WORK

In a preface to the second edition of the *Twice-Told Tales* which appeared in 1851, the author declared that he might justly feel ashamed if he could not "after so many sober years ... criticise his own work as fairly as another man's." This he proceeded to do though it would seem, as a critic has noted, that it could hardly be profitable either for him or for his publisher, in view of the fact that he was rather inclined to understatement than the reverse when judging himself. As it stands, we owe a debt to the publisher as well as to the author for the fact that the preface was printed. It is the earliest of the rather few direct self-confessions we have from Hawthorne's pen, and its evidence stresses the fact that any student of his work must soon see: that the only way to know this author, so reticent about himself, leading such an uneventful life, is through his work. To the bulk of it the same words apply as Hawthorne utters about his first tales: "They are ... attempts ... to open an intercourse with the world."

By character, inheritance, and environment, Hawthorne was a recluse. The contrast between his yearning for solitude, and his equally strong impulse to be publicly acknowledged as a literary man, constitute one of the tensions from which his work derives. It would be unfair to use the word vanity to characterize his firm conviction that he belonged to the few chosen to interpret to the world the spirit of his country. Though he developed a searching selfcritical attitude towards this "pride," as he termed it, he was aware of his powers without overestimating them; he also knew that he lacked most other qualifications that might have paved the way for him to the American Parnassus: money, influential connections, enterprise. The frustration connected with his modest beginnings, his isolation, and the sparse recognition he received find an expression in the very first, frequently quoted paragraph of the preface referred to above:

"The Author of 'Twice-Told Tales' has a claim to one distinction which, as none of his literary brethren will care about disputing it with him, he need not be afraid to mention. He was, for a good many years, the obscurest man of letters in America."[1]

This sense of frustration doubtless goes far to explain the perseverance with which the ambitious recluse continued on his way towards an ever increasing mastery of his means of expression, a wider knowledge of history, literature, and contemporary human conditions, a deeper insight into the life and laws of the soul.

One of the foremost characteristics of the recluse is an inveterate shyness. Contemporary evidence agrees in stressing this feature in Hawthorne's character. Few persons ever came into close inner contact with him. He formed some friendships at college, among which the lifelong tie which united him with Horatio Bridge — a marine officer and author of a book of travel, *An African Cruise*, to which Hawthorne wrote a foreword — was the most intimate. Most of Hawthorne's friends belonged, like Bridge, to active life, viz. William B. Pike, a businessman, or Franklin Pierce, the President, and he always kept his predilection for the haunts of plain and everyday people, as testified by Caroline Ticknor, the daughter of Hawthorne's publisher and near friend, George Ticknor of Boston. She says in her memories of Hawthorne:

"That he could reach, pounce upon, and draw wisdom from beneath commonplace exteriors and everyday doings, was the explanation of many things which the casual thought strange or unbecoming. His reluctance to participate in the elegant hospitality pressed upon him was derived from no taste for ignoble company, but because at the Old Province House Tavern of Master Waite, he could see and feel, beyond the common men who came to wet their clay in its bar-room, its true ghosts that still qualified the atmosphere of its chambers and stairways, while in the long dining-room of the Bromfield House, where sturdy Crockett stood and carved for his oldfashioned table d'hôte, were to be met stout and shrewd Boston men, through whom were to be traced back, for record and use, traits of person, demeanor and character, which no fine social gathering could have supplied him ... He liked best to be taken to such plain miscellaneous hotels as the Astor or

---

[1] *Works* I, p. 13.

Bixby's, to be entered anonymously as 'a friend' of his companion, to carry no money, to know nothing of the details of the journey, to make only chance acquaintances whom he could anatomize, but who could have no clue to him, and to be brought back home as mutely as he had been taken away."[1]

Hawthorne also cherished this kind of acquaintanceship on the long excursions which he was wont to make every year, and which have been described in some of his tales such as *The Seven Vagabonds*, *Sketches from Memory*, or *Passages from a Relinquished Work*, of which the last-mentioned was intended to link together the stories in a collection, pretending that they were told by two wayfarers.

But Hawthorne also had friends and acquaintances of a definitely intellectual order. At college, he associated with Longfellow, though the poet never belonged to the circle of his intimate friends. He was on friendly terms with his first publisher, Samuel Goodrich, and a close friend of George Ticknor, as is evident from the work by the latter's daughter already mentioned. During the Brook Farm episode, he came into contact with the leading intellectual and literary men and women of his time, and later, in Concord, he associated with Emerson, Ripley, Channing, and Alcott. Hawthorne, however, never belonged to any group. His attitude towards the Transcendentalists was detached and critical, and the social experiment at Brook Farm was sooner rejected by him than by the other participants. The American author who came closest to him was Melville who lived in the vicinity of Lenox, when the Hawthornes stayed there. It is a great loss to the literary historian that the correspondence between the two authors and visionaries was lost or destroyed at an early date. But there are proofs enough of their close and friendly relations and sympathy — apart from the statements each made in public of mutual appreciation and understanding — to enable us to proclaim Melville as the literary friend who personally meant most to Nathaniel Hawthorne.

Edgar Allan Poe, who is doubtless the American of his generation best known in Europe, and in his work treats much the same kind of subjects as Hawthorne, was no personal acquaintance of Haw-

---

[1] Caroline Ticknor, *Hawthorne and his Publisher*, Boston & New York, 1913, p. 8.

thorne's. At first sight it may seem likely that both authors influenced each other, and Poe even suggested something of the kind in a critical article on Hawthorne's Tales written in 1842.[1] But a closer knowledge of the work of both will show that though they were under the spell of the same trends in thought and literature, their manner of treating their subjects is different, owing to social and temperamental dissimilarities. In Hawthorne, there was nothing of Poe's morbidity; in Poe, nothing of Hawthorne's sternness. Their separate developments make an interesting study of parallels, but the two lines rarely meet.

During his English sojourn, Hawthorne — as we have seen — made few literary friendships, both because he was burdened with consular work, and because of his invincible shyness. In Italy, his best friends were not authors, but other artists. He became rather intimate with the sculptor William Story, whose work and ideas we glimpse in *The Marble Faun*.

The human relationship of really decisive importance to Hawthorne was his engagement and marriage to Sophia Peabody. Through her he managed, at last, to approach the surrounding world. His letters to her tell us as much as can be told by a man who — constitutionally and by upbringing and milieu — was as reticent as Hawthorne. As material for psychological studies or research concerning literary sources the notebooks are no more illuminating than his printed works. Hawthorne's diaries were to him no outlet for personal reactions or sentiments. They were simply records of events, encounters or scenes that might later on be wrought into stories. They have great interest for the student of his methods of work: his ideas may be traced, as those of few other writers, from the very germ to their full development. But Hawthorne did not — or at least very rarely — like Emerson or the Goncourts, write down anything about his own inner life or the forces that worked on it, about literature, philosophy or religion. The reader is left to make his own inferences.

We have mentioned the review by a contemporary French critic, E. Montégut, who considered that Hawthorne's analytical powers were typical of a descendant of the Puritans.[2] The French perspicacity in admiring the eerie dexterity shown by Hawthorne in

---

[1] *Graham's Magazine*, May, 1842.
[2] Cp. p. 60 of the present work.

unravelling the threads of the unconscious or repressed processes in the souls of men and women points to one of the factors in Hawthorne's analytical equipment. There was the Puritan strain, the methodical and severe examination of the conscience that belonged to the spiritual régime of the Calvinist dissenters; but there was, also, a detached, sceptical and alert psychological interest of the kind that characterized French thinkers such as Montaigne and Voltaire. Shakespeare's intuitional character-probing has sometimes been mentioned when discussing Hawthorne.[1] To the present writer, the affinity with Montaigne appears much closer. To return to the preface to the *Twice-Told Tales*, this self-confession contains some lines which express, in an succinct form, the very ideal of that French philosopher's writing:

"The sketches are not, it is hardly necessary to say, profound; but it is rather more remarkable that they seldom, if ever, show any design on the writer's part to make them so. They have none of the abstruseness of idea, or obscurity of expression, which mark the written communication of a solitary mind with itself. They never need translation. It is, in fact, the style of a man of society. Every sentence, so far as it embodies thought or sensibility, may be understood and felt by anybody who will give himself the trouble to read it, and will take up the book in a proper mood."[2]

This passage is not so easily endorsed by a more superficial reader. There is little of the man of society in the narrator of the tales from the early Puritan days in New England, or the interpreter of the *Rill from the Town Pump* in the small-town America of those days. But the expression affords a key to the aims of this author who was, by cultural standards, a man of the world, and a representative of literary society of prime importance. From his ancestors he had inherited a keen religious sense. Even if Hawthorne never belonged to any church organization, he retained throughout his life a true veneration for the Christian tradition. To this view of life belonged his interest, which sometimes seemed to amount to an *idée fixe*, in exploring the depths of human conscience.

---

[1] *e.g.* by Herman Melville. Cp. above p. 56. See also Julian Hawthorne, *Problems of the Scarlet Letter*, The Atlantic Monthly, April, 1886, J. V. Cheyney, *The Golden Guess*, Boston, 1892, p. 281, and H. S. Canby, *Classic Americans*, New York, 1931, p. 247.

[2] *Works* I, p. 17.

For his methods, he was deeply indebted to the French authors —
as was, in a measure, Calvin too — with their acute psychological
sense, their ever questioning scepticism, and unbiassed searching
for truth. This was a feature which definitely separated Hawthorne
from his Transcendentalist colleagues who were caught in the
nets of thought woven at Koenigsberg and Craigenputtock.

Emerson was an admirer of Montaigne, to whom he devoted
the chapter in his *Representative Men*, entitled *The Sceptic*. He
had read his works — curiously enough with the exception of the
Apologie de Raimond Sebond where Montaigne's scepticism reaches
its most poignant expression[1] — and he tried to interpret him, as
he interpreted other philosophers to his countrymen. But when
he had to accept or decline the sceptical attitude, Emerson made
a stand against the ideal of Montaigne, and his final resolve was to
reject the way of thinking for which the French author stands.

Hawthorne, on the other hand, never discussed the subject of
sceptical philosophy. He imbued it early in life, and made it one
with himself. He became, not an unbeliever, but a severe judge,
the kind of "candid thinker" of which Emerson speaks in his essay
on *The Sceptic*. One of the characteristics of Hawthorne is the
very emblem of the true sceptic: the suspended judgment, the
ataraxia of the Greek thinkers, signifying that truth is not yet
attained but must still be sought. Even this attitude, the device of
leaving two or more issues open for the reader at the end of a tale,
or an essay on a moral subject, is one of the features most typical
of Hawthorne's manner of writing.

A direct proof of Hawthorne's early and intimate knowledge of
Montaigne is given in a letter to Miss Delia Bacon, who had
submitted a work for his verdict. In this letter he also expresses
his views on the mutual influences of writers, and the conscious or
unconscious impressions that may be given or received. In writing
this, Hawthorne had foremost in his mind the relations between
Shakespeare (or Bacon) and Montaigne, but it is not impossible
that he was also thinking of himself in the same connotation:

"You seem to me to have read Bacon and Montaigne more pro-
foundly than anybody else has read them. It is very long (it was
in my early youth, indeed) since I used to read and re-read Mon-

[1] See C. L. Young, *Emerson's Montaigne*, New York, 1941.

taigne; and in order to do any justice to your views I ought to re-
peruse him now — and Bacon also — and Shakespeare too . . .
We find thoughts in all great writers (and even in small ones) that
strike their roots far beneath the surface, and intertwine themselves
with the roots of other writers 'thoughts; so that when we pull up
one, we stir the whole, and yet those writers have had no conscious society with one another. I express this very shabbily, but
you will think it for me better than I can say it."[1]

Hawthorne's critical attitude toward Emerson and his brethren
in the domain of thought has found several, and very clear expres-
sions, notably in the passage in his foreword to *Mosses from an Old
Manse*, where he speaks of those "strange moral shapes of men"
that were attracted to Concord by the "widespread influence of
a great original thinker":

"People that had lighted on a new thought, or a thought that
they fancied new, came to Emerson as the finder of a glittering
gem hastens to a lapidary, to ascertain its quality and value. Uncertain, troubled, earnest wanderers through the midnight of the
moral world beheld his intellectual fire as a beacon on a hill-top,
and climbing the difficult ascent, looked forth into the surrounding
obscurity more hopefully than hitherto. The light revealed objects
unseen before — mountains, gleaming lakes, glimpses of a creation
among the chaos; but also, as was unavoidable, it attracted bats
and owls and the whole host of night birds, which flapped their
dusky wings against the gazer's eyes, and sometimes were mistaken
for fowls of angelic feather. Such delusions always hover nigh
wherever a beacon fire of truth is kindled."[2]

In the paraphrase of *Pilgrim's Progress*, called *The Celestial
Railroad*, we find this significant description of Giant Transcendentalist:

" . . . into their deserted cave another terrible giant has thrust
himself, and makes it his business to seize upon honest travellers
and fatten them for his table with plentiful of smoke, mist, moonshine, raw potatoes, and sawdust. He is a German by birth, and
is called Giant Transcendentalist; but as to his form, his features,
his substance, and his nature generally it is the chief peculiarity

---

[1] Letter to Miss Delia Bacon, dated June 21st, 1856. Cited from a copy in
the Yale University Collection.
[2] *Works* II, pp. 41—42.

of this huge miscreant that neither he for himself, nor anybody for him, has ever been able to describe them. As we rushed by the cavern's mouth we caught a hasty glimpse of him, looking somewhat like an ill-proportioned figure, but considerably more like a heap of fog and duskiness. He shouted after us, but in so strange a phraseology that we knew not what he meant, nor whether to be encouraged or affrighted."[1]

On the other hand, we may truly say that Hawthorne, as well as Melville, treated subjects of a transcendental kind: truths, and morals, beyond the everyday appearance of things. The inner happenings in the soul of man were the subjects common to both authors, and the outward appearances were but what Melville termed "pasteboard masks." But this very personal intensification of the transcendental current of thought rather removed than approached them to men of the stamp of Bronson Alcott.

During his not too successful sojourn at Brook Farm, Hawthorne had practical proof of the social philosophy of the Transcendentalists. It was not much to his taste. Neither was he an admirer of its theory. His wife tells us of his reading Fourier in a letter to her mother, April 6th, 1845:

"It was not a translation of Fourier that I read, but the original text — the fourth volume; and though it was so abominable, immoral, irreligious, and void of all delicate sentiment, yet George Bradshaw says it is not so bad as other volumes . . . My Husband read the whole volume and was thoroughly disgusted."[2]

Thus, Hawthorne stands alone, spiritually as well as socially, among the intellectuals of his country. In his methods of composition, too, he differed widely from his American contemporaries. The bulk of his work is conspicuously small. But it contains specimens of perfect workmanship. From the beginning his style was limpid and pure, but he was never satisfied till his work was chiselled and polished in every detail. And the subjects of his stories were as conscientiously worked out with regard to psychological and realistic detail. His sense of allegory which has been investigated by so many authors with so various results, was not only the love of allegory which belonged to Romanticism and appeared in so many

---

[1] *Works* II, p. 224.
[2] Cited from a copy in the Yale University Collection.

contemporary novels and stories of European authors. It was more
than a technical device, it was an ingrained craving. W. C. Brownell,
the American arbiter of the last decade of the 19th century,
described him as allegory-mad. In our days, F. O. Matthiessen
has interpreted this love of allegory as a characteristic of the New
England mind which is obviously linked to later authors like Henry
James and T. S. Eliot. The background of Hawthorne's allegory
is, in Mr. Matthiessen's opinion, common to all American art of
the time:

"No art that sprang from American roots in this period could
fail to show the marks of abstraction . . . The tendency of American
idealism to see a spiritual significance in every natural fact was far
more broadly diffused than transcendentalism. Loosely Platonic,
it came specifically from the common background that lay behind
Emerson and Hawthorne, from the Christian habit of mind that
saw the hand of God in all manifestations of life, and which, in the
intensity of the New England seventeenth century, had gone to the
extreme of finding 'remarkable providences' even in the smallest
phenomena, tokens of divine displeasure in every capsized dory
or runaway cow."[1]

Matthiessen separates allegory and symbolism, using the generally
accepted distinction that "symbolism expresses a mysterious connection between two ideas, allegory gives a visible form to the conception of such a connection,"[2] and in his following discussion
points to Melville as the carrier of symbolism, while Hawthorne
stands for allegory. Newton Arvin, in his preface to his collection
of Hawthorne's Tales[3], notes that Hawthorne might be regarded as
a precursor to the symbolists, had he been known in France at their
time, but that he really occupies a place mid-way between the two, a
region all of his own. Leaving these problems that belong to a
later period than that of Hawthorne and Melville themselves, we
may use the term allegory of Hawthorne's parables and symbols,
the main tools in his artistic equipment.

The Christian frame of mind was, however, not the only source
of Hawthorne's allegorical bent. Much of it derived from the
Romantic currents that pervaded the literary atmosphere around

[1] F. O. Matthiessen, *American Renaissance*, New York, 1941, p. 243.

[2] *Ibid.*, p. 249.

[3] Newton, Arvin, *Hawthorne's Tales*, New York, 1946.

him. Allegory was one of the Romanticists' most cherished means of expression, used by Coleridge and Leigh Hunt in England, Tieck and Fouqué in Germany, as well as by Musset and Hugo in France. Part of Hawthorne's predilection for symbols was, too, the natural outcome of a delicacy of feeling that was one of the contributing causes of his personal shyness, and which appeared, moreover, in his relation to the figures he created in his books. He expects much from his reader in the way of understanding mere suggestions, in the art of studying fictive beings as he would study personal acquaintances in real life, and still regard them as personifications of ideas. To a critic who had mentioned the shadowy character of the plot in *The Marble Faun*, Hawthorne writes: "As for what you say of the plot I do not agree that it has been left in an imperfect state. The characters of the story come out of an obscurity and vanish into it again, like the figures on the slide of a magic lantern; but, in their transit, they have served my purpose, and shown all that it was essential for them to reveal. Anything further, if you consider it rightly, would be an impertinence on the author's part towards the reader."[1]

He also derived much of his allegorical bent from his early reading of Spenser, Milton, and Bunyan. In discussing these influences which have been treated in detail by several authors, Matthiessen joins hands, over the intervening century, with the literary men of America of the eighteen-forties, in regretting, on his literary countrymen's part, "the scantiness of material and atmosphere," the "lack of plastic experience." Speaking of Hawthorne's avowed liking for realistic writers like Anthony Trollope[2], Mathiessen

---

[1] Letter to Henry Bright, dated Brunswick Court, April 4th, 1860. Cited from a copy in the Yale University Collection.

[2] On February 11th, 1860, Hawthorne wrote to Fields: "It is odd enough that my own individual taste is for quite another class of novels than those which I myself am able to write . . . Have you ever read the novels of Anthony Trollope? They precisely suit my taste; solid and substantial, written on the strength of beef and the inspiration of ale, and just as real as if some giant had hewn a great lump out of the earth." (Cited from a copy in the Yale University Collection.)

That Hawthorne was not the only one of the great contemporary novel-writers to be impressed by the work of the popular Englishman is shown by an entry in Tolstoy's diary during his writing *War and Peace*: "Trollope kills me by his mastery . . . I console myself that he has his and I have mine." On

74

finds the reason for his inability to emulate the European patterns of realism in the fact that

"with all the feverish activity of America around him, there was not the social solidity that Fielding knew, or the manifold gradations between classes that Balzac could analyze."[1] [2]

Mr. Granville Hicks, on the other hand, finds the fault not in the American social scene of the time, but in what he calls the author's inability to come to terms with his generation:

". . . between his art and his deepest interests on the one hand, and these vivid scenes and active lives on the other, his imagination could establish no effective contact."[3]

Mr. Hicks' verdict is that

"when he was a representative American, he was not an artist; when he was an artist, he was not a representative American."

Mr. Sargent Hall holds an entirely opposite view. In his recent work[4], he joins Mr. Matthiessen and Mr. Hicks in considering Hawthorne's melancholy to be a result of the maladjustment of the individual to the behaviour pattern regulating his relations with his fellow individuals, but he views even this as a representative feature of the America of his day. An American tragedy like Hawthorne's, says Mr. Hall, discussing *The Scarlet Letter*, could have come from none but a democratic writer, and "at the present time it represents about the most satisfactory expression in art of the

the other hand, Trollope was deeply impressed by Hawthorne: "He will have plunged you into melancholy, he will have overshadowed you with imaginary sorrows; but he will have enabled you to feel yourself an inch taller during the process. Something of the sublimity of the transcendent, something of the mystery of the unfathomable, something of the brightness of the celestial, will have attached itself to you, and you will all but think that you too might live to be sublime, and revel in mingled light and mystery." (A. Trollope, *The Genius of Hawthorne*, *The North American Review*, Sept., 1879.)

[1] F. O. Matthiessen, *American Renaissance*, New York, 1941, p. 235.

[2] To such a view might be opposed Herbert Read's comment (in *The Sense of Glory*, Cambridge (England), 1929, p. 165) on Henry James' Hawthorne biography, that "a province, though it lacks many of the positive virtues of a metropolis, has some rather negative virtues of its own." Read points to the achievements of English provincial authors, contemporary to Hawthorne, like the Brontës or Wordsworth.

[3] Granville Hicks, *The Great Tradition*, New York, 1935, p. 6.

[4] Lawrence Sargent Hall, *Hawthorne Critic of Society*, New Haven, 1944.

basic morality of democratic life." Besides Hawthorne's candid and at the same time imaginative probing into the depths of contemporary American life, Whitman, to Mr. Hall, seems picturesque, Emerson visionary, and Thoreau crabbed. To him, Hawthorne's romances are not so much romantic tales as social documents. *The Scarlet Letter* is the story of the isolation of the human heart, but Dimmesdale's isolation depends not on crime against human nature and a personal love-conflict, but on the sense of the growing rift between him and society. Dimmesdale is lost because he has rejected the true relationship to society, whereas Hester is saved because she made no secret of her sin. Donatello in *The Marble Faun* is, to Mr. Sargent Hall, "the product of American social thought during an era which was trying to determine, as Whitman put it, how much liberty men were able to bear." Hawthorne's conception that ideal democracy should comprise no state supervision is, in Mr. Sargent Hall's opinion, the reality behind the allegory that no policemen were dogging the steps of Donatello. Mr. Sargent Hall stresses the practical vein in Hawthorne, his strong sense of duty when working in the U. S. Customs service or during his consulship at Liverpool, his conscientiousness in money matters. After his venture in Transcendental idealism, Hawthorne would, according to this author, have subscribed, in a measure, to the doctrine of opportunism in practical life, and his acceptance of the consulship would represent a candid adoption of the practice and doctrine of utilitarianism.

Mr. Sargent Hall's analysis is acute and extremely interesting as showing Nathaniel Hawthorne mainly from a sociologist's point of view. There is no denying that some of Hawthorne's works — the biography of Pierce, and *Our Old Home* — may be regarded as social documents, the one perhaps with a bias of opportunism, both with political aims. The Pierce biography, which stands in direct opposition to the liberal ways of thought of the Brook Farm group, is taken by another critic, Mr. Newton Arvin, as a typical example of Hawthorne's manner of isolating himself, of the attitude that "kept him from orienting himself humanly and, so to say, socially; from expanding on all sides as a personality, and multiply his fruitful contacts with reality."[1] To Mr. Arvin, Hawthorne's

---

[1] Newton Arvin, *Hawthorne*, Boston, 1929, p. 177.

isolation is the core of his "pride." Hawthorne's intense experience
of loneliness has, according to this writer, made him aware of the
close connection between secrecy and guilt, and his tales and novels
are a dramatization of his social and psychological reactions, which
led to a final disunion and fragmentation, as shown in his latest
work.

To the present writer, there is no doubt that Hawthorne himself considered literature to be a far more important element in
life than politics, or even his private finances or social standing.
In spite of later experiences, there always remained in him something of that conviction which found an early expression in a letter
to his fiancée of May 4th, 1891: "I want nothing to do with politicians — they are not men; they cease to be men in becoming
politicians. Their hearts wither away and die out of their bodies.
Their consciences are turned to India-rubber — or to some substance as black as that, and which will stretch as much."[1]

In accordance with this attitude, which Hawthorne shared with
many of his distant Romantic brethren on the other side of the
Atlantic, is his later judgment of organized reform as personified in
Hollingsworth in the *Blithedale Romance*. His candid personal
attitude to the consulship in Liverpool must at least sometimes
have been such as is shown in a letter to George Ticknor written
in July, 1855, during a vacation trip to Lake Windermere:

"Well, I am sick of America, and feel it a relief to escape all knowledge of its affairs, for a week or two; for I have been more bothered
with my own countrymen and their troublesome peculiarities,
since coming to England, than ever before in my life. I shall need
a residence of two or three years on the Continent, to give me a
sense of freedom."[2]

And his notebook contains, on January 3rd, 1858, this eloquent
exclamation:

"Thank Heaven, I am a sovereign again, and no longer a
servant."[3]

According to such evidence as this, Hawthorne's main purpose
in life was hardly to become a social servant of his country, not

[1] Letter to Sophia, dated 15.3. 1840. Cited from the manuscript in the Huntington Library.
[2] Cited from a copy in the Yale University Collection.
[3] *Works* VIII, p. 601.

even a valuable member of his own family, but to serve his people and Humanity by becoming an American "Artist of the Beautiful."[1] He *was* a good social servant, and an ideal husband and father, but he always reproached himself for nurturing in his heart of hearts another and stronger ambition, for being, in the circle of colleagues, among his own kin, always an "Ambitious Guest."[2] His fiction was not intended to be a political message. It was the outcome of his moral philosophy and artistic inspiration. He might have subscribed to Emerson's lines about the writer who "lent his hand to the Great spirit that over him planned." But, unlike Emerson, he did not content himself with suffering the spirit to direct him, he was greatly concerned with controlling the artistic quality of his work. Hawthorne's writings are never rhapsodical outbursts of the moment, never immediately enthusiastic or indignant. They are the mellow fruit of long cogitation and careful work. To Hawthorne himself, one of their most important qualities was that they were original — the work of a selfdependent American writer. In this fact may be found an explanation of Hawthorne's reluctance to make literary acquaintances both in America and Europe, and also of his aversion from even mentioning his reading or making any direct quotations in his note-books. In his heart he knew that this craving for originality went too far, that it originated in an exaggerated individual and national pride. Nevertheless, he persisted, and the knowledge of his pride — one of the seven deadly sins of old — remained as a stigma on his inner life and as the recurring subject of his best work. Hawthorne has too often been termed a puritan. Puritanism is, in itself, hostile to art, and no conscious artist can be a conscious Puritan. On the other hand, Hawthorne used all the paraphernalia of Puritanism as artistic media. And he had inherited from his stern forefathers a sensitive conscience, an ever alert inclination to detect sin or the vestiges of sin in himself and others. Sin is his great theme, and foremost the "unpardonable sin," that pride of which he was so consciously guilty himself. He told of it in allegory upon allegory, and the interpretation of them is manifold. The reader is induced to ponder over the author's own relation to that unpardonable sin. Did he

---

[1] *Works* II, p. 504.
[2] *Works* I, p. 364.

really regret it? Did he not rather, coldly and proudly too, develop it — the very incitement to work, to artistry, that lived in his heart like a "Bosom Serpent"?[1] Was he not too preoccupied with his art, really and personally to care for any ethics? From an outward point of view, his life was unpretentious. His material conditions were average, sometimes even below that standard. His relations to women were of an exemplary kind, and his marriage seems to have been exceptionally happy. He appears to have had no ambition to earn more money or to acquire a more exalted position — except when his income was actually too small for the subsistance of his family. But in regard to literary fame and originality, his aspirations were unlimited. In order to attain artistic effects within the rather limited domain he had chosen, to convey his spiritual messages in a new and poignant way, everything was permitted. To this end, he used his intimate knowledge of the history of his own country and of the world; he availed himself of devices borrowed from religion and philosophy, and drew on the different experiences gathered from practical life that he had stored in his notebooks. There is less certainty, whether he was conscious of the use he also made of literary reminiscences. Sometimes he might parade them, as in *P's Correspondence*[2], or *A Virtuoso's Collection*[3]. He likes openly to refer to Milton, to Spenser, or to Bunyan, his great models of allegory. But he also uses devices borrowed from authors he never mentions by name. Some of them we know through the letters and library lists mentioned in a previous chapter. Others may be added by future research. Hawthorne's work as a whole, affords, however, evidence of so great learning, of so wide reading, that a closer knowledge of his reading is of prime importance. The use he made of it cannot be termed borrowing, but the influence is there, and the significance of this element in his art is too great not to be explored in detail. Nathaniel Hawthorne's position as one of the first great representatives of the culture and literature of a continent warrants every attempt to unravel the threads that link him to other authors, temperaments, artistic methods and manners of thought, to throw a light over the dynamic work in the mind of this great writer of early American fiction.

The basic influence exercised on Hawthorne by the history of

---

[1] *Works* II, p. 303.   [2] *Works* I, p. 407.   [3] *Ibid.*, p. 537.

his country and by his reading of early American literature, like
the Mathers, and English classics like Milton and Spenser, will be
disregarded here. Attention will be centred less on the Transcendental trend than on the reverberations of European Romanticism that reached the New World. Fielding and Balzac have been
mentioned as authors with kindred aims to those of Hawthorne,
but with the advantage of a more varied social environment.[1] They
represent a tradition to which Hawthorne's work may, from one
point of view, be counted, that of the realistic novel. He himself,
by calling his works romances, acknowledged the ties that bound
him to another tradition, that of the Romantic school. Many traits
in his attitude to life are common to contemporary Romanticists
in all countries. We mention the favourite Romantic theme of the
solitude of genius, which received its classic expression in the exclamation of Alfred de Vigny's *Moïse*: "Vivrai-je donc toujours
puissant et solitaire?"

In Europe, the poet's general sense of isolation from other individuals and from the social and political world at large, belonged to
the sense of frustration that followed the Napoleonic wars, and
that has a parallel in the literature of the present day. The heightened sensibility that is the root of such deep suffering was connected with the reaction that followed upon the cult of the intellect
which had characterized the 18th century and its literature. But,
in America, that former cult had never been felt so keenly. The
minds of the young American literati occupied themselves just as
much with building up a theory of life which would be in harmony
with the demands of the heart — that became, as a result, more
of an irrational, emotional, and religious order than of a philosophical — as with that pampering of the feelings, which was such
an important concern of their European contemporaries. In
Nathaniel Hawthorne, these trends merged in an original way, and
were meditated in an isolation that made the final result a unique
and fascinating product.

A well-known modern authority on Hawthorne, Mr. Austin
Warren, finds his works "not romantic in any of the most current
senses. They minimize picturesque background, minimize love,
are deeply serious; and as he avers, they may not 'swerve aside

---

[1] Cp. p. 74 of the present work.

from the truth of the human heart'."[1] The present writer allows herself to advocate a contrary opinion. Picturesque backgrounds abound in Hawthorne's works, as will be further shown in the chapter on his connections with the tradition of Gothic Romance. It may be true that love in itself is not so much his subject as the causes and consequences of love, and that deep theme, the "truth of the human heart," which is not less essentially Romantic. Hawthorne's very seriousness, his preoccupation with moral truths is entirely in keeping with the literary school that made the individual its main concern. There is much in Hawthorne that belongs to Romanticism, though he may not be included in any group. He stands alone, an heir to European literary traditions as well as to the rich and unexploited resources of his own continent, reaching out to unexplored areas of his art, thus foreshadowing later developments in his country's literature. He was full of contradictions: a Romanticist, yet using the most realistic of observations; a descendant of the Puritans, retaining their keen insight into the workings of the conscience, yet viewing the moral problems also with the detachment of the born and trained sceptic; a consummate artist, fastidious in his choice of motives and means, yet not refraining from the use of devices borrowed from the arsenals of the popular authors of stories of terror and wonder; a scion of several generations of New Englanders with New World ideals and New World aspirations, yet bound — through ties of ancestry and keen literary insight — to the cultural traditions of the Old World.

The study of this deeply interesting literary personality has proved a great attraction for critics and students of succeeding generations, especially in the United States. Hawthorne's ties with the old history of his own country, with its literature, and its contemporary politics, his relations to contemporary American philosophical, literary, and social trends have been analyzed in their different aspects, and the story of his life has been told and retold. English influences have been unearthed, and so have possible influences from German authors. The remainder of the present work will be devoted to the task of finding out the extent to which Nathaniel Hawthorne has, consciously or unconsciously, worked under the impression of the Gothic school, and of two French authors, Mme de Staël and Balzac.

[1] Austin Warren, *Nathaniel Hawthorne*, American Writers Series, New York, 1934, p. LXII.

HAWTHORNE AND THE TRADITION
OF GOTHIC ROMANCE

Horace Walpole's Italian castle, this "croquant féodale" as it has been called by a French critic[1] a century after its creation, cannot boast of any structural beauty of a classical kind, and as little of any artistic elevation or historical truth. And yet it remains a literary monument of high importance that reflects itself even in the novels of today. The mysteriousness, the ghostly atmosphere, appeal to kindred depths in the human soul, and there are few authors belonging to the generation that grew up during the golden age of the Gothic novel, who have escaped being consciously or subconsciously impressed by its potent if somewhat ridiculous pathos.

Critics specializing in the field of Gothicism[2] have found it convenient to classify the principal attributes of these novels, and the same method, using a different classification and an exemplification derived from works most of which Hawthorne is known to have read, will be applied in the present study of the Gothic influence on Nathaniel Hawthorne's art.

1. THE MANUSCRIPT

The authors of the novels of terror and wonder have a great predilection for the trick of telling a story at second hand. One of the characters of an introductory story gives an account of his experiences, or, better still, produces an old manuscript, where the happenings are written down. By supposing parts of the manuscript to be unreadable, the author may evade difficult or unexplicable

---

[1] Charles de Rémusat, *Horace Walpole*, *Revue des deux mondes*, April 15th, 1852.

[2] Helene Richter, *Geschichte der englischen Romantik*, Halle, 1911.

Alice M. Killen, *Le roman terrifiant ou roman noir de Walpole à Anne Radcliffe*, Paris, 1924.

passages in his tale, as is the case in Mathurin's *Melmoth*; he may even pass off the whole of his work as a translation of an old document, as Walpole did when he first brought out *The Castle of Otranto*.

2. THE CASTLE

The Gothic castle of Walpole forms the gloomy background of most Gothic novels. It contains numerous secret cabinets and corridors and a labyrinthine network of subterranean passages. Sometimes it is transformed into a convent or the abode of an alchemist or of an erudite inventor of some miraculous or fatal elixir. The castle and its effect on the beholder may be illustrated by an example from *The Mysteries of Udolpho*:

"Another gate delivered them into the second court, grassgrown, and more wild than the first, where, as she surveyed through the twilight its desolation, its lofty walls, overtopt with briony, moss and nightshade, and the embattled towers that rose above — long suffering and murder came to her thoughts . . . The sentiment was not diminished when she entered an extensive Gothic hall, obscured by the gloom of evening."[1]

3. THE CRIME

The principal theme consists of a mysterious crime, not infrequently illicit or incestuous love, and at times perpetrated by a person in holy orders. Of all the sin-laden culprits who people the world of the Gothic novel, the Abbot of Matthew Gregory Lewis is the most encumbered. Of him it is said that he was finally accused "not only of rape and murder: the crime of sorcery was laid to his charge."[2]

4. RELIGION

One or several of the dramatis personae are often monks or have some kind of tie with religion. Lewis's abbot may also serve as an example here. The Inquisition plays a prominent part. The phenomenon of stigmatization which not infrequently occurs, also has affinities in religion.

---

[1] Ann Radcliffe, *The Mysteries of Udolpho*, p. 109.
[2] M. G. Lewis, *The Monk*, Vol. II, p. 243.

5. ITALIANS

The villain of the piece is generally an Italian. This device follows an old tradition, going back to the influence of the Catholic excommunication of Machiavelli.[1] Sometimes a Spaniard may be substituted for the Italian. Italians are, for example, Schedoni in Radcliffe's *The Italian*, and Montoni in *The Mysteries of Udolpho* by the same author. Spaniards are Lewis's monk, Ambrosio, and Monçada in *Melmoth*. The villains have often pledged themselves to the devil. They are tempted by him and are finally claimed by him. Such is the case in *Vathek*, where Carathis ends her life in the subterranean domains of the giaour, where her heart becomes a "receptacle of eternal fires" and she "continues to revolve without intermission,"[2] and in *The Monk*, where the scene expands into one of the most effective and terrifying canvasses ever painted by a Gothic master:

"The devil: . . . 'Thus, I secure my prey.'

"As he said this, darting his talons into the monk's shaved crown, he sprang with him from the rock. The caves and mountains rang with Ambrosio's shrieks. The demon continued to soar aloft, till reaching a dreadful height, he released the sufferer. Headlong fell the monk through the airy waste; the sharp point of a rock received him; and he rolled from precipice to precipice, till bruised and mangled, he rested on the river's banks. Life still existed in his miserable frame; he attempted in vain to raise himself; . . . Blind, maimed, helpless and despairing, venting his rage in blasphemy and curses, execrating his existence, yet dreading the arrival of death destined to yield him up to greater torments, six miserable days did the villain languish. On the seventh a violent storm arose: the winds in fury rent up rocks and forests; the sky was now black with clouds, now sheeted with fire; the rain fell in torrents; it swelled the stream; the waves overflowed their banks; they reached the spot where Ambrosio lay, and when they abated, carried with them into the river the corpse of the despairing monk."[3]

Melmoth meets a similar fate: " . . . he fell, and falling grasped

[1] Cp. the Machiavelli figure in Marlowe's *Jew of Malta* and Richardson's declaration that he classed his figures as "men, women, or Italians."

[2] W. Beckford, *Vathek*, p. 120.

[3] C. R. Mathurin, *Melmoth the Wanderer*, p. 329.

at aught that might save him. His fall seemed perpendicular —
there was nought to save him — the rock was as smooth as ice —
the ocean of fire broke at its foot . . . he fell — he blazed — he
shrieked. The burning waves boomed over his sinking head, and
the clock of eternity rung out its awful chime: — Room for the soul
of the Wanderer."[1]

6. Deformity

Another attribute of the villain, which appears a little later, possibly caused by the Romantic predilection for motives from folklore,
is a deformity of some kind or other. Quasimodo, the dwarf of
Notre Dame in Victor Hugo's novel, is such a figure.

7. Ghosts

Ghosts abound in the stately chambers and subterranean passages of the Gothic mansions. They may be real spirits of a supernatural kind, like the huge helmet in the *Castle of Otranto*, or the
model ghost from Clara Reeve's *Old English Baron*, which appears
to the enemies of the hero when they one night keep watch in a
haunted room: "As they stood with their fists clenched, on a sudden
they were alarmed by a dismal groan from the room underneath.
They stood like statues, petrified by fear, yet listening with trembling
expectation. A second groan increased their consternation; and
soon after a third completed it. They staggered to a seat, and sank
down upon it ready to faint; presently, all the doors flew open, a
pale glimmering light appeared at the door from the staircase, and
a man in complete armour entered the room; he stood with one
hand extended, pointing to the outward door."[2] They may also be
arrayed in shrouds like the mother of Antonia in *The Monk*:
" . . . suddenly she [Antonia] fancied that she heard a low sigh
draw near her . . . Gracious God, she said to herself, what could be
that sound? Was I deceived, or did I really hear it? Her reflections
were interrupted by a voice at the door scarcely audible; yet the
bolt she knew to be fastened, and this idea in some degree assured
her. Presently the latch was lifted up softly, and the door moved
with caution backwards and forwards . . . Slowly and gradually
the door turned upon its hinges, and standing upon the threshold

---

[1] *Op. cit.*, Vol. II, p. 263—264.

[2] Clara Reeve, *The Old English Baron*, p. 99.

she beheld a tall thin figure, wrapped in a white shroud which covered it from head to foot . . . The figure pointed to the ground with one hand, and with the other raised the linen which covered its face."[1]

The apparitions may also be false ghosts, *viz.* phenomena that seem supernatural to the beholder, but are afterwards rationally explained. Regularly of such a character are the ghosts and other mysteries evoked by Mrs. Radcliffe, who takes pains to explain, for example, certain blue lights as electrical phenomena.

To this section also belong the sepulchral and graveyard mysteries, conveying the sinister and tragic atmosphere so essential to Romantic poetry.

8. MAGIC

Witches and sorcerers are often met with in these novels, perhaps oftener in the Oriental variety and in the later German short stories of terror and wonder than in the English Gothic romance. Carathis, the mother of Vathek, is a witch, and gives the following self-characterization to show the legitimacy of her claims to the title: " . . . I myself have a great desire to . . . visit the subterranean palace, which no doubt contains whatever can interest persons like us; there is nothing so pleasing as retiring to caverns; my taste for dead bodies and everything like mummy is decided."[2] Enchanted objects, magic potions, amulets, etc., are to be found in great profusion.

9. NATURE

For the purpose of evoking sensations of terror, the authors of these novels frequently avail themselves of natural phenomena, sometimes rather surprisingly stressed to serve the terrifying purpose. A deep darkness often attends the crucial events. Rain is falling, wind is blowing, lightnings are flashing and thunders rolling. The pale glimmer of the moon has quite another function for the Gothic authors than for the elegiac poets: its dim light only enhances the prevailing terror. It is night when Mathilda (*The Monk*) leads Ambrosio to the subterranean cavern: "A profound

---

[1] *Op. cit.*, Vol. II, p. 114.

[2] *Op. cit.*, p. 43.

obscurity hovered through the void; damp vapours struck cold the friar's heart, and he listened sadly to the blast while it howled along the lonely vaults."[1]   When Lucifer appears, we find that "the lightning flashed around him, and the thunder with repeated bursts seemed to announce the dissolution of nature."[2] Cp. also the example from *The Monk* under (5).

Apart from these more or less regular phenomena, prodigies of different kinds also occur. When the Indian magician after having undergone most uncivil treatment has transformed himself into a great ball and rolled away, the irritated Vathek, in exasperation regards the stars and reproaches them with treachery: "but lo! On a sudden the clear blue sky appeared streaked over with streams of blood, which reached from the valley even to the city of Samarah."[3]

10. ARMOURED KNIGHTS ETC.

As has already partly been seen in the example of ghostly appearances in *The Old English Baron* (7), the stage-properties of the Gothic scene include numerous sets of armours, shields, helmets, etc. It is well known that, according to Walpole's own statement, he had got his original inspiration for his novel in a dream of an iron-clad fist, and in *The Castle of Otranto* we find objects like the huge helmet which has fallen down from the clouds into the courtyard of the castle and plays a strange and decisive part in the action of the novel. When Manfred shows his intention of pursuing Isabella, once the intended bride of his son, it is said that "the moon, which was now up and gleamed[4] in at the opposite casement, presented to his sight the plumes of the fatal helmet, which rose to the height of the windows, waving backwards and forwards in a tempestuous manner, and accompanied with a hollow and rustling sound."[5]

11. WORKS OF ART

The mysterious influence of works of art is related to the previous section, and presents themes of endless variability. Portraits en-

---

[1] *Op. cit.*, Vol. II, p. 66.   [2] *Ibid.*, p. 234.   [3] *Op. cit.*, p. 22.
[4] Cp. No. (9).   [5] H. Walpole, *The Castle of Otranto*, p. 13.

dowed with a life of their own that step out of their frames or content themselves with rolling their eyes or uttering some fateful words, belong to the best beloved supernatural appearances of this kind. We remember the walking portrait in *The Castle of Otranto*: "Manfred . . . had advanced some steps after her, still looking backwards on the portrait, when he saw it quit its pannels, and descend on the floor with a grave and melancholy air."[1] In *The Old English Baron*, two portraits of the same lively kind form part of the furniture of the room where the spectres appear, and when the hero in *Melmoth* first catches sight of the fatal family portrait, Mathurin describes the impression he receives by saying that, had he known them, he would have cited Southey's lines from Thalaba:

"Only the eyes had life,
They gleamed with demon light."[2]

In Mrs. Radcliffe's *Mysteries of Udolpho* there is also to be found a veiled picture that inspires the poor heroine with indescribable horror. Like all the mysteries of Mrs. Radcliffe's this one, too, is finally given a natural explanation. Even pieces of sculpture may show signs of life. In *The Castle of Otranto*, there is a marble statue that is suddenly seen to bleed. Later on, optical illusions partly supplanted the rôle of the animated works of art.

In this connection the mirrors, which play an important part in many magic tricks and illusions, must also be mentioned. Where human eyes are deceived, the looking-glass may show the truth. It may also possess visionary virtues, like Mathilda's mirror (*The Monk*), when she tempts Ambrosio by showing him the picture of Antonia: "She put the mirror into his hand. Curiosity induced him to take it, and to wish that Antonia might appear. Mathilda pronounced the magic words. Immediately a thick smoke arose from the characters upon the borders, and spread itself over the surface. It dispersed again gradually; a confused mixture of colours and images presented themselves to the friar's eyes, which at length arranging themselves in their proper places, he beheld in miniature, Antonia's lovely form."[3]

[1] *Ibid.*, p. 14.   [2] *Op. cit.*, Vol. I, p. 20.   [3] *Op. cit.*, Vol. II, p. 61.

12. BLOOD

Quantities of blood ooze through the whole of this literature. In the subterranean passages, heroes and villains find their way by tracing more or less mysterious trails of blood. Persons long deceased show a strong tendency to bleed, preferably through the nostrils — a phenomenon which every contemporaneous reader knew to constitute an accusation of murder. Should a corpse show signs of life, there are also strong reasons for suspecting a case of suspended animation, caused by some magic draught. It may also happen that statues begin to bleed, as mentioned above (11). When Manfred in *The Castle of Otranto*, in the presence of Alfonso's statue, announces his intention of divorcing his lawful wife in order to marry Isabella, Walpole tells us that "As he spoke those words, three drops of blood fell from the nose of Alfonso's statue ... Behold, said the friar; mark this miraculous indication that the blood of Alfonso will never mix with that of Manfred."[1] We also recall the prodigy in *Vathek*, which consisted of bloody streaks in the sky.[2]

Over the terrifying or wonderful dramas played on the stages of Gothic romance, with their sinister walls and turrets silhouetted against backgrounds dyed in a bloody red, chance sways a pretty omnipotent sceptre. Time or place never constitute any impediments to the most incredible coincidences and encounters. However high the difficulties of the heroes and heroines may pile up, the reader may look forward with almost unerring certainty to the final appearance of some *deus ex machina* conferring liberation and rewarding virtue. Neither the composition nor the psychological development of the Gothic novel can boast of anything very like logic, and humour is altogether unknown to its authors. Its machinery is, as we have found, rather simple, and the success of each work depends on the author's resourcefulness and fantasy, his talent for conveying a weird and ghostly atmosphere, and his flair for nerveracking effects. From comparatively unimportant beginnings, as a reaction against the rationalism and formal severity of the eighteenth century, Gothic romance grew into one of the most powerful currents in the general literature of the nineteenth century.

*

---

[1] *Op. cit.*, p. 118.   [2] Cp. p. 86.

The scenery and the whole machinery of Gothic Romance became, just like Puritanism or Spiritualism, one of Hawthorne's
media of artistic expression. He called all his whole-length stories
romances[1], and has given reason for this in the introduction to
The House of the Seven Gables:

"When a writer calls his work Romance, it need hardly be
observed that he wishes to claim a certain latitude, both as to its
fashion and material, which he would not have felt himself entitled
to assume had he professed to be writing a Novel. The latter
form of composition is presumed to aim at a very minute fidelity,
not merely to the possible, but to the probable and ordinary course
of man's experience. The former — while, as a work of art, it
must rigidly subject itself to laws, and while it sins unpardonably
so far as it may swerve aside from the truth of the human heart —
has fairly a right to present that truth under circumstances, to a
great extent, of the writer's own choosing or creation. If he think
fit, also, he may so manage his atmospherical medium as to bring
out or mellow the lights and deepen and enrich the shadows of the
picture. He will be wise, no doubt, to make a very moderate use
of the privileges here stated, and especially to mingle the Marvellous rather as a slight, delicate, and evanescent flavour, than
as any portion of the actual substance of the dish offered to the
public. He can hardly be said, however, to commit a literary
crime, even if he disregard this caution."[2] [3]

In the present study I shall treat 15 of Hawthorne's short stories,
his youthful romance *Fanshawe*, his four great romances, and the
four posthumous manuscripts. According to Quinn[4], 19 of Hawthorne's 79 short stories deal with supernatural themes, but as has
already been mentioned, Hawthorne broached subjects related
to spiritism or mesmerism which will not be touched upon here.

---

[1] Cp. above p. 25.

[2] *Works* III, p. 13.

[3] Hawthorne's literary ideal has been in a certain measure foreshadowed by
Leigh Hunt who once wrote, "A ghost story, to be a good one, should unite
as much as possible objects such as they are in life with a preternatural spirit.
And to be a perfect one — at least to add to the other utility of excitement a
moral utility." Hunt was one of the few British authors Hawthorne met while
in England.

[4] Quinn, *Some Phases of the Supernatural in American Literature*. PMLA
XVIII, 1910.

Thanks to E. Lathrop-Chandler's excellent study[1] of the chronology of Hawthorne's early productions, I have been able to take up the stories according to the order in which they were originally written.

The first pages we possess by Hawthorne — except his first notebooks — are the fragments of the story called *Alice Doane's Appeal*.[2] When Hawthorne re-edited the tale he had invented at 16 years of age, he gave it a congenial setting, placing himself as a narrator, accompanied by two beautiful ladies on Gallow's Hill, where he produces his manuscript. The story begins with a murder, and is then traced back to the description of how the beautiful and virtuous Alice Doane and her brother Leonard, who is obsessed by a diseased imagination, make the acquaintance of Walter Brome, a young man who has formerly led a reckless and ungoverned life in Europe (cp. *Melmoth*). There is a striking resemblance between Walter, who falls in love with Alice, and Leonard who hates the stranger and feels a strong jealousy on behalf of his sister. Leonard murders Walter, and in the same moment recognizes in him his own brother. Then follows a fantastic description of a moon-lit winter's night, and suddenly the reader is led on to a graveyard: " . . . each family tomb had given up its inhabitants, who, one by one, through distant years, had been borne to its dark chamber, but now came forth and stood in a pale group together . . . The whole miserable multitude, both sinful souls and false spectres of good men, groaned horribly and gnashed their teeth, as they looked upward to the calm loveliness of the midnight sky, and beheld those homes of bliss where they must never dwell. Such was the apparition, though too shadowy for language to portray; for here would be the moonbeams on the ice, glittering through a warrior's breastplate, and there the letters of a tombstone, on the form that stood before it . . . This company of devils and condemned souls had come on holiday to revel in the discovery of a complicated crime."

The narrator suggests that his manuscript contains an explanation of how the whole horrible story of the incestuous love between sister and brother and the fratricide was due to the machinations

---

[1] Elizabeth Lathrop-Chandler, *A Study of the Sources of the Tales and Romances written by Nathaniel Hawthorne before 1853*, Smith College Studies, 1926, Vol. 7, No. 4.

[2] *Works* XII, p. 279.

of a wizard, "a small, grey, withered man, with fiendish ingenuity in devising evil, and superhuman power to execute it."

In this early literary attempt of Hawthorne's, we find no less than five of the elements in our scheme represented. There are two crimes, of which one is of an incestuous nature (3), there is the scene with the spectres assembled in the graveyard (7), the wizard (8) who is a dwarf (6), and the typically Romantic description of a moon-lit night (9). Though the manner of telling the story in the form of repetition from a manuscript does not belong to its original version, and the manuscript is not an old parchment but only some sheets of paper from the author's own drawer, we may also add point (1) of our list of Gothic characteristics.

The next work under consideration here is *Fanshawe*, the youthful novel that Hawthorne later on wanted to suppress. It is a story from a college, behind which the contours of Bowdoin may readily be traced. The Rector, whose name is Melmoth (sic!), receives in his home a young girl, Ellen Langton, daughter of one of the friends of his youth. Two students, the death-haunted and melancholy Fanshawe — whom one might be tempted to call a Werther if such a likeness did not prevail between him and the young author himself — and the buoyant Walcott, both fall in love with her. A mysterious fisherman, another edition of the Melmoth figure, who has, during his wandering life, become "irrevocably ruined and irreclaimably depraved," appears and takes advantage of a letter he brings from Ellen's father to get an interview with her. The fisherman, Butler, believes Ellen's father to be dead, but does not tell her this. Instead, he tries to elope with her, assisted by the local innkeeper, who has formerly been his companion in pirate adventures. Ellen is saved from his first attempt to abduct her. Afterwards, Melmoth receives a letter from her father, who has been miraculously saved from an impending shipwreck. Ellen disappears anew and is taken by Butler to a cave on the seashore. Walcott and Fanshawe search for the elopers, and Fanshawe catches sight of them from the top of a rock. Butler tries to climb the cliff in order to wrestle with Fanshawe, but slips and is hurled down into the abyss: "When within a few feet of the summit, the adventurer grasped at a twig too slenderly rooted to sustain his weight. It gave way in his hand and he fell backwards down the precipice. His head struck against the less perpendicular part of the rock, whence

the body rolled heavily down to the detached fragment, of which
mention has heretofore been made. There was no life left in him.
With all the passion of hell alive in his heart, he had met the fate
that he intended for Fanshawe."[1] The melancholy Fanshawe lacks
the courage to make a serious attempt at conquering Ellen's heart
and hand. He dies in his twentieth year, and Ellen, as might be
expected, marries the more robust Walcott.

This novel displays a whole set of definite reminiscences from
the reading of *Melmoth*. We find them in the motto of one of
the chapters, in the headmaster's name, in the description of the
mysterious traveller Butler and his catastrophic end.[2] Barring the
romance of the Rev. Mathurin, the predominant influence of Walter
Scott, namely *The Antiquarian*, and *Waverley* is discernible in
several features of Hawthorne's first novel.[3]

Fanshawe was begun in August, 1816 and published in December,
1827. The short story of *The Hollow of the Three Hills* was com-
menced as early as 1824, but published for the first time in 1830,
and afterwards included in the *Twice-Told Tales*. In the shadow
of a majestic oak on a mantling pool, at a spot that has been known
from time immemorial as the resort of the powers of evil, there
meet two women: one is old and withered; the other is young,
beautiful, pale, and unhappy. The young one puts her head in the
old woman's lap, and the latter murmurs a sort of incantation. By
faint sounds arriving to her from an illimitable distance of space
and time, the young woman then perceives the things that have
happened to the people closest related to her, but severed from her
by an evil fate.

In this sketch from the early immigration period, we find as
instances of our categories: (8), the witch and her magic power,
and (9), the description of the surrounding landscape with its
traditional weirdness. In his criticism of the stories, Poe has drawn

[1] *Works* XI, p. 208.

[2] The descriptions of men falling into abysses are quoted at some length
because they give one of the best illustrations to be found of the strong impressions Hawthorne received from his reading of novels of terror and of the tena-
city with which they persisted from boyhood till late in his life.

[3] G. Harrison Orians points out in Ellen "the romantic indistinctness of
Scott's aristocratic women," and the figure of the hostler Crombie who has,
moreover, such a Scottish name. (G. Harrison Orians, *Scott and Hawthorne's
Fanshawe, The New England Quarterly*, 1938.)

attention to Hawthorne's original manner of remoulding one of the traditional forms of witchery: "It has been the fashion to describe, in such cases, a mirror in which the images of the absent appear; or a cloud of smoke is made to arise, and thence the figures are gradually unfolded. Mr. Hawthorne has wonderfully heightened the effect by making the ear, in place of the eye, the medium by which the fantasy is conveyed."[1]

Young Goodman Brown[2] (written in 1828—29, included in *Mosses from an Old Manse*) is a fantastic, legend-like tale of 17th century Salem, and one of Hawthorne's most suggestive stories. The whole atmosphere of the period and the scene were extremely familiar to the author — both the village street basking in the clear sunshine of the morning, and the picture which a superstition-ridden imagination draws of the witch-sabbath in the depths of the dense woods.

There is very little action in the story. It describes how, one morning, young Goodman Brown takes farewell of his young wife in order — but for a single time — to make an excursion into the wood, driven by his curiosity as to the midnight revels that the devil is said to hold there. He soon chances to meet the personage in question, "a man in grave and decent attire," owner of a quaint staff that bears the likeness of a great wriggling snake. They advance into the wood, and are by and by overtaken by different well-known people from the little town. There are the minister and Deacon Gookin, there is old Goody Cloyse, the pious teacher of catechism to the small children; now she vanishes into the air, and it is understood that, having lost her own broomstick, she is riding on the mysterious rod of the Devil. In the heart of the wood, the witch sabbath is celebrated. The Devil mounts a sort of pulpit and below him assemble the honest citizens and pious widows and housewives of the town, its ancient spinsters and fair young girls, mixed with women of bad reputation and men of dissolute lives, even criminals. "Bring forth the converts," somebody cries, and Goodman Brown recognizes his Faith among the crowd, whose otherwise veiled crimes appear in the shades of the unhallowed night. They are all baptized in blood in a font which nature has formed in the rock. Goodman Brown staggers

---

[1] *Graham's Magazine*, May, 1842.
[2] *Works* II, p. 89.

home to Salem, where the street lies calm and peaceful in the light of the morning sun, where the morning prayer of the minister is to be heard through an open window and Goody Cloyse is catechizing a little girl. Faith greets him, but he cannot answer her as before. Never will Goodman Brown regain his joy in living. Was his experience real or only a bad dream?

Here we find, fully developed, Hawthorne's method of creating parables around his constant theme: the question of the rôle of sin in human life. The setting he has chosen is the Puritan environment of his ancestors, with its religious severity and its wealth of superstition. The gloomy atmosphere that surrounds the wanderers in the dark forest is skilfully evoked: Goodman Brown and his companion hear human voices belonging to invisible people on their way to the witches' sabbath, or they see how the moon is obscured though there is no wind, and infer that some human form must have passed through the air. Goody Cloyse possesses all the traditional attributes of a witch. Somebody has stolen her broomstick, "and that too, when I was all anointed with the juice of smallage, and cinquefoil, and wolf's bane," etc. The Devil, who, by his baptism, makes both men and women "partakers of the mystery of sin, more conscious of the secret guilt of others, both in deed and thought, than they could now be of their own," causes the leaves on a bough which he takes in his hand to shrivel and die. The whole thing is a rather exquisite pastiche in the style of Dürer; Hawthorne has already attained perfect mastery of his means of expression.

When now passing on to scrutinize the story in relation to our scheme, we might dwell both on the mention of a mysterious crime and on the religious atmosphere; but these ingredients are not used here in a strictly Gothic sense. They rather form an integrating part of Hawthorne's personal message, though they certainly intensify the gloominess of the story. But our category (8) is strongly represented, as is also (9) in the moonlight and the supernatural lull in the wood. Further, we remark the blood (12) of the font in the rock.

The life and manners of the old 17th century Puritans form the environment of several of Hawthorne's best tales from the late twenties, such as *The Grey Champion* (1828—29) and *The May-pole of Merry Mount* (1828—29). Possessing certain claims of being founded on historical tradition, they are rather to be referred to Hawthorne's historical sketches, and, though they certainly have a somewhat ghostly atmosphere, they will not be further treated here. We pass on instead to *The Great Carbuncle* (1832—33, *Twice-Told Tales*).[1]

The theme of this story is taken from a sphere which otherwise does not belong to Hawthorne's stock-in-trade. The great advance towards the West, the Frontier, the life of settlers and Indians, is one of the chief themes on which American literature is founded, and was of an immense importance to many of Hawthorne's contemporaries. To Hawthorne himself it was of less vital consequence. Legends and superstitions based on life in the Western wilds did not captivate his imagination as intensely as did tales about mysterious happenings in a more cultured contemporary environment, or dealing with early days in New England, or with mediaeval Europe. Nevertheless, we find here and there glimpses of Indian romance in Hawthorne's works; it is often coloured by dark and primitive magic. *The Great Carbuncle* is derived from the Indian legend of a jewel of supernatural splendour and beauty that is said to exist in the virgin forest but has never been seen by human eyes. Hawthorne introduces his readers to a little party of seven persons who have all departed from their homes in quest of the treasure. The story is of the semi-allegoric, "Hawthornesque" kind; it illustrates human striving in different forms. One of the seekers is a merchant, another is a poet. The eldest of them, who is only called the Seeker, is clad in the skins of wild animals and is described as follows: "He was one of those ill-fated mortals, such as the Indians told of, whom, in their early youth, the great Carbuncle smote with a peculiar madness, and became the passionate dream of their existence." At his side sits a doctor Cacophodel, "who had wilted and dried himself into a mummy by continually stooping over charcoal furnaces, and inhaling unwholesome fumes during his researches in chemistry and alchemy. It was told . . . that he had drained his body of all its richest blood, and wasted it . . . in an unsuccessful experiment." There is also an English nobleman "who, when at home, was said to spend much of his time in the burial vault of his dead progenitors, rummaging among their

---

[1] *Works* I, p. 173.

mouldy coffins in search of all the earthly pride and vainglory that was hidden among bones and dust." Lastly, the author presents Hannah and Matthew, a young, newly-married couple, who in their natural simplicity seem rather out of place among all the dreamers in the quaint company. The seekers all tell us legends about the mysterious gem, and of the Indian spirit which is said to keep watch over it.

When morning comes, the pilgrims wander about in different directions in search of the Carbuncle — the merchant intending to sell it at an exorbitant price, the lord aiming to give it a fitting place in his ancestral castle, etc. The young couple only want it for embellishing their humble abode, which they want to make as pleasant and comfortable as possible for each other. After many hours, Hannah and Matthew find themselves surrounded by a dense mist, through which a faint light is gleaming. The light shows itself to be the Great Carbuncle, glowing from the brow of a cliff on the other side of a lake. At the base of the cliff, they perceive the dead body of the Seeker with his arms extended towards the goal. Hannah and Matthew catch fright at the sight. To them the blessed sunshine and the quiet moonlight suffice. And so they return to their cottage — without the Great Carbuncle. And the fate of the marvellous gem? "It is affirmed that, from the hour when two mortals had shown themselves so simply wise as to reject a jewel which would have dimmed all earthly things, its splendour waned." But there are also some few who believe that the Great Carbuncle is still blazing as of old.

In this fully developed allegory, Hawthorne has made skilful use of the mysteriousness of Indian folklore, which he has interwoven with ideas and events that are well known to readers of the Gothic novels. The description of the Seeker reminds one of many magicians (8), and also the misshapen scholar at his side apparently derives his origin from the long descent of deformed villains in the same kind of literature (8, 6). The carbuncle itself is a still more brilliant variety of the Carbuncle of Giamschid, which is promised to the beautiful Nourounihar if she forsakes her childish betrothed Gulchenrouz for Vathek. The subtitle of the story, *A Mystery of the White Mountains*, itself shows that Hawthorne was quite consciously appealing to his readers' appreciation of the supernatural when, in this modern parable, he tried to depict the vanity of human strivings.

The Wedding Knell (1835, *Twice-Told Tales*)¹ is told as a true story, but nevertheless it has a strong allegorical purport. The author tells of a New York wedding in the young days of his grandmother. Neither of the parties were young any longer, but they had once in their youth been engaged to each other. He had spent forty years in solitude and become an eccentric old bachelor. She had been married twice, first to an aged gentleman with a fortune and, secondly, to a southerner considerably younger than herself. Though widowed anew, she still tried to play the part of a young woman, and entered the church at the head of a bridal party made up of youth and gaiety. The bridegroom was late, and meanwhile the churchbells began to sound — but it was not the tinkling of the gay wedding-bells but the heavy toll of the funeral knell. At the same moment, a hearse with a train of several coaches approached, and to the great fright of the bridal party, there entered through the church door a strange crowd: ". . . a dark procession paced into the church. First came an old man and woman, like chief mourners at a funeral attired from head to foot in the deepest black, all but their pale features and hoary hair." Thereupon followed a whole train of aged people dressed in mourning. They formed a circle around the altar, and the bridegroom appeared in their midst: ". . . a form, that had been worthily ushered in with all this gloomy pomp, the death knell, and the funeral. It was the bridegroom in his shroud . . . Come, my bride, said those pale lips, the hearse is ready . . . Let us be married, and then to our coffins." The bride is as frightened as the merry wedding-guests, but the bridegroom makes a speech and proves that it is he who wears the proper garb for a wedding like this. The spring-time of life is past, and both of them must prepare for the grave. The bride concedes that he is right, and her worldliness disappears. The couple are united, and the organ's peal of solemn triumph mingles itself with the tolling of the deathbell.

Once more, Hawthorne has here endowed his moral lesson with impressive force by mingling the mysteriousness of death and funeral rites with his story. The contrast between the gay and youthful bridal party and the sinister funeral procession produces a very striking effect. That the bridegroom in his shroud is fairly directly drawn from the sepulchral chambers of the novels of terror and wonder (7) is clear. When, in a hollow voice, he tells his bride:

"Then to our coffins," he repeats a late echo of the first modern literary ghost ballad, the *Lenore* of Bürger, which, in a way, constitutes the beginning of literary Romanticism in Germany. Hawthorne tells us in an item in his note-book that he is busy translating this piece of poetry from the German, but as the item is entered in 1843[1], it may not be surmised with certainty that he knew *Lenore* as early as 1836. Still, it is reasonably plain that the sinister summons can be traced back through unknown intermediaries to the ghostly horseman of Bürger, who, in the stormy night, whispers to his beloved on the pommel of his saddle:

"Graut, Liebchen, auch? Der Mond scheint hell.
Hurra. Die Toten reiten schnell ..."

From 1835 also originates *The Prophetic Pictures* (*Twice-Told Tales*).[2] The author declares in an introductory note that he has got the motive of the story from Dunlap's *History of the Art of Design*. The principal figure is a painter, as is so often the case in the novels of terror and wonder. He has no name in the story, and the only thing that is known of his origin, is that he has been born and educated in Europe — the Continent that had also fostered the painter Francesco, master of the picture of Rosalie in Hoffmann's *Elixiere des Teufels*. He is a master of his art, and even more than that: " ... he paints not merely a man's features, but his mind and heart. He catches the secret sentiments and passions, and throws them upon the canvas, like sunshine — or perhaps, in the portraits of dark-souled men, like a gleam of infernal fire." He also possesses knowledge in other fields, partly to be classified as magic: he not only excels in his peculiar art, but possesses vast acquirements in all other branches of learning and science. "He talks Hebrew with Dr. Mather, and gives Lectures in anatomy to Dr. Boylston." This European has come to America, where he later on travels about in order to detect the charm of the New World: " ... the stern dignity of Indian chiefs, the dusky loveliness of Indian girls; the domestic life of wigwams ... The glow of perilous moments ... love, hate, grief, frenzy; in a word, all the wornout heart of the old earth had been revealed to him under a new form." Here we chance upon one

---

[1] Cp. p. 58 of the present work.
[2] *Works* I, p. 192.

of the rare cases of frontier romance in Hawthorne. But the principal theme of the story is formed by the two portraits, which this painter paints of Walter Ludlow and his young wife Elinor. His technique is a strange one: he paints them both at the same time, adding strokes alternately in a sort of queer interplay, and, according to his own words, the two pictures are the best things he has hitherto made. Here, Hawthorne inserts a brief meditation on the character of portraits and portrait-painting in general, which we repeat because of the interest it will acquire in our study of his later works: "Nothing, in the whole circle of human vanities, takes a stronger hold of the imagination than this affair of having a portrait painted. Yet why should it be so? The looking-glass, the polished globe of andirons, the mirror, like water, and all other reflecting surfaces, continually present us with portraits, or rather ghosts, of ourselves, which we glance at, and straightway forget them. But we forget them only because they vanish. It is the idea of duration — of earthly immortality — that gives such a mysterious interest to our portraits."

The painter goes away on his great American journey, and the two portraits are given their places of honour in the new home of Elinor and Walter. They soon begin to exert a sinister influence, and rumours are whispered about them in the town. Slowly, the features of the pictures change — and the observer will find the same alterations in the faces of their models: " . . . had the picture itself been a mirror, it could not have thrown back her present aspect with stronger and more melancholy truth." Finally they are covered with a curtain. The painter returns, and goes to visit the house and look at the pictures, and it is said that "he seemed to hear the step of Destiny approaching behind him, on its progress towards its victims." The young couple are standing before the pictures, the malignant influence of which now decides their fate. Walter draws a dagger and aims it at Elinor's bosom.

Even if Hawthorne here likewise tries to point a sort of moral — if the result of our actions could be set before us, would we then abstain from the ominous ones? — the chief motive of the story is not at all a moral one. It consists in the gradually increasing suspense by the inherent magic of the pictures (11), and it has been treated with great skill and beauty. The painter, as has already been mentioned, is a figure often found in the works of romantic novelists.

The magic of pictures is a popular theme. It was one of the subjects most often treated by Washington Irving (*The Adventure of
My Aunt, The Young Italian*), though, in the works of that author,
the mysteries are always given some plausible explanation. Although most points in our scheme are not applicable to this story,
the atmosphere and the whole conception of the theme of *The
Prophetic Pictures* is nevertheless one of the most manifest examples
of Hawthorne's close connection with the novel of terror and
wonder.

Doctor Heidegger's Experiment (Twice-Told Tales)[1] was written
in 1836. The old scientist here portrayed, and his surroundings,
are repeatedly to be met with in Hawthorne's later productions.
He is busy with chemical and magic experiments in his study, "a
dim, old-fashioned chamber, festooned with cobwebs, and be-
sprinkled with antique dust." There is a mirror, of which it is
rumoured that all the doctor's deceased patients dwell within its
verge and "would stare him in the face whenever he looked thither-
ward." We here find a further development of the idea expounded
in the passage cited in the preceding paragraph. — There are
also a bust of Hippocrates, a skeleton and a portrait of a young
lady. Most marvellous of all, however, is Dr. Heidegger's book:
"There were no letters on the back, and nobody could tell the title
of the book. But it was well known to be a book of magic; and once,
when a chambermaid had lifted it, merely to brush away the dust,
the skeleton had rattled in its closet, the picture of the young lady
had stepped one foot upon the floor, and several ghastly faces had
peeped forth from the mirror; while the brazen head of Hippocrates
frowned and said — 'Forbear!'"

In this room, we find, apart from the host, four guests of his,
a lady and three gentlemen of his own age. All four of them are
described in Hawthorne's accurate and amusing manner, and we
likewise get an analytic description of their reactions when the
host, producing a withered rose, dips it into a mysterious liquid
that changes the shrivelled flower into a fresh bud and afterwards
asks his guests to taste of the elixir that he has procured from the
Fountain of Youth in Florida. The first glass changes the four old
people into middle-aged ones, the second transforms them into

---

[1] *Works* I, p. 258.

youths. They laugh and dance, and in the rivalry of courtship, the vase containing the precious fluid is dashed onto the floor. The whole scene is reflected in the mirror, which shows four elderly people in an unseemly intoxicated state. Gradually, the rose withers again, and three aged gentlemen and a matron are once more sitting round the table of their host. Dr. Heidegger's guests have taught him a lesson. He will never taste the water from the Fountain of Youth.

There is no small part of the machinery of the Gothic novel to be found in this story. Dr. Heidegger must be viewed as a sort of modernized wizard (8), and his elixir as a witch beverage (8). In his room are to be found a skeleton (7), a magic mirror (11), a moving portrait, and a bust endowed with the power of speech (11). The whole of this didactic fantasy is built on a Gothic foundation. In a foot-note, Hawthorne meets certain accusations of having plagiarized the idea of the story from a chapter in one of the novels of Alexandre Dumas. He shows that his own tale was written several years before the publication of the work of the Frenchman. When speaking of the four unpublished posthumous manuscripts of Hawthorne, we shall have cause to revert to Dr. Heidegger and his cobwebby study.

In 1838, Hawthorne wrote four tales of old Boston and published them under the joint title of *Legends of the Province House* (*Twice-Told Tales*).[1] The Province House was the former mansion of the English governors of the town, and had, in Hawthorne's day, been adapted as a public-house. We have already mentioned Washington Irving as a predecessor of Hawthorne's and the introducer of the Romantic short story into American literature. Like many of his European models, Irving liked to join the short stories together in a framework tale. According to Hawthorne's principal editor, G. P. Lathrop[2], Hawthorne originally intended to provide such a framework for the *Twice-Told Tales*, but gave up the plan. The four stories from the Province House, are, however, bound together in this way. Hawthorne tells us, how, on a summer's evening, he discovers the old house and enters it with a view to sightseeing. The detailed description of the house, which covers several pages, would do credit to the author of a guide-book; the whole manner

[1] *Works* I, p. 272.
[2] The Riverside Edition.

reminds the reader of Hawthorne's English notebooks and of *Our Old Home*, the work through which Hawthorne wanted to make his fellow-countrymen familiar with their mother-country. Hawthorne finally takes a seat in the bar-room, where Mr. Tiffany, an old customer and gossip, tells him the story of the festivity celebrated by Governor Howe during the siege of Boston. "It is," says Hawthorne, "desperately hard work, when we attempt to throw the spell of hoar antiquity over localities with which the living world, and the day that is passing over us, have aught to do." But his attempt at evoking before the reader's eyes the last festival given by a British governor in the town of Boston, is a great success. Sir William Howe was the name of this dignitary, and the party he gave was a masquerade. The British guests were all very merry, but among them there was also to be discovered a very serious personage: old Colonel Joliffe, who belonged to the Whig party, had, strangely enough, accepted the governor's invitation. Eleven strokes had pealed from the old clock, when an unexpected music was heard from outside the house. The host frowned at the sound of the funeral march which had been played at the death of George III., but when he found that it was not his own orchestra that played it, he did nothing to stop the music. In a little while, a strange procession was seen to descend the great staircase. The foremost was a man in the old Puritan garb with a steeple-crowned hat and a skull-cap. — Endicott! it was whispered among the crowd, and after there followed all the deceased governors and rulers of the old original democracy of Massachusetts, such as they had once wandered about in their lifetime. Astonishment reached its peak, when Howe's predecessor, Gage, advanced, just at the moment when the light of the lamps began to flicker. After him followed a shape, drawing up his military cloak over his face — the likeness of Howe himself! The governor took a step forward, but checked himself. It is said that the gesture made by his double in that moment was exactly the same as the one Sir William made some hours later when, for the last time, he passed through the portal of the Province House. It was a departed power that was commemorated by the ghostly procession.

Hawthorne makes the reader suspect that the whole event may have been a bitter jest, arranged by old Joliffe. But the description wholly tallies with the legend that Hawthorne had also heard, that on each anniversary of the British defeat, all the former governors of Massachusetts still glide through the portal of the Province House. The flickering of the lamplights, the sinister funeral march, and the procession itself, have a decidedly supernatural character, not far removed from the world of Mrs. Radcliffe. The reader is free to choose: either to believe in a ghostly apparition, or to view the whole pageant as a macabre warning jest played by the Boston Whig party. The method reminds one of Irving's manner, and some parts of this story may also make the reader remember *The Masque of the Red Death* by Edgar Allan Poe, which has certain affinities with it.

The ghost-like atmosphere also pervades the three other stories of the Province House. Number two of them, which is also told by the elderly gentleman of the bar-room, is called *Edward Randolph's Portrait*, and is centred round an old picture which has formerly hung in the Province House: "The canvas itself was so dark with age, damp, and smoke, that not a touch of the painter's art could be discerned. Time had thrown an impenetrable veil over it, and left to tradition and fable and conjecture to say what had once been there portrayed." Some people state it to be an authentic portrait of the Evil One, others believe that a familiar spirit abides behind the blackness of the canvas and has shown himself, at seasons of calamity, to the governors. The governor who inhabits the house at the time of the story, Hutchinson, believes the picture to represent Edward Randolph, the builder of the house and the man who obtained the repeal of the first provincial charter, thus depriving the Bostonians of their democratic privileges. One evening, he tells this view to a young relative of his, Alice Vane, a pale, young lady who has been educated in Europe, and, among other things, has learned all the secrets of the art of painting. She suggests that it might be possible to remove the black surface of the canvas, but the discussion passes on to other subjects: the governor's decision to make British troops that are still on board a ship in the harbour, occupy a neighbouring fortress in order to subdue the rebellious colony. When Alice Vane bids her companions good night, her air and mien are "such as might have belonged to one of those spirits of fable — fairies or creatures of a more antique mythology — who sometimes mingled their agency with mortal affairs, half in caprice, yet with a sensibility to human weal or woe."

On the following morning, the landing of the troops, which is expected to cause serious trouble, is discussed in the Province House. Just as the governor lifts his pen to sign the fatal order, Alice Vane steps forward and draws aside a curtain that she has hung over the mysterious portrait. "By heaven," cries the governor, "if the spirit of Edward Randolph were to appear among us from the place of torment, he could not wear more of the terrors of hell upon his face."

In spite of this warning, Hutchinson signs the order — and burdens his conscience with a great guilt: "As, far over the ocean, his dying hour drew on, he gasped for breath, and complained that he was choking with the blood of the Boston Massacre." In his face there are traces of the same desperate expression that had characterized Randolph's portrait. It was afterwards rumoured, that, during the night following upon the fatal decision, the portrait had stepped out of its frame and spoken face to face with the governor. But if such a miracle had taken place, it had left no trace, and the portrait was soon afterwards once more covered with the impenetrable cloud that had always veiled it. The effect of Alice Vane's method of removing it — was it a painter's trick learnt in Italy, or some witchery? — lasted only a few brief hours.

In this tale, which likewise leaves the reader to choose between belief in miracles and scepticism, we thus find a mysterious portrait (11) that has been dexterously used to draw a historical parallel. We further remark the words cited about the governor's feeling of being "choked with blood" (12) at the memory of his guilty action, and the suggestion that Miss Vane's manipulations with the picture might be of a supernatural kind (8). But, on the other hand, what charming young lady might not in the eighteen thirties be likened to a fairy?

Lady Eleanor's Mantle is the title of the third tale, which is also told by the aforesaid Mr. Tiffany at a first-class oyster supper in the Province House. Lady Eleanor was a young lady belonging to the English aristocracy, who, at the beginning of the 18th century, arrived on a visit to her relative, Colonel Shute, at the time the resident in the Province House. Lady Eleanor was a beauty, and her arrival was looked forward to with a certain excitement, partly because it was said that an embroidered mantle in her possession "was invested with magic properties, so as to lend a new and untried

grace to her figure each time that she put it on." The garment was,
according to rumour, embroidered by a woman who had been
waiting for her own impending death. The governor arranged a
festivity in Lady Eleanor's honour, and the gorgeous mantle was
admired by everybody, while its bearer lost ever more sympathy
through her malicious sarcasms and haughty manner. Among the
guests at the party appeared a young man, Jervase Helwyse, whose
suit Eleanor had refused in England, and who had now followed her
to the New World. He offered her a cup of wine as "a symbol that
you have not sought to withdraw yourself from the chain of human
sympathies." He also asked her to throw off the mantle. She
refused, and he was led away. A short time afterwards, an epidemic
disease broke out in the town; contrary to the normal course, it
seemed at first to confine itself to the higher circles of society.
Gradually, the infection was traced back to — Lady Eleanore's
mantle. Jervase Helwyse went to see her, disfigured by the illness,
and snatched away the fatal garment. Afterwards the people formed
a procession, at the head of which was carried a puppet bearing
the mantle. It is told that the plague disappeared when the puppet
and the mantle had been burned, and that a mysterious woman
bearing a wide mantle is still seen of nights in the Province
House.

The witchery of this story of the magic mantle has travelled
rather far from the manner of Washington Irving, and bears the true
Hawthornesque stamp. It is not so far from the embroidered mantle
to the embroidered A on Hester Prynne's breast. The theme is
here less the historical ghost than the story of how the proud Lady
Eleanor, who could feel no compassion with Jervase Helwyse,
became in her turn the victim of somebody stronger than herself.
The mantle becomes a symbol of her pride and of the punishment
that the sinner carries with him. Still, we note number (7) of our
list — the ghost of Lady Eleanor — and (8), her bewitched mantle.

Old Esther Dudley, the fourth story of the Province House,
tells of the last loyal British subject left in Boston after the departure
of the last governor. Old Esther is a decayed descendant of an old
English family who has found a refuge in the Province House and
stays on there after Governor Howe and the British troops have
left the town. She takes care of the old house and its treasures,
among which there is a mysterious old mirror of which people tell

that "old Esther could cause the Governors of the overthrown
dynasty, with the beautiful ladies who had once adorned their
festivals, the Indian chiefs who had come up to the Province House
to hold council or swear allegiance, the grim Provincial warriors,
the severe clergymen — in short, all the pageantry of bygone days —
all the figures that ever swept across the broad plate of glass in
former times — she could cause the whole to reappear and people
the inner world of the mirror with shadows of old life." It was
rumoured that if she felt lonely, she was wont to summon a black
slave from the mirror and send him to fetch company from the
churchyard: "forth went the sable messenger with the starlight
or the moonshine gleaming through him, and did his errand in the
burial ground, knocking at the iron doors of tombs or upon the
marble slabs that covered them."

But the guests that are dearest to Old Esther Dudley are the
children of the town. She talks to them of bygone days, and when
they return to their homes, they will, in their turn, tell stories of
people of the past, as if they were still living. They claim to have
met a governor long since dead, but, they say, "when old Esther
Dudley had done speaking about him he faded away out of his
chair."

Time passes, and the Republican governor Hancock is appointed
and takes possession of the Province House. Old Esther Dudley
perceives that a festival occasion is at hand. She arrays herself in
her best silk and descends the great staircase to kneel to the new-
comer. "God save King George" is her strange greeting when
giving him the keys. And so the representative of another era dies
as the new age crosses the threshold of the Province House.

The ghostly atmosphere of this story is not as strong as in the
other three. The light over it has rather a sad lustre. It is the
superstition of her environment that partly isolates old Esther
Dudley. The old woman, who lives wholly in the past, is understood only by the children: "Thus, without affrightening her little
guests, she led them by the hand into the chambers of her own
desolate heart, and made childhood's fancy discern the ghosts that
haunted there." But the machinery is easily recognized. The
magic mirror (11), the moon that shines through the ghostly negro
(9), the whole idea of nocturnal banquets where the whole party is
called forth from the mirror and have their domiciles in the church-

yard (7), all these conceptions are so many borrowings from the world of terror and wonder. "Weird" is the word used by Lathrop about these historical tales, which are typical of Hawthorne's attempts to invest the past of his country with life. Unlike the European Romanticists or their great model, Shakespeare, he had no medieval history to revive, but the same dim and mysterious twilight that they had borrowed from age-old legends and popular superstition in their countries was searched for by him in the comparatively recent beginnings of the New World and spread over his tales.

The sorcerers of the Middle Ages, with their alchemy and their faculty of infusing life into the pictures they painted, might seem to an imaginative person of the eighteen thirties to be reborn in the chemists and photographers of the new time. That the practitioners of both these professions were, in Hawthorne's opinion, surrounded by a radiance of mysticism, is proved over and over again by his works. I have chosen two representative short stories to illustrate this fact: *The Birthmark* (1843) and *Rappaccini's Daughter* (1843), both included in *Mosses from an Old Manse*.

The Birthmark[1] is the tale of the beautiful Georgiana, the perfect woman, who, at the end of the 18th century, just "when the comparatively recent discovery of Nature seemed to open paths into the region of miracle" has been married to Aylmer, the eminent man of science. Georgiana's beauty has but one blemish: a birthmark in the shape of a tiny hand appears on her cheek when she blushes. In order to be absolutely faultless in the eyes of Aylmer, Georgiana suffers him to make her the object of a scientific experiment to remove the stain on her beauty. Georgiana is introduced into Aylmer's laboratory, where his assistant Aminadab, a sort of Caliban, is working: "With his vast strength, his shaggy hair, his smoky aspect, and the indescribable earthiness that incrusted him, he seemed to represent man's physical nature." Georgiana is placed in a beautiful apartment, specially arranged for the occasion, and unconsciously becomes the object of mysterious influences from the adjoining laboratory. Finally, Aylmer offers her the magic potion. Georgiana falls asleep, and the birthmark slowly fades away. When she awakes, however, it is only to find that she is going to die. The fatal hand has grappled with the

---

[1] *Works* II, p. 47.

mystery of life in her. Aminadab chuckles hoarsely. The gross being of the earth knows well that men cannot with impunity seek perfection in human existence.

The second tale, *Rappaccini's Daughter*[1], is in the introduction said to be written by a Frenchman, Monsieur de l'Aubépine — an intentionally transparent pseudonym. The story itself has its setting in Padua, whither a young Italian, Giovanni Guasconti, comes in order to pursue his medical studies. When he has moved into his lodgings, he discovers in the garden of the adjoining house a beautiful young maiden who wanders about among the most wonderful flowers. Her father is Professor Rappaccini, a scientist who lives isolated from his colleagues because his scientific zeal is so ruthless that he shows no regard for human considerations when he wishes to obtain scientific results. In his garden he cultivates strange and venomous plants. He dare not touch them himself, but his daughter Beatrice has grown up among them and is wholly imbued with their fragrant potency. Guasconti and Beatrice fall in love with each other, and often meet in the garden, in spite of the warnings of Guasconti's old teacher. One day, this old man tells the youth everything about Rappaccini and his perilous experiments, and Guasconti is horrified to find that he, too, has been imbued with the poisons of Rappaccini's garden. Flowers fade in his hands, insects die when they meet his breath. He descends to keep a tryst with Beatrice, carrying with him a flagon with a strong antidote. Beatrice seizes it, drinks the liquor and sinks down upon the ground. "Thus the poor victim of man's ingenuity and of thwarted nature, and of the fatality that attends all such efforts of perverted wisdom, perished . . ."

Both of these stories are enacted in a world of quasi-scientific experiments that is rather remote from the Gothic novel. But in the later varieties of it, *e.g. Melmoth*, we find the man of science, who has plighted himself to the devil, who occupies himself with alchemy or the interpreting of old documents and in whose study skeletons and crystal globes are to be found. Features of the Faust figure, of Machiavelli and the Wandering Jew are to be traced in these old magicians. In spite of his youth, Aylmer is a typical sorcerer of this kind (8). His subordinate Aminadab has, apart from his name,

---

[1] *Works* II, p. 107.

other features drawn from the Oriental novel, while in outward
appearance he resembles the misshapen villain (6). Rappaccini himself is not only a deeply immoral scientist but, furthermore, an
Italian (3, 5). The devil's elixir (8) has acquired a new and original
shape in this story[1], and the old manuscript (1) is nothing less than
the collected works of Monsieur de l'Aubépine. If Hawthorne was
elsewhere fully conscious of using the machinery of Gothic romance,
it is possible that in this case he was not aware of it.

The story which has given its title to the collection *The Snow
Image and Other Tales* (1847)[2], also contains an element of wonder,
which must not be left out in the present connection. It bears the
sub-title "A Childish Miracle," and describes how a snow figure,
modelled by two little playing children, is endowed with life and
becomes their playmate. Hawthorne got the idea of this story when
he saw his own children romping in the snow, and it is one of the
most charming examples of his exceptional talent for depicting
children. It possesses both humour and poetry, and a slightly
pathetic moral. The little snowgirl is not allowed to remain in her
own element: the kind and sensitive father of the children drags her
into the house to get her warm in front of the fire. The lesson to
be learned is "that it behoves man, and especially men of benevol-
ence, to consider well what they are about, and, before acting on
their philanthropic purposes, to be quite sure that they comprehend
the nature and all relations of the business in hand." There is no
gloomy Gothic mysticism in this airy play of fantasy. It is a fairy-
tale, in which the children introduce into the every-day life of
quite a common family a miracle, in the person of the enchanting
little snow-image. When the mother looks out through the window,
there is "a small figure of a girl, dressed in white with rose-tinged
cheeks and ringlets of golden hue, playing about the garden with

---

[1] *Rappaccini's Daughter* has much in common with E. T. A. Hoffmann's
Datura Fastuosa, a tale in which a wonderful flower reared by a mysterious
Spaniard, who is a sorcerer and has formerly been the inmate of a Jesuit con-
vent, plays an important rôle. The sorcerer in Hoffmann's tale prepares a po-
tent powder for enhancing the beauty of the flower and eventually killing a
human being. For other suggestions concerning E. T. A. Hoffmann see H.
Arlin Turner, *Hawthorne's Literary Borrowings*, PMLA, June, 1936, and A.
Jessup and H. Canby, *The Book of the Short Story*, New York, 1907, p. 10.

[2] *Works* III, p. 391.

the two children . . . airily as she was clad, the child seemed to feel not the slightest inconvenience from the cold, but danced so lightly over the snow that the tips of her toes left hardly a print on its surface." Real though the charming little image is, she never opens her lips to utter a word, and when she enters and is placed in front of the hearth, she simply thaws, dissolving into a little puddle of water.

We here find ourselves far removed from armour, Gothic castles, and blood-stains. The supernatural feature of the story is the fact that the little image awakens to life. A similar motive, worked out in a far more traditional manner, is employed in *Feathertop* (1848, *Mosses from an Old Manse*).[1] Its sub-title is "A Moralized Legend," and the structure and manner of the story remind the reader of old European popular stories of the kind collected by the brothers Grimm. "Upon my word," says Hawthorne in the introductory paragraph, "if the legend were not one which I heard on my grandmother's knee, and which had established its place among things credible before my childish judgment could analyse its possibilities, I question whether I should have the face to tell it now."[2]

The contents of the story are as follows: Mother Rigby calls for her invisible servant Dickon to get a coal to light her pipe. She then begins to create or rather manufacture a scarecrow out of a broomstick, a flail, a puddingstick, a meal bag, and a pumpkin. When it is ready, it is named Feathertop, and acquires life through a puff at Mother Rigby's pipe. And so she sends Feathertop out into the world to make his own fortune. His life depends on the pipe; he must constantly puff at it, and now and then get it lighted anew by calling Dickon. Feathertop arrives in the town, where he is very much honoured, and under the name of Lord Feathertop he pays his respects to Master Gookin and his pretty daughter Polly, who is on the verge of falling in love with him. But suddenly she catches sight of him in a mirror, and shrieks. Feathertop likewise looks towards the mirror, and there beholds "not the glittering mockery of his outside show, but a picture of the sordid patchwork of his real composition, stripped of all witchcraft." Mother Rigby

[1] *Works* II, p. 253.

[2] Concerning the lively discussion of Hawthorne's dependence on Tieck in this special case, I refer the reader to the results of the researches made by Schönbach, Belden and Just. Cp. p. 58 of the present work.

is sitting at her hearth, puffing away at her pipe, when Feathertop returns. He does not feel like living any longer. The fault is not Polly's, nor anybody else's: "I've seen myself for the wretched, ragged, empty thing I am," he says. And so Feathertop becomes at last only a scarecrow.

Here we find once more a rich flora of elements from the world of the Gothic novel and the supernatural world. Mother Rigby is a hag (8) with an invisible servant of a devilish nature. Feathertop is admired by many people, akin with the good citizens of the town where H. C. Andersen's emperor with the invisible clothes lived: they are willing to be swindled, though the dog barks at Feathertop, and a little child prattles "some unintelligible nonsense about a pumpkin." The mirror, which is incapable of flattery, exposes Feathertop's whole pitifulness (11).

After *Feathertop*, Hawthorne wrote only two more short stories before passing over to the romances. To the reader of to-day, the short stories of Hawthorne often seem to have retained more of their freshness than his longer works. This may certainly be partly explained by his manner of applying the machinery of Gothic romance in the different instances. The very details that may in a short and artistic pastiche be of good effect, even because of their fantastic nature, will easily make his larger canvases appear affected and give them an antiquated stamp. But though one may be tempted to smile at the supernatural fancies and the host of reminiscences from Radcliffe and Mathurin in the novels of Hawthorne, one ends by finding them indispensable. They form an integral and essential element of his artistic method, and a great part of his originality consists in his completely unprejudiced manner of using old, worn-out ideas and figures abstracted from Gothic literature which had entered into the common imagination of the reading public. That the philosophical character of the romances must inevitably make them less palatable to a wide public was clear to Hawthorne, as is shown by a letter to the *International Monthly Magazine*, dated December 15th, 1851, in reply to a request concerning serial publication:

"I doubt whether my romances would succeed in the serial mode of publication; lacking, as they certainly do, the variety of interest and character which seem to have made the success of other works, so published. The reader would inevitably be tired to death of the one prominent idea, if presented to him under different aspects for a twelve-month together. The effect of such a story, it appears [to] me, depends on its being read continuously."[1]

Rather than acquire a wide public by abandoning his "one prominent idea," Hawthorne went his own way, sticking to his favourite subject: the rôle of sin in human life. It formed the main theme of *The Scarlet Letter* which appeared in 1850. A short synopsis will make clear the action of this novel.

In one of the earliest immigration years, Hester Prynne has arrived, alone and unknown, in the town of Boston. After some time it becomes known that she is expecting a child, but she refuses to reveal the identity of its father. She is put into prison and there gives birth to a girl, who is called Pearl. The romance opens with Hester's coming out of prison. According to the sentence of the magistrates, she has to stand on the scaffold as a penitent, and afterwards she must always wear on her bosom a red letter A (signifying Adulteress) sewn on to her dress. Hester submits to the judgment, but endeavours to render the token of her sin as beautiful as possible. Her fingers are deft and skilful, and the red letter, which estranges her from her intolerant environment, glows in brilliant red and golden hues of silk embroidery. As gorgeous as the letter is little Pearl. The children are in general exempted from the Puritan insistance on black clothing, and the girl is beautifully dressed in the same colours as the token on her mother's bosom. Time passes, and Hester Prynne leads an exemplary life, taking care of the sick and earning her living as a seamstress.

On the very day when Hester came out of prison, there arrived in the town an elderly man, who turns out to be a skilful physician and calls himself Chillingworth. Among his patients is the young minister of the town, Dimmesdale, who has a great reputation as a future spiritual leader, as well on account of his sermons, where penitence for hidden sins is one of the most frequent themes, as because of his ascetic way of life. In the description of all these things, the chief stress is put on the slow inner process through which Dimmesdale, who is the father of Hester Prynne's child, is driven to public confession. Under the pretence of medical attendance, Chillingworth, who, in fact, is Hester's husband, with a devilish mixture of deep-rooted ill-will and scientific thoroughness,

---

[1] Cited from a copy in the Yale University Collections.

drives him on to increasing self-torture. The principal persons are, consequently, the two sinners, Hester and Dimmesdale, and the victims, Chillingworth and Pearl.

According to the traditional Puritan view, the course of events ought to be arranged so that the sinners are punished, and the victims obtain satisfaction. But to Hawthorne's mind, the greatest guilt does not belong to those who have sinned against the commandments of the moral code. "What we did had a consecration of its own," says Hester to Dimmesdale. To Hester, the isolation caused by the red letter on her bosom becomes the spur to a richer development of her personality. If the well-to-do and robust people around her shut their doors to the excommunicated sinner, the poor and sick instead open theirs to the modest and skilful nurse. She has found her life's path, and when, after the confession, she chooses to remain in New England, continuing her work of charity there, she becomes, in spite of the red letter, a generally esteemed woman — Hawthorne shuns overstatements, but the reader may possibly feel tempted to discern a faint halo around her saint-like head.

Dimmesdale follows another course. Without confessing his crime, he tries to atone for it by continuing and intensifying his religious work. But here, it seems that the commandment of first removing the beam from one's own eye must be applied with Puritan severity. He does not feel at peace with himself till he has publicly ascended the scaffold of the pillory together with Hester and little Pearl. It is Dimmesdale's route from the pulpit to the pillory that occupies the greatest space in the book, and engrosses most of the author's interest. With unyielding and minute exactitude he follows the development of Dimmesdale's consciousness of sin, which is also symbolized by an A, branded on his bosom but concealed from the eyes of the multitude. Many readers and critics have expressed their dissatisfaction with the lack of explanation of the real nature of this letter. Was it a form of stigmatization, as palpable to other humans as to Dimmesdale himself, or was it a fantasy, produced by his sick conscience? Was it perhaps the symptom of a physical disease, which had, by a whim of fate, taken a form resembling Hester Prynne's scarlet letter? Or was it the effect of the treatment which Chillingworth had given the minister? These questions are never answered. The scarlet letter is a symbol, or perhaps rather an allegory, that pervades the whole book. It is to be found on Hester Prynne's garment, it burns on Dimmesdale's breast, it flames as a menacing omen in the sky during the scene by night when Hester and Dimmesdale meet at the scaffold, and it is personified in little Pearl, who, in her clothes of red and gold, seems to be not an earthly child but some elfish, or rather impish, sprite.

In fact, little Pearl, who is one of the victims of the sin, is nothing but a living accusation. There exists a mysterious connection between her and the letter on her mother's bosom, not only visible in her own appearance, but also inherent in her demeanour; as a baby she reaches for it, and when a little older, she often looks at the letter when speaking to her mother, and likes to draw attention to it. When Hester and Dimmesdale finally meet in the forest and Hester tears away the sign and throws it away among the trees, Pearl finds it again and carries it back to her mother. Pearl does not become a real human child till the confession has taken place. We are told that afterwards she grows up and becomes a beautiful young lady in a far-off country, where she even marries a nobleman and naturally always keeps up contact with her mother in the little Puritan town over the Ocean.

The fourth principal person, Chillingworth, plays the darkest rôle in this gloomy story. He is also the bearer of a guilt which consists in his having married Hester not because of her personality but because of her beauty. The conception that beauty is a great difficulty and danger, not to say a misfortune, to a woman, especially if she chance also to possess brains and heart, is peculiar to Hawthorne, and has been stressed by his French biographer.[1] But Chillingworth does not choose the path of confession and atonement. Instead, he sinks deeper and deeper in dark thoughts of implacability and vengeance, and the consequence is his own disaster.

The student who leaves out of consideration the chief problems concerned with the development of characters — which would otherwise constitute a tempting theme for a closer investigation — and concentrates his attention on the traces of Gothic romance to be found in *The Scarlet Letter*, will be able to gather a not incon-

---

[1] Dhaleine, *N. Hawthorne, sa vie et son œuvre*, Paris, 1905. Cp. Zenobia (*The Blithedale Romance*) and Miriam (*The Marble Faun*).

siderable fund of observations.[1] In the preface to the book, which is regarded as a masterpiece of satire, where Hawthorne has unburdened himself of the disgust and irritation that had accumulated in his mind during the years spent in the Customs House at Salem, he states that he got the idea for the novel from an old manuscript found among a heap of rubbish in an attic in the Customs House. In the roll of parchment, there was also "a certain affair of fine red cloth, much worn and faded"[2] — nothing less than the famous Scarlet Letter. Hawthorne even tells us that he tried to fasten it on his own breast, and thereby "experienced a sensation not altogether physical, yet almost so, as of burning heat: and as if the letter were not of red cloth but red-hot iron."

Here, then, we find the classical source of the Gothic novel: the manuscript (1), and an amulet with more or less pronounced magical qualities (8). Looking for an equivalent to (2) in our list, the Gothic castle, to our astonishment we discover such a one in the heart of seventeenth-century Boston. When Hester and Pearl one day go to visit Governor Bellingham, the man is found residing in a house that is built of wood, but covered by a kind of stucco in which fragments of broken glass are intermixed and where "cabalistic figures and diagrams"[3] have been engraved. There are also narrow towers on each side of the arched entrance. The interior, likewise, reveals many tokens of medieval times. The huge hall is illuminated by a bow-window with a deep and cushioned seat, the table and chairs are heirlooms "of the Elizabethan age or perhaps earlier," on the walls there hangs a row of stern portraits, and, finally, we find a suit of mail with a burnished breastplate standing before the oak panelling. Here, we recognize the traditional armour (10), which also serves another end: little Pearl uses it as a lookingglass (11) where "owing to the peculiar effect of this convex mirror" Hester's scarlet letter is "represented in exaggerated and gigantic proportions, so as to be greatly the most prominent feature of her appearance."[4] Number (3) — the mysterious crime — is represented by the guilt of Hester and Dimmesdale, and Dimmesdale's position

---

[1] For the results of my investigations concerning the reminiscences of Gothic Romance to be found in *The Scarlet Letter* and *The House of the Seven Gables*, I am indebted to impulses and observations given by Professor S. B. Liljegren in his lecture on *The American Novel of Terror*, October 12th, 1944.

[2] *Works* V, p. 49.　　[3] *Ibid.*, p. 129.　　[4] *Ibid.*, p. 132.

as a minister invests the crime with the religious character so dear to Gothic romance. The mental sapping work of Chillingworth may also be counted as a crime (3). His deformity (6) has already been mentioned. Hawthorne repeatedly takes his readers to the cemetery of Boston (7). There, Chillingworth finds some of his mysterious herbs: "I found them (answered the physician) growing on a grave, which bore no tombstone, nor other memorial of the dead man, save these ugly weeds, that have taken upon themselves to keep him in remembrance. They grew out of his heart, and typify, it may be, some hideous secret that was buried with him, and which he had done better to confess during his life-time."[1] Little Pearl feels very much at home in the burial ground. She speaks of the Black Man who is coming to fetch her mother and the minister. "So she drew her mother away, skipping, dancing and frisking fantastically, among the hillocks of the dead people, like a creature that had nothing in common with a bygone and buried generation nor owned herself akin to it. It was as if she had been made afresh, out of new elements . . ."[2] Hags (8) are mentioned in several instances. The sister of the Governor, Mrs. Hibbins, is a hag, a fact that is repeatedly and expressly stressed.[3] Mrs. Hibbins is wont to speak of the witches' meetings in the forest: "Ha, ha, ha, cackled the old witch-lady, still nodding her high head-dress at the minister . . . Well, well, we must needs talk thus in the day-time. You carry it off like an old hand. But at midnight, and in the forest, we shall have other talk together."[4] Chillingworth's rôle as a magician is proved by his interest not only in healing herbs but also in alchemy: "Old Chillingworth arranged his study and laboratory not such as a modern man of science would reckon even tolerably complete, but provided with a distilling apparatus and the means of compounding drugs and chemicals which the practised alchemist knew well how to turn to purpose."[5] During his Indian captivity he has also "enlarged his medical attainments by joining in the incantations of the savage priests; who were universally acknowledged to be powerful enchanters, often performing seemingly miraculous cures by their skill in the black art."[6]

---

[1] *Ibid.*, p. 160.   [2] *Ibid.*, p. 164.

[3] Concerning the influence of John Winthrop's Journal, see H. Arlin Turner, *Hawthorne's Literary Borrowings*, PMLA, June, 1936.

[4] *Works* V, p. 265.   [5] *Ibid.*, p. 154.   [6] *Ibid.*, p. 156.

We have already spoken of the magic letter A, which must also be included under (8), and about its appearance as an omen in the sky, which must belong under (9) of our list. The A on Dimmesdale's breast is never fully explained, but there are hints that it might be regarded as a case of stigmatization (4). Concerning the mirrors (11) there are some further observations to be added. When Hester longs to see her own image reflected in Pearl's eye, she perceives "not her own miniature portrait, but another face ... fiend-like, full of smiling malice, yet bearing the semblance of features that she had known full well, though seldom with a smile, and never with malice in them. It was as if an evil spirit possessed the child, and had just then peeped forth in mockery."[1] With his accustomed evasiveness, Hawthorne shuns a closer analysis of what Hester really saw. Perhaps it was a revelation of a likeness between the child and her father, which made her think of his constant remorse. However, this mirror effect is very impressive. Another effect of the same kind is attained when Hawthorne describes little Pearl impishly playing about in the wood. The child stands before a little pool which reflects her figure: "This image, so nearly identical with the living Pearl, seemed to communicate somewhat of its own shadowy and intangible quality to the child herself."[2]

The examples of the use of Gothic machinery in *The Scarlet Letter* might be multiplied, but these specimens of ten of the twelve items on our list seem to suffice for supporting the assertion that Hawthorne in his first full-length novel shows himself to be heavily indebted to the authors of the old novels of terror and wonder.

As early as 1851, Hawthorne published his second novel, *The House of the Seven Gables*. Reminiscences from his native town and old stories from the family chronicle of the Hawthornes provide a great deal of the material for this work, the theme of which is the psychological study of a supposed crime and its consequence for members of two families.

The old house that forms the scene of the action, and at the same time is a symbol of the disastrous power and influence of family tradition, was built in the seventeenth century by the hard and ruthless Colonel Pyncheon on a piece of soil which he had wrongfully usurped from the poor carpenter Matthew Maule. When, some

[1] *Ibid.*, p. 122. [2] *Ibid.*, p. 249.

years later, Matthew Maule was accused of sorcery and hanged, he cursed the whole family of the Pyncheons and prophesied that the Colonel would "get blood to drink." The Colonel, who was said to have acquired a large and fertile piece of land from an Indian tribe, later died under dramatic circumstances, with a stream of blood trickling from his mouth. His heirs in vain sought for the document by which the purchase had been confirmed. Of the Maule family it was only known that Matthew's son had assisted at the building of the House of the Seven Gables, and it was believed that the family became extinct at his death. The Pyncheon family, on the other hand, flourished during two centuries more. Once, about thirty years before the beginning of the story, an old bachelor, who was of an eccentric turn of mind, wanted to restore the house to its rightful owners, if any members of the Maule family were to be found; but before he had been able to realize these plans, the old man was found dead, possibly the victim of a murderer. His nephew Clifford was accused of the deed, and he received the death-sentence, later on commuted to imprisonment for life. Another nephew, who showed in his character all the traditional ruthlessness of the Pyncheons, and who was also an image of the old Colonel as to his outer appearance, inherited the fortune of his uncle. At the beginning of the story, twenty years after the violent death of the old man, this nephew of his, Judge Pyncheon, has become an important citizen in the little town, and Clifford's sister, Hepzibah, resides in the family mansion. In order to earn her living, she has sublet a couple of rooms to a young daguerrotypist, Holgrave, and she also opens a little cent-shop in the basement story of the house, some days before she expects her brother Clifford, who has been released, to return home. Just at that moment she receives an unexpected visit from a distant relative, the young Phoebe Pyncheon. Phoebe is as gay and lively as she is simple and charming; she fills the old house with life and runs the cent-shop in a splendid manner. When Clifford arrives, tired and worn-out by the long prison years, she becomes indispensable to him, and Holgrave falls in love with her.

After some time, Phoebe departs, and a little later, Judge Pyncheon presents himself and asks to see Clifford, stating that the old man must possess some knowledge of where the family fortune is to be found, thereby alluding to the lost Indian contract. The Judge places himself in an old family chair, according to tradition the very

one in which the Colonel was once found dead, and under a portrait
of that ancestor, which is strikingly like himself. Clifford has disappeared, but then suddenly presents himself, and at this surprise,
the Judge gets such a shock, that he collapses in the chair and dies.
Clifford and Hepzibah are very much frightened — Clifford has
once before been accused of the murder of a member of the family
who died in the selfsame room — and they depart on a fantastic
flight by railway.

Phoebe returns and finds the house locked, but is let in through
a back door by Holgrave. This young man now shows himself to
be a descendant of Matthew Maule, from whom he has inherited
something of the "mesmerism" that made the old "wizard"
suspected of sorcery. He is also filled with radical ideas and interested in scientific experiments. He now declares that the judge, as
well as his uncle previously — who had not really been murdered,
but only severely frightened — and very likely the Colonel Pyncheon
of yore, had all died from a hereditary disorder. Through a mis-
understanding, the reason for which was known only to the Judge,
Clifford had been accused of the murder of the old bachelor, and
afterwards sentenced to imprisonment. Hepzibah and Clifford
return, and everything is cleared up. Holgrave and Phoebe become
engaged, and he builds a new house for them to live in. One day,
he discloses the secret of his family. The carpenter Maule, who
assisted at the building of the house of the seven gables, had hidden
the Indian document, that would have procured so great riches
to the Pyncheon family, in a secret niche behind the old family
portrait. It is now so old as to have lost its validity. The old family
feud is ended, and Phoebe and Holgrave begin their life in their
new home with Hepzibah and Clifford, who also move from the
dismal old house of the seven gables.

As is shown by this synopsis, the action of the novel is very in-
significant. The dramatic events have taken place before the opening of the story, and the interest is centred on the character-drawing.
There is no principal character in the proper sense of the word, if
Clifford, the sensitive, unjustly accused victim, who late in life
recovers his liberty, but must be considered a broken man, is not
to be viewed as such. Holgrave, the representative of the new age
and at the same time possessor of the personal magnetism that
characterized his ancestor, the sorcerer, is an attempt to amal-

gamate old beliefs in magic with the interest in the secret faculties
of the soul that was so generally prevalent in Hawthorne's time.
Phoebe personifies the unspoilt freshness of youth, Hepzibah is a
dried-up branch of an old tree. Judge Pyncheon embodies selfish
greed and ruthlessness. The whole of the action is laid in modern
times. Is it then possible to find any traces of Gothic romance in
this story of an American family mansion of 1850? We shall pass
on to a closer investigation of this interesting question.

The old house where the story is enacted and which has given
the book its title is a dark and gloomy edifice. According to G. P.
Lathrop[1], there are in Salem at least three houses with claims to the
honour of being the original of Hawthorne's house of the seven
gables. But, as Hawthorne declares in his introduction, the mansion
is first and foremost an edifice "of materials long in use for con-
structing castles in the air."[2] According to the description in the
opening chapter of the book, it rises in pride, not modesty, and its
whole exterior is "ornamented with quaint figures, conceived in
the grotesqueness of a Gothic fancy, and drawn or stamped in the
glittering plaster, composed of lime, pebbles, and bits of glass,
with which the woodwork of the walls isoverspread."[3] The medieval
impression is enhanced as well by the seven pointed gables, which
present "the aspect of a whole sisterhood of edifices," as by the
principal entrance, which has "almost the breadth of a churchdoor."
The psychic atmosphere of the house is perhaps best described by
citing Clifford's assertion that "the greatest possible stumbling-
block in the path of human happiness and improvement are these
heaps of bricks and stones, consolidated with mortar, or hewn
timber, fastened together with spike-nails, which men painfully
contrive for their own torment, and call them house and home . . .
Morbid influences, in a thousand-fold variety, gather about hearths,
and pollute the life of households. There is no such unwholesome
atmosphere as that of an old home, rendered poisonous by one's
defunct forefathers and relatives . . . a rusty, crazy, creaky, dry-
rotted, damp-rotted, dingy, dark and miserable old dungeon."[4]
It is not only the word dungeon that is here fetched from the Gothic
mansions; also the peaked pinnacles and the quaint figures, ex-

---

[1] G. P. Lathrop, Introductory note to *The House of the Seven Gables*,
Works III, p. 10.

[2] *Ibid.*, p. 15.   [3] *Ibid.*, p. 24.   [4] *Ibid.*, pp. 309—10.

pressly termed Gothic, are devised to awake reminiscences from the reading of Gothic romance and catch something of the weird atmosphere belonging to it. Thus, we here note an instance of point (2) in our scheme.

The mysterious crime (3) appears in a very central position in this novel. It is represented by the repeated, unexplained deaths in the Pyncheon family, which for a long time remain unsolved riddles engendering evil deeds like Matthew Maule's hanging or Clifford's imprisonment. Colonel Pyncheon's acquisition of poor Maule's soil and the selfish and ruthless, not to say criminal, way in which the Judge takes possession of his uncle's papers and fortune are also actions fraught with disastrous consequences which may be included in this category.

The house of the seven gables and the happenings within its walls naturally give birth to a number of rumours, and even if Hawthorne declares that he is speaking of local sayings, he delights in describing the ghostly happenings that are said to occur in the old building. An eighteenth century member of the family, who was the first to open the little shop in the basement, is, according to tradition, sometimes still visible there: "It used to be affirmed, that the dead shop-keeper in a white wig, a faded velvet coat, an apron at his waist, and his ruffles carefully turned back from his wrists, might be seen through the chinks of the shutters."[1] It is also averred, that the whole company of deceased members of the family sometimes honour the house by visiting it: "First comes the ancestor himself, in his black cloak, steeplehat, and trunk-breeches, girt about the waist with a leathern belt, in which hangs his steel-hilted sword ... So decided is his look of discontent as to impart additional distinctness to his features, through which, nevertheless, the moonlight passes, and flickers on the wall beyond ... Here come other Pyncheons, the whole tribe, in their half a dozen generations ..."[2] The beautiful Alice Pyncheon who fell into a tragic dependence on a witchcraft-practising member of the Maule family, is also supposed to haunt the house — "especially when one of the Pyncheons was to die, she had been heard playing sadly and beautifully on the harpsichord"[3] and, true enough, Hepzibah catches a strain of music immediately before the decease of Judge Pyncheon. The ghostly music is a trait beloved especially

---

[1] *Ibid.*, p. 45.   [2] *Ibid.*, p. 330.   [3] *Ibid.*, p. 108.

by Mrs. Radcliffe. The woods around the French châteaux in *The Mysteries of Udolpho* resound ever and anon to harmonies of the same melancholy and ghostly character as the preludes of Alice Pyncheon's harpsichord.

We need not hesitate in classifying the members of the Maule family with the community of sorcerers and magicians (8). Even Holgrave's modern profession, that of a photographer, is endowed with a magic and prophetic touch when Hawthorne speaks of it.[1] It is said of the Maules, that "their companions . . . grew conscious of a circle round about the Maules, within the sanctity or the spell of which, in spite of an exterior of sufficient frankness and good-fellowship, it was impossible for any man to step . . . Among other good-for-nothing properties and privileges, one was especially assigned them — that of exercising an influence over people's dreams."[2] This characterization may be stretched a point to include also the mesmerism which appertains to the late descendant of the Maules, Holgrave. But every possibility of linking popular sayings with reality is excluded when it comes to the excellent specimens of ghosts drawn by Hawthorne in another description of the peculiarities of the Maule family, which is put in the mouth, or rather included in the manuscript, of Holgrave: "Their graves, in the crevices of rocks, were supposed to be incapable of retaining the occupants, who had been so hastily thrust into them. Old Matthew Maule, especially, was known to have as little hesitation or difficulty in rising out of his grave as an ordinary man in getting out of bed, and was as often seen at midnight as living people at noonday."[3] It would be difficult to find a more accurate and at the same time humourously sceptical description of a real, old-time wizard ghost than this. Holgrave's sorcery is of a more modern kind. He makes pictures out of sunshine by means of his camera. But his pictures have a wonderful character of their own; there is, he says, "a wonderful insight in Heaven's broad and simple sunshine. While we give it credit only for depicting the merest surface, it actually brings out the deepest secret character with a truth that no painter would ever venture upon, even could he detect it."[4] The young man also possesses other mysterious qualities. "I am," says he to Phoebe, "somewhat of a mystic, it must be confessed.

<hr />

[1] Cp. p. 107 of the present work.   [2] *Works* III, pp. 41—42.
[3] *Ibid.*, p. 226.   [4] *Ibid.*, p. 116.

The tendency is in my blood, together with the faculty of mesmerism, which might have brought me to Gallow's Hill, in the good old times of witchcraft."[1] A better expression of Hawthorne's view of oldtime sorcery could not be found. He clearly perceived the identity of what his ancestors had termed witch-craft with phenomena that in his own days had found a scientific or at least pseudo-scientific explanation. But he preferred by far to use the old and romantic words and view-points in order to describe them and thus create the mysterious twilight in which his personages felt best at their ease and best could express the truths that he wanted to impress upon his readers.

An important rôle is also played by the ancestral chair (8) of the Pyncheons, of which it is once said that "it really seems to be enchanted like the one in Comus."[2] Sitting in that same chair, the Colonel, the old unmarried uncle of Clifford, and Judge Pyncheon all get their mysterious attacks, or, as expressed in the language of superstition, "get blood to drink."

Above the chair hangs the picture of Colonel Pyncheon, the stern, unmitigable features of which "seemed to symbolize an evil influence, and so darkly to mingle the shadow of their presence with the sunshine of the passing hour, that no good thought or purposes could ever spring up and blossom there."[3] In telling the legend of Alice Pyncheon, Holgrave also recounts what is rumoured of the old portrait: "This picture, it must be understood, was supposed to be so intimately connected with the fate of the house, and so magically built into its walls, that, if once it would be removed, that very instant the whole edifice would come thundering down in a heap of dusty ruin. All through the foregoing conversation between Mr. Pyncheon and the carpenter [Maule], the portrait had been frowning, clenching its fist, and giving many such proofs of excessive discomposure ... And finally ... the ghostly portrait is averred to have lost all patience, and to have shown itself on the point of descending bodily from its frame."[4] Here, Hawthorne has given a free rein to his Gothic imagination and has gone almost as far as Walpole did in *The Castle of Otranto*. But it must be remarked that this is not done in his own story, but in the old legend, which he makes Holgrave read aloud to Phoebe. We note, however, here a reminiscence of number (11) of our list.

---

[1] *Ibid.*, p. 259.   [2] *Ibid.*, p. 324.   [3] *Ibid.*, p. 36.   [4] *Ibid.*, p. 236.

Hawthorne's predilection for mirrors (11) is also visible here. The saying goes that in one room of the old house there hangs "a large, dim-looking glass ... which was fabled to contain within its depths all the shapes that had ever been reflected there — the old colonel himself and his many descendants."[1] Hawthorne states that "the posterity of Matthew Maule had some connection with the mystery of the looking-glass, and that, by what appears to have been a sort of mesmeric process, they could make its inner region all alive with the departed Pyncheons." We recognize here a mirror of exactly the same kind as the one in the old Province House, where Esther Dudley used to surround herself with a mirror-bred society of bygone generations. In the novel of the Pyncheon family, however, the mirror never comes to play the rôle which seems designed for it in the description cited above.

The ancestral portrait has a central importance of a different kind for the plot of the book. In its frame there is a secret spring devised by the carpenter of the Maule family. The spring is known only to members of that "mesmeric" race, and it is by touching it that Holgrave finally brings forth the old document of the Indian sagamores, by which the Colonel had become entitled to such wide domains, now irreparably lost to his descendants. The portrait and the mirror may amply suffice to illustrate number (11) in our tabulation.

Number (12) is also represented in *The House of the Seven Gables*. The blood which God gives the members of the Pyncheon family to drink as a retribution for their sins is of a decidedly Gothic brand. The reader of Hawthorne's short stories may remember that Hutchinson, the British governor depicted in *Edward Randolph's Portrait*, when his dying hour drew on[2] "gasped for breath, and complained that he was choking with the blood of the Boston Massacre."

The House of the Seven Gables has more of a ghostly atmosphere than any other of the full-length stories that Hawthorne published during his life-time. The musty, dark, morbid and melancholy air throughout the book is temporarily blown away only by Phoebe's gay and girlish figure. The hatred of family oppression which pervades the whole work has certainly something to do with Hawthorne's own seclusion in his maternal home. But realism

---

[1] *Ibid.*, p. 35.   [2] Cp. p. 104 of the present work.

had not yet come into its own, and Hawthorne chose the tools that were at hand. The effects that he achieved by using parables and hints drawn from his reading as a schoolboy of the blood-curdling ghost-stories, are still impressive in their subtle toning down and perfection of style.

A Blithedale Romance is the literary outcome of Hawthorne's stay at Brook Farm and his closer contact with the group of Transcendentalists who there sought the realization of a socialistic ideal. As has already been mentioned, Hawthorne found that for him rural labour was incompatible with literary activity. He was a dreamer who shrank from practical life and soon tired of hard physical labour, however attractive the accompanying intellectual environment might seem to him. But his disillusion was even deeper. He was a greater sceptic than most of the idealistic "farmhands" in the community and saw clearly that the experiment could not be a lasting one. The *Blithedale Romance* is perhaps first and foremost a settling of his account with Brook Farm and with an exaggerated reformatory zeal, such as he has embodied it in the person of Hollingsworth. His contemporaries believed the fictitious persons to be portraits of members of the Transcendentalist group. Such insinuations were, however, consistently rejected by Hawthorne.

When the narrator of the story, Miles Coverdale, who has not a few features in common with Hawthorne himself, arrives at Blithedale, he is met by the host, Silas Foster, and Zenobia, the feminine soul of the enterprise. Zenobia's origin is obscure, but she has created a position and a name for herself as an authoress and an artist in conversation. She is also very rich and strikingly beautiful. Even in the simple dress that she is wearing in this rural surrounding, her appearance is that of a queen, and she gives a personal touch to her attire by always wearing a sumptuous flower stuck into her black curls. Contrasting with her stands the gloomy figure of Hollingsworth, a simple and uncultivated blacksmith, obsessed by a philanthropic idea — a rather unrealistic project for the rehabilitation of criminals. He is in need of money for the realization of his plans, and he does not hesitate to exploit for these ends the affection that Zenobia feels for him, but that he does not reciprocate. To the Blithedale farm comes also Priscilla, a frail and delicate little creature. She is a seamstress by profession and daughter of Old

Moodie, a rather decayed individual. Priscilla attaches herself to Zenobia, but the latter's friendship changes into jealousy when she sees that Hollingsworth is attracted by the pale charm of the little seamstress. And so Zenobia surrenders Priscilla into the hands of Westervelt, a mysterious person, half hypnotizer, half criminal, who has formerly exploited Priscilla and made her appear during his séances in the rôle of The Veiled Lady. Hollingsworth assists at such a séance, and suddenly realizing the nature of his feelings for Priscilla, he takes her away from Westervelt. Zenobia, who is really the elder sister of Priscilla — the daughter of Old Moodie in a previous and wealthier existence — disappears, exasperated by jealousy, and is later on found drowned by Foster, Hollingsworth and Coverdale.

It may seem a difficult business to introduce any Gothic romance in the description of a rural socialistic experiment in New England during the eighteen forties. The instances of such an influence are, indeed, rarer here; but Hawthorne's innate predilection for reminiscences of a Gothic character nevertheless found their way into the *Blithedale Romance*.

In his introduction to the book, Hawthorne himself says that his stay at Brook Farm was "certainly the most Romantic episode of his own life," and it seems that his intention was to content himself with writing a romance of reality, without introducing any supernatural machinery. But he was unable to keep his imagination from playing with the thought of how this reality might be metamorphosed into a regular romanticized, or rather gothicized, version. When Priscilla enters the story, accompanied by Hollingsworth, Zenobia gives a mockingly scornful description of how the happenings of the evening might be turned into a ballad: "It is a grand subject, and worthy of supernatural machinery. The storm, the startling knock at the door, the entrance of the sable knight Hollingsworth and this shadowy snow-maiden, who, precisely at the stroke of midnight, shall melt away at my feet in a pool of ice-cold water and give me my death with a pair of wet slippers."[1] This may sound like a jest, but there is something of a sinister prophecy in the facetious words: Priscilla will give Zenobia her death in ice-cold water, though she does not at the moment suspect anything of the kind. On another occasion, Zenobia is likened to a tragic actress

---

[1] *Works* V, p. 357.

"fumbling in her bosom for a concealed dagger or mingling the ratsbane in her lover's bowl of wine."[1] That such a thing would be impossible to imagine in New England, but, to Hawthorne's romantic mind, a quite natural occurrence south of the Appenines, is shown by the words which immediately follow: "And, besides, had we been in Italy, instead of New England, it was hardly yet a crisis for the dagger or the bowl" (5).

The mysteriousness of *A Blithedale Romance* consists chiefly in the mesmeric faculty possessed by Priscilla and utilized by Wester-velt. Hawthorne's attitude towards these matters is shown in a comment referring to the public at the séance where Priscilla appears as the Veiled Lady: "The epoch of rapping spirits, and all the wonders that have followed in their trails — such as tables upset by invisible agencies, bells self-tolled at funerals, and ghostly music performed on jew's harps — had not yet arrived. And, my countrymen, methinks we have fallen on an evil age. If these phenomena have not humbug at the bottom, so much the worse for us."[2] Still, Hawthorne uses the effects of Westervelt's magnetism or mesmerism much in the same way as he earlier used the Gothic machinery. And into his description of this very mod-ern kind of superstition, there enters not a little of the weirdness remembered from the Gothic Romance.[3] Westervelt may logically be counted among the wizard types of Hawthornesque Romance. He is a handsome man of a type decidedly Italian or Spanish (5): "His hair, as well as his beard and mustache, was coal-black; his eyes, too, were black and sparkling, and his teeth remarkably bril-liant."[4] Other traits are rather to be assigned to category (8): he has a "metallic laugh," Coverdale says, and continues: "in the excess of his delight he opened his mouth wide, and disclosed a gold band around the upper part of his teeth, thereby making it apparent that every one of his brilliant grinders and incisors was

---

[1] *Ibid.*, p. 409.   [2] *Ibid.*, p. 545.

[3] Cargill remarks that Hawthorne may have been influenced by a passage in M. Fuller's *At Home and Abroad* where she represents the Germans, the Norwegians, and the Swedes as the carriers of Old World mysticism into the New World. Hawthorne got the name Westervelt from the list of drowned seamen on board a Swedish vessel Elisabeth. (Oscar Cargill, *Nemesis and Na-thaniel Hawthorne*, PMLA, 1937, No. 3.)

[4] *Works* V, p. 424.

a sham. This discovery affected me very oddly. I felt as if the whole man were a moral and physical humbug: his wonderful beauty of face, for aught I knew, might be removable like a mask; and, tall and comely as his figure looked, he was perhaps but a wizened little elf, gray and decrepit, with nothing genuine about him, save the wicked expression of his grin."[1] The artfulness of this mixture of romantic folklore and modern scientific sham is exquisite. Using the gold band round Westervelt's sham teeth as a medium, Hawthorne obtains the same effect as do the old Nordic tales of the forest witch who has no back to her lovely form.

Just as Zenobia foreshadows her own fate in the jesting words mentioned above, she tells her audience of Priscilla's peculiar nature, when she narrates the story of the silvery veil. It is, says Coverdale expressly, "undeniable nonsense," but nonsense of a very clear-sighted and not altogether kindly nature, with an undertone of menace. When finally Zenobia interrupts her tale by throwing the piece of gauze she holds in her hand, over Priscilla's head, the meaning stands quite clear to the reader: Zenobia is going to deliver the girl into Westervelt's hands. Zenobia, though in all her gorgeousness perhaps the most intense flesh-and-blood figure Hawthorne ever created, has nevertheless something magic in her being. "Zenobia is an enchantress," whispers Coverdale to Hollingsworth. " . . . the flower in her hair is a talisman. If you were to snatch it away, she would vanish, or be transformed into something else."[2]

But if Zenobia is, on the whole, a creature of earthly clay, Priscilla has all the more supernatural qualities. "Hidden things were visible to her . . . and silence was audible . . ." These strange faculties were explained by the modern magicians in their own way: "It was a period when science . . . was bringing forward a new board of facts and imperfect theories, that had partially won credence in elder times, but which modern scepticism had swept away as rubbish . . . Yet . . . the busy tongues . . . averred . . . that the strange gentleman (Westervelt) was a wizard, and that he had taken advantage of Priscilla's lack of earthly substance to subject her to himself, as his familiar spirit, through whose medium he gained cognizance of whatever happened, in regions near or remote" (8).[3]

That is the nearest Hawthorne ever comes to Gothic reminiscence

[1] *Ibid.*, pp. 427—28.　　[2] *Ibid.*, p. 371.　　[3] *Ibid.*, pp. 533—34.

in his *Blithedale Romance*. He has endeavoured and on the whole succeeded, in creating with this book a work mainly of his own age. But, even though Zenobia lends to the novel the whole glamour of her vivid and dynamic personality, of all Hawthorne's novels this remains the one that makes the faintest impression on the reader nowadays. It is possible that Hawthorne took the same view of his own writings. In the evolutionary curve that may be traced of the dependence on Gothic art in Hawthorne's work, *A Blithedale Romance* stands as the point of maximum independence between the starting-point of recently imbibed youthful impressions and the harking back to old sources in the works of his later years. It is possible that this development would have taken place even if Hawthorne had stayed in America all his life. But undoubtedly his years as Consul at Liverpool and his acquaintance with English monuments from earlier epochs, with old legends and with living historical tradition in Britain did much to accelerate it. In his notebooks, and in *Our Old Home* we find many references to more or less fantastical stories that have much in common with the Gothic tradition. During these years, however, Hawthorne wrote no fiction in the proper sense of the word. When he finally reverted to this field, it was under the liberating influence of another intellectual and physical climate, during a prolonged stay in Italy, the home of Romance, where many half-forgotten figures and scenes from the world of the Gothic tales rose to the surface of his mind petitioning a place in his creations. *The Marble Faun* was regarded by Hawthorne himself as his best work, and in his Preface he states the rôle of Italy in this "fanciful story, evolving a thoughtful moral." The author's intention is not to portray Italian manners and the Italian character: "Italy as the site of his Romance was chiefly valuable to him as affording a sort of poetic or fairy precinct, where actualities would not be so terribly insisted upon as they are, and must needs be, in America. No author, without a trial, can conceive of the difficulty of writing a romance about a country where there is no shadow, no antiquity, no mystery, no picturesque and gloomy wrong, nor anything but a commonplace prosperity, in broad and simple daylight, as is happily the case with my dear native land . . . Romance and poetry, ivy, lichens, and wall-flowers, need ruins to make them grow." [1]

---

[1] *Work* VI, p. 15.

9 – 47370 *Jane Lundblad*

This description of the appropriate setting for a romance might have been given by Mrs. Radcliffe herself. It shows better than anything else that Hawthorne's ideal, though morally and in many respects also artistically so very superior to those of the "Gothic" authors, still had very much in common with them. We shall find further proofs of this fact by studying the composition and some details of his story of Rome: *The Marble Faun.*

The Marble Faun vies with *The Scarlet Letter* for the honour of being the most widely read of Hawthorne's romances. Apart from its literary value, it has a certain topographical interest for the tourist in Italy, and the volume is still to be found in book-shops in Rome beside Madame de Staël's *Corinne* and Zola's *Rome.*

This story traces its inception to a visit to the Capitoline Museum, where Hawthorne, who was otherwise seldom captivated by sculpture, immediately took a great interest in the so-called Faun of Praxiteles. In his Italian note-book he himself tells us of the occasion: "We afterwards went into the sculpture gallery, where I looked at the Faun of Praxiteles, and was sensible of a peculiar charm in it; a sylvan beauty and homeliness, friendly and wild at once. The lengthened but not preposterous ears, and the little tail, which we infer, have an exquisite effect, and make the spectator smile in his very heart. This race of fauns was the most delightful of all that antiquity imagined. It seems to me that a story with all sorts of fun and pathos in it, might be contrived on the idea of their species having become intermingled with the human race; a family with the faun blood in them, having prolonged itself from the classic era till our own days. The tail might have disappeared, by dint of constant intermarriages with ordinary mortals; but the pretty hairy ears should occasionally reappear in members of the family; and the moral instincts and intellectual characteristics of the faun might be most picturesquely brought out, without determent to the human interest of the story."[1]

Such a figure was just what Hawthorne needed to illustrate his now yet further developed theory about the rôle of sin in man's mental and intellectual development. Donatello, the chief personage of the story, is a scion of such an old Italian family as was described in the note-book. He is beautiful, healthy and gay, an

---

[1] *Hawthorne's Italian Note-book*, April 22nd, 1858.

unsophisticated child of nature without any higher development of character. In Rome, he makes the acquaintance of a coterie of young artists and falls in love with the beautiful and mysterious Miriam, a lady of unknown origin whose past life remains a riddle to the reader throughout the book. Some sort of connection with Miriam's past is, however, traceable in a model, a sort of demoniacal lazzarone, who follows everywhere in her wake. One evening, he appears when Miriam and Donatello are standing just at the edge of the Tarpeian precipice, and, in a fit of passion, Donatello seizes the man and holds him above the abyss. With a glance, he consults Miriam, before he lets him fall to be crushed against the stones at the foot of the rock. Thus Donatello has come to know sin and is going to be familiar with the sense of guilt — a guilt that he shares with Miriam, because it is she who has given him the final sanction for accomplishing the deed. A shadow of guilt also falls on Hilda, Miriam's friend, a young girl who is a perfect specimen of the idealized "American womanhood" that Hawthorne often praises. She is beautiful, pious and pure of heart. Each day, when she has finished her work, which consists in copying the works of the old masters, she returns to her attic, in front of which she keeps alive the lamp before an image of the Virgin Mary, and feeds white doves that assemble there. The continuation of the story is enacted partly in Rome, partly on Donatello's family estate in the vicinity of Florence. It is a description of how Donatello and Miriam, like two damned spirits, roam about separated, in quest of a peace which neither of them shall ever be able to find. Donatello is no longer in possession of the mysterious contact with nature that has formerly been his greatest joy as well as the most salient feature of his character. Miriam cannot free herself from her gloomy mood, even though she has been delivered of her persecutor. At last they meet at Perugia, and after having spent some time together in Rome during the carnival, they part for ever. Donatello gives himself up to justice in order to expiate his crime. The fate of Miriam remains unknown to the reader. Hilda, who has also made a confession — in spite of her Protestantic faith uttered in a whisper in a confessional at St. Peter's — achieves peace after an inner struggle, and finally marries Kenyon, the fourth member of the set.

Here, we are not concerned with the personal development of these three personages. The substance of Hawthorne's message in this book is expressed in the following words, uttered by Kenyon on the last page of the work: "Sin has educated Donatello, and elevated him. Is sin then — which we deem such a dreadful blackness to the universe — is it, like sorrow, merely an element of human education, through which we struggle to a higher and purer state than we should otherwise have attained? Did Adam fall that we might ultimately rise to a far loftier paradise than his?"[1] In *The Marble Faun*, we watch Donatello's development from a pagan and carefree youth, full of animal spirits, into a grown-up man with a deep sense of responsibility who uprightly and consciously aspires towards a righteous life. His confession is not the result of external pressure, like Dimmesdale's, but the outcome of a free inner development — a transformation.

The Gothic trick of presenting the story as if found in an old manuscript has here been discarded by Hawthorne. But otherwise, it is rather amazing how many of the old patterns appear when he proceeds to write a romantic story from the enchanted country of Romance. He tells it, of course, in his usual, sceptical way; but, to a higher degree than elsewhere, it is felt that he assumes the reader to be inspired by a romantic feeling which makes all sorts of supernatural and wonderful things quite plausible. Proceeding with our tabulation, we now arrive at item (2), the Gothic castle, and we soon recognize it without any difficulty, standing in the Florentine landscape and free of all disguise.

The title that Hawthorne first gave to his novel was *The Romance of Monte Beni*, and it was under this name that the book was first printed in America. Monte Beni is the ancestral castle of Donatello — for which the Villa Montauto near Florence, where Hawthorne had been staying some time in 1858, was the model — and the description of the building leaves little to be desired as to age, loneliness, and other traditional attributes of the Gothic castle. It possesses ancient battlements and an "owl tower" with a prisoner's cell, where in olden days a necromancer was kept prisoner. It is now converted into a chapel, with a crucifix, a Bambino, and a human skull carved in alabaster as chief adornments. The castle also contains a big entrance room, which Hawthorne likens to an "Etruscan tomb," and "an almost interminable vista of apart-

---

[1] *Works* VI, p. 519.

ments . . . reminding him [Kenyon] of the hundred rooms in Blue Beard's castle, or the countless halls in some palace of the Arabian nights."[1]

Still more weirdly Gothic is the description of the catacombs of St. Calixtus, where Miriam has a mysterious and frightening interview with her strange and awe-inspiring follower. These ancient subterranean passages possessed an atmosphere of dark mystery, corresponding fairly exactly to Hawthorne's conception of the ideal surroundings for a ghostly interview. To him they must have been a great find — the very scenes of the beloved books of his boyhood come true. Conscientiously he records the itinerary for the tourists: "Sometimes their gloomy pathway tended upward, so that, through a crevice, a little daylight glimmered down upon them, or even a streak of sunshine peeped into a burial niche; then again they went downward by gradual descent, or by abrupt, rudely hewn steps, into deeper and deeper recesses of the earth . . ."[2] Further on, "they found two sarcophagi, one containing a skeleton, and the other a shrivelled body, which still wore the garments of its former lifetime." Reality such as this more than equals the most terrific descriptions of subterranean cellars belonging to Italian convents or Spanish castles to be met with in the original Gothic novels.

Passing on to item (3) on our list, we find the mysterious crime as the chief secret of Miriam's dark destiny. The connection between her and the model, who is later found to be a Capuchin friar, is never made quite clear, but Hawthorne hints several times at a parallelism between Miriam's fate and that of Beatrice Cenci, whose portrait is copied by Hilda. Here we thus find the religious character of the crime, which is also possibly of incestuous nature[3] — the very model of the crimes of Gothic romance. The second crime in the novel — the murder of the model by Donatello — is of a different kind, chiefly meant to illustrate Hawthorne's idea of sin and its consequences.

Number (4) is represented, as has already been pointed out, by the model, who is found to be a Capuchin monk. He is the central figure of the event which forms the climax of the action: the murder. The beggar — who is really a monk — is hurled down

---

[1] *Ibid.*, p. 255.   [2] *Ibid.*, p. 40.

[3] Beatrice Cenci was, according to the legend, violated by her father.

the Tarpeian rock and crushed at its foot. The fall is not described
from a visual point of view. As often elsewhere[1], Hawthorne contents himself with giving the auditive effects: "Along with it [the
struggle], or closely succeeding it, was a loud, fearful cry, which
quivered upward through the air, and sank quivering downward
to the earth. Then, a silence."[2] We hardly err, if we see in this
downfall a reminiscence of Lewis's monk when he is precipitated
down a rock by the devil, or of Melmoth, whose fall is so obviously
copied in Hawthorne's first literary attempt *Fanshawe*. These men,
who are hurled down craggy precipices, appear abundantly throughout Romantic literature. The real Count Victorin tumbles down
a steep rock before Medardus assumes his rôle[3], and a little later
Claude Frollo falls headlong from the towers of Notre Dame.[4]
It is tempting to try to picture the immediate reaction of Hawthorne
when he stood for the first time on the edge of the Tarpeian Rock.
He described the occasion in his Italian notebook.[5] He and his
wife had been to tea with Fredrika Bremer, who was at the time
staying in Rome, and afterwards the party went out to look at the
precipice. The note-book contains no reference to any future
literary application of the motive. Hawthorne only notes that he
has seen "the famous precipice, down which the old Romans used
to fling their traitors, or sometimes, indeed, their patriots,"[6] but
perhaps just at that moment, before the dispassionate gaze of the
unsuspecting little Swedish lady, was born the strange hybrid between a satyr, a ghost, and a monk, which in Hawthorne's last great
romance, was to find his death at the foot of the Tarpeian Rock.
Other passages relating to the Church are not of any immediate
interest for the theme analyzed here.

The rôle of Italy in the story is clearly that of presenting the
action under a more romantic aspect as taking place beneath the
sky of southern Europe and among historical ruins and antiquities
of different kinds. But, to Hawthorne, Italy is not only a storehouse
of antiquities. It is also the centre of the Old World, filled with

[1] Cp. p. 93 of the present work.
[2] *Works* VI, p. 202.
[3] E. T. A. Hoffmann, *Die Elixiere des Teufels*.
[4] Victor Hugo, *Notre Dame de Paris*. Cp. Killen, *Le roman terrifiant*, p. 183.
[5] May 22nd, 1858.
[6] *Notebook*, May 22nd, 1858.

memories of hoary crimes and iniquity. We recall his words about its value as a setting cited from the Preface of the book.[1] Speaking of the Villa Borghese, he once says: "Just an instant before it was Arcadia and the Golden Age. The spell being broken, it was now only that old tract of pleasure-ground close by the people's gate of Rome — a tract where the crimes and calamities of ages, the many battles, blood recklessly poured out, and deaths of myriads, have corrupted all the soil, creating an influence that makes the air deadly to human lungs."[2] This impression of Rome as something positively corrupted goes through the whole narrative, culminating in a passage likening the Eternal City to a "long-decaying corpse,"[3] an uncomfortable and inhospitable-seeming abode to a citizen of the New World, but still possessing its own inimitable fascination.

The spectres (7) of the Gothic novel are also embodied in the person of Miriam's model. Another instance, showing Hawthorne's trust in his readers' readiness when it comes to accepting ghost-like effects, is given in the description of the nightly visit paid by a company of tourists to the Coliseum. Here the sculptor Kenyon acts as the author's mouthpiece when he says: "Fancy a nightly assemblage of eighty thousand melancholy and remorseful ghosts, looking down from those tiers of broken arches, striving to repent of the savage pleasures which they once enjoyed, but still longing to enjoy them over again." Whereupon Hilda rejoins: "You bring a Gothic horror into this peaceful moonlight scene."[4] A few moments afterwards, the real spectre, the model, makes his appearance. The character of this very compound figure is certainly partly spectral (7), but it is perhaps still more that of a sorcerer (8): Miriam appears to be a bewitched person, as soon as he approaches. When catching sight of him, "fancying herself wholly unseen, the beautiful Miriam began to gesticulate extravagantly, gnashing her teeth, flinging her arms wildly abroad, stamping with her feet. It was as if she had stepped aside for an instant, solely to snatch the relief of a brief fit of madness." Even though Hawthorne gives a sort of psychological explanation of her demeanour, stating that she wished to "relieve her nerves in this wild way," the similarity between her gestures and the traditional witch dances is nevertheless striking. Elsewhere,

---

[1] Cp. above p. 129.
[2] *Works* VI, p. 111.   [3] *Ibid.*, p. 372.   [4] *Ibid.*, p. 185.

too, Miriam is depicted as a woman with a bent towards the supernatural: "She has . . . a suggestive power, a magnetic influence,
a sympathetic knowledge."[1]

The model is, indeed, a strange mixture of different romantic
types. In the chapter entitled "The Spectre of the Catacombs,"
he is mentioned as an artist's model "of exceedingly picturesque
and even melodramatic aspect." His costume is that of a Roman
peasant, but under his broad-brimmed hat "a wild visage was
indistinctly seen, floating away, as it were, into a dusky wilderness
of mustache and beard. His eyes winked, and turned uneasily from
the torches, like a creature to whom midnight would be more congenial than noonday." When he speaks, his voice is hoarse and
harsh: "Inquire not what I am, nor wherefore I abide in the darkness," he says, ". . . She [Miriam] has called me forth, and must
abide the consequence of my reappearance in the world."[2] And so
begins his sinister influence "such as beasts and reptiles of subtle
and evil nature sometimes exercise upon their victims . . . That
iron chain . . . must have been forged in some such unhallowed
furnace as is only kindled by evil passions and fed by evil deeds."[3]
We might here point to item (5) in our tabulation, the Italian villain
in pact with the Devil, as well as to (7), spectres, and (8), magicians.
Hawthorne has used all the resources of Gothic machinery to sug-
gest the same impression of fright as the old novels of terror had
once awakened. At the same time, his use of them is as sceptically
circumspect as possible, taking care not to run the risk of an
accusation that he belonged to the Gothic school himself. To a
modern reader, the attraction of these Gothic mysteries remains
incomprehensible, but that the flavour bestowed was heartily
relished by contemporary readers is shown by a letter to the
author from Motley, cited by Lathrop in an introductory note
to *The Marble Faun*: "I like those shadowy, weird, fantastic
Hawthornesque shapes flitting through the golden gloom which is
the atmosphere of the book. I like the misty way in which the
story is indicated rather than revealed."

An equivalent to the magic potions of the sorcerers (8) is also
described in the novel. In the grounds around Donatello's ancestral
castle, the peasants cultivate and press a wine, the manufacture of

---

[1] *Ibid.*, p. 369.   [2] *Ibid.*, pp. 45—46.   [3] *Ibid.*, p. 115.

which has from time immemorial been a family secret. The wine is called Sunshine, and it possesses "hidden peculiarities and subtle exquisiteness"; the drinking of it is "more a moral than a physical enjoyment."[1] But all these properties would — just as is really the case with so many excellent Italian wines — vanish and evaporate if it were sent to the market, i.e. transported some distance. Once more, Hawthorne has found the wonderful in a quite ordinary fact.

The magic of the fine arts (11) also plays a rôle in this book, in which Hawthorne has stated his view of imitative art on the whole. He had no very great comprehension of it; sculptured figures in the nude seemed to him as unnatural as indecent, and the picture galleries wearied him. It is rather characteristic that the painter who found most favour in the sight of Hawthorne was Guido Reni with his sugary sweetness: two of the works of this artist play a certain rôle in the action of the novel. One of them is the picture of the Archangel Gabriel putting his foot on the monster of evil, hung in the Capuchin monastery. The significance of this picture chiefly belongs to the discussion of certain ethical problems in the book, but some importance may be ascribed to the fact that the demon, on which the Archangel is setting his foot and which is commonly reputed to ressemble Cardinal Pamfili, is found to bear a striking likeness to Miriam's model. The fact is acknowledged both by Kenyon and by Hilda "and it added not a little to the grotesque and weird character which, half playfully, half seriously they assigned to Miriam's attendant, to think of him as personating the demon's part in a picture of more than two centuries ago."[2] The second picture is the portrait of Beatrice Cenci, which is connected in some way or other with Miriam's destiny. During a conversation between Miriam and Hilda, who has copied the portrait, a faint light is thrown over Miriam's mystery: "It was," says Hawthorne, "a sorrow that removed this beautiful girl out of the sphere of humanity, and set her in a far-off region, the remoteness of which — while yet her face is so close before us — makes us shiver as at a spectre."[3] Hilda considers Beatrice sinless, but Miriam asserts that "Beatrice's own conscience does not acquit her of something evil, and never to be forgiven."[4] It is in this way that

[1] *Ibid.*, p. 258.   [2] *Ibid.*, p. 168.
[3] *Ibid.*, p. 82.   [4] *Ibid.*, p. 84.

Hawthorne suggests the real nature of Miriam's mysterious past (3) and explains the sadness that surrounds her.

But the magic of art is not inherent only in pictures. We have seen that Hawthorne got the inspiration for his book while admiring the Faun of Praxiteles, and the inward and outward resemblance between the statue and Donatello is stressed throughout the story. Many readers have complained that they never got to know whether Donatello's ears were pointed and hairy like those of the real faun — not as many have expressed their curiosity as to the little tail. These are secrets that Hawthorne has kept to himself, leaving the problem, with an amused smile, to be conned by people whose imagination is not of his own lofty kind. But in the story we find also other sculptures, more or less akin to the wandering statues of Gothic romance. Kenyon, when staying at Monte Beni, models a bust of Donatello. During his work, "Kenyon gave up all preconceptions about the character of his subject, and let his hands work uncontrolled with the clay, somewhat as a spiritual medium, while holding a pen, yields it to an unseen guidance other than that of her own will." It is just at the time when Donatello undergoes his transformation, and the bust, after having first shown a beautifully spiritual expression, is changed, by some accidental handling of the clay by the sculptor, so as to show "a distorted and violent look, combining animal fierceness with intelligent hatred."[1] Had Hilda or Miriam seen the bust, says Hawthorne, they might have recognized Donatello's face as it was when he flung the model down the Tarpeian precipice. But the final result is different: "It gives," says Hilda of the sculpture, when it is later on shown to her, "the impression of a growing intellectual power and moral sense . . . it is the Faun, but advancing towards a state of higher development."[2] Thus, the bust of Donatello shows his spiritual development in a way not altogether different from the way in which the prophetic pictures reflected the evolution of the destinies of young Walter Ludlow and his wife.[3]

When Donatello and Miriam are united for the first time after the period of purification, they meet alone by the statue of Pope Julius III. at Perugia. They soon separate again, in order to proceed on their ways to Rome, and in that moment, "Miriam, Donatello,

---

[1] *Ibid.*, pp. 313—14.   [2] *Ibid.*, p. 433.
[3] Cp. pp. 98—100 of the present work.

and the sculptor, all three imagined that they beheld the bronze pontiff endowed with spiritual life. A blessing was felt descending upon them from his outstretched hand."[1] The description may be understood as an interpretation of the power inherent in every great work of art. Perhaps there is also contained in it some reminiscences of the sort of mysteries included under (11) in our scheme.

When Miriam and Donatello have perpetrated their crime, they feel that they have been united by a new, strange bond. The life of the model has strung them together for all times to come, their affinity is, as Donatello expresses himself, "for evermore cemented with his blood." Saying this, Donatello starts, and tells himself that it is "cemented with blood, which would corrupt and grow more noisome forever and forever, but bind them none the less strictly for that."[2] The truth of the uniting power of a crime perpetrated in common has here found an expression founded on the traditions of Gothic romance and the strange faculties ascribed to blood that had been admitted into the general consciousness (12). Another and far more conspicuous specimen of "Gothic" blood is met with in the scene where the dead monk — or model — is lying on his *lit de parade* in the church of the Capuchin monastery. "As the three friends stood by the bier, they saw that a little stream of blood had begun to ooze from the dead monk's nostrils: it crept slowly towards the thicket of his beard, where, in the course of a moment or two, it hid itself." The obvious inference is immediately drawn by the sin-oppressed Miriam: "How can we tell but that the murderer of this monk may have just entered the church?"[3] she asks. This is one of the passages which make it impossible for the present-day reader to take this book quite seriously. The familiar and current superstition that Hawthorne here treats as a matter of course has, in the course of the intervening century, become an antiquated and ridiculous conception.

As has been shown by the above analysis, Hawthorne has introduced a great number of recollections from the world of Gothic romance into this novel of 1859. In subsequent products from his pen, he was to continue his experiments with this machinery and move still further away from the firm ground of reality. At his death, he left four unfinished manuscripts, all of them dealing with two themes. One was the vivifying elixir of youth, which had

---

[1] *Works* VI, p. 371.   [2] *Ibid.*, pp. 206—7.   [3] *Ibid.*, p. 221.

long been occupying his imagination. The other motive had presented itself to him on a visit to Smithell's Hall, an English manorhouse. There, a footprint on a flagstone was shown to him, that was said to have been left by the bloody foot of a murderer. At Hawthorne's visit to the place, his hostess asked him to "write a ghost-story for her house," and in his note-book he jotted down that the legend was "a good one."[1] The first sketch of a romance located to England and treating this theme is *The Ancestral Footstep*, of which a couple of notes, arranged in the form of a diary, have been published after the author's death. He then abandoned the theme of the bloody imprint for a time, writing *The Marble Faun* and *Dr. Grimshawe's Secret* and editing his English notebooks. Afterwards, he reverted to it in the unfinished novel called *Septimius Felton*, and finally he once more began to rewrite the story. Of this last version only three chapters exist and have been published under the name of *The Dolliver Romance*. The theme of the elixir of life occurs in *Septimius Felton* and *The Dolliver Romance*. These unfinished novels will here be treated in their chronological order.

Already in 1886, the German scholar Anton Schönbach made the four manuscripts the subject of a careful analysis[2]; starting from an investigation of Hawthorne's note-books and manuscripts, he first examined his working method, and then proceeded to disentangle other problems such as the influence of German literature on Hawthorne's productions. In the following I shall avail myself of his results as to dates and certain other facts.

The Ancestral Footstep is nothing more than a preparatory sketch. In 1858, Hawthorne drew these outlines of the English Romance that had haunted his mind ever since his visit to Smithell's Hall. Strangely enough, the English family legend has traits in common with an idea jotted down in his notebook five years before his visit to England[3]: "The print in blood of a naked foot to be traced through the street of a town." The outlines of the story are written in the form of a diary and give a disconnected, sometimes contradictory summary of the projected tale. The final version is as follows:

[1] *Hawthorne's English Note-book*, August 25th, 1855.

[2] Anton Schönbach, *Beiträge zur Charakteristik Nathaniel Hawthornes*, *Anglia*, 1886.

[3] *Hawthorne's American Note-book*, December 19th, 1850.

Middleton is the descendant of a family that has long been resident in America. His ancestor had left England after a bitter dissension with a brother of his. Both brothers had loved the same girl, and she had been prevailed upon to marry the elder one. On the wedding-day, however, the bride and the younger brother both disappeared. The elder brother never married and left his title and estate to a third brother who had been wounded in a quarrel between the brothers before the flight. He had then left a bloody trace on the stone steps in front of the house.

Middleton has some old family documents in his possession and takes them with him to England, where he meets an old man, inmate of a hospital. The estate is now owned by a Mr. Eldredge, who "shall have an Italian mother and shall have the personal characteristics of an Italian... Dark suspicion of past crime, and of the possibility of future crime, may be thrown around him."[1] Middleton, who has in the meantime been appointed American minister to one of the minor Continental courts, is invited to spend some days at the castle. There he opens an old cupboard, to which he has brought the ancestral key, and finds some old documents. Eldredge tries to murder Middleton by offering him a goblet of poisoned wine — a repetition of a crime perpetrated two hundred years earlier — but does not succeed. Middleton marries Alice, niece of the aged inmate of the hospital.

This short summary only gives the chief outlines of the action. Hawthorne had originally meant to have the story told by a gentleman whom he had first met during his years as Consul at Liverpool. Thus, the introduction would have assumed something of the same character as the famous prefatory sketch to *The Scarlet Letter*, with its description of his life as a custom officer at Salem.

In this rough draught for another great romance, we recognize, to begin with, the artifice of telling the story from another person's point of view (1), and further the castle (2), the Italian villain (5), and the bloody imprint (12). It would seem that Hawthorne met with certain difficulties in the further development of the intrigue and therefore abandoned the manuscript while busying himself with other tasks. During one of the following years, he composed his next story, which we possess in the form of an undated manu-

---

[1] *Works* XI, p. 512.

script edited by his son, Julian Hawthorne, under the title of *Dr. Grimshawe's Secret.*

Dr. Grimshawe is "an elderly person of grim aspect," who lives about the beginning of the 19th century in a small New England town together with two adopted children, Ned and Elsie. The house, which stands on the outskirts of a graveyard, is of a strange appearance, especially Dr. Grimshawe's study is "overlaid with dust, that in lack of a visiting card, you might write your name with your forefinger upon the tables: and so hung with cobwebs, that they assumed the appearance of dusky upholstery."[1] The Doctor has a quaint predilection for spiders, of which he possesses many varieties, but, in particular, one huge specimen. The Doctor tells the children legends of old times in England; there often recurs a story about a family, one member of which had assisted at the beheading of King Charles I., and therefore always afterwards left a bloody track behind him wherever he went. He was imprisoned in his ancestral castle, but escaped, and finally came over to New England.

The old Doctor is a very unpopular man, and is once assailed by a mob in the street. He is saved by a delicate-looking stranger, Colcord, who afterwards comes to live in the Doctor's house for some time. Colcord is a schoolmaster, and the descendant of an old English family. One night he mysteriously disappears. Some time afterwards, Grimshawe dies. Ned preserves some old documents of which the Doctor has often spoken.

Many years later, a stranger named Redclyffe comes to England. He meets an old man who turns out to be none other than Colcord. Redclyffe is the boy Ned, now a grown-up man and a successful American civil servant. The master of a neighbouring castle, Braithwaite, is half Italian. He and Redclyffe, who has in the meantime been appointed American Minister to a European court, meet at a dinner in the Hospital, and Redclyffe is invited to the castle. There, he finds a Jesuit priest, who shows him the library, where are to be found not only a book-worm but also a huge spider of the kind that Dr. Grimshawe cherished. Later on, Braithwaite offers him a strange wine. Redclyffe faints away and awakes in a closed chamber. Opposite him sits a strange figure, and he remembers the family legend told him by Dr. Grimshawe, about "the undying

---

[1] *Works* XIII, p. 1.

one" of the manor-house, a former Edward Redclyffe who had been treacherously imprisoned. When he speaks to the figure, it sinks down in a rattling heap on the floor, "as if a thing of dry bones had been suddenly loosened at the joints."[1] Colcord and the warden of the hospital go to the castle to ask for Redclyffe, but are told that he has already left. This Colcord refuses to believe. "Dark, murderous man," says he to Braithwaite, "your course has not been unwatched; the secrets of this mansion are not unknown. For two centuries back, they have been better known to them who dwell afar off than to those resident within the mansion. The foot that made the Bloody Footstep has returned from its long wanderings, and it passes on straight as destiny — sure as an avenging Providence — to the punishment and destruction of those who incur retribution."[2] Saying this, Colcord advances through a previously unseen door in the panels of the wall, into a narrow, dark passage. He opens a segment of the floor, which gives access to a flight of small, dark stairs. Followed by the other members of the party, he arrives in a gloomy cell where they find Redclyffe and an old coffer to which Redclyffe has the key, given him once by Dr. Grimshawe. When the coffer is opened, it is found to contain "golden ringlets, abundant, clustering through the whole coffer, and living with elasticity."[3] These are the only remains of the whole bodily substance of a legendary person, known as the Beauty of the Golden Locks. Colcord possesses such a lock, and thus can show himself to be the rightful heir of the mansion. Redclyffe has been educated by Dr. Grimshawe, who hated the old family, in order to enable the doctor to impose a foundling on them.

This story is much better worked out than *The Ancestral Footstep*, though it contains, likervise, several inconsistencies. Here, we shall only trace its connection with the tradition of Gothic Romance. We thus find the old castle (1) with its secret passages and even a family ghost (7), the dark crimes, both that of a bygone generation and that of the present owner of the mansion (2). There is an Italian priest in the castle, a person possessing "a mildness, gentleness, softness, and asking-of-leave, in his manner, which he [Redclyffe] had not observed in persons so well assured of their position as the Church of England clergy"[4] (4). Braithwaite is partly

---

[1] *Ibid.*, p. 331.　　[2] *Ibid.*, pp. 338—39.　　[3] *Ibid.*, p. 342.　　[4] *Ibid.*, p. 286.

of Italian birth: "There have been three descents of this man's branch in Italy," says the warden of the Hospital, "and only one English mother in all that time... His civility is Italian, such as oftentimes among his countrymen has offered a cup of poison to a guest, or insinuated the stab of a stiletto into his heart"[1] (5). Dr. Grimshawe has many traits in common with the magicians of the novels of terror and wonder (8). A speciality of his is his collection of spiders, which we have met before in Hawthorne's productions as symbols of mystery and evil thoughts.[2] The graveyard outside the Doctor's house contains some specimens of common English garden flowers "which could not be accounted for, — unless, perhaps, they had sprung from some English maiden's heart, where the intense love of those homely things, and regret of them in the foreign land, had conspired together to keep their vivifying principle, and cause its growth after the poor girl was buried."[3] But otherwise this cemetery has little in common with item (7) in our schedule: "So far as ever came to the present writer's knowledge, there was no whisper of Doctor Grimshawe's house being haunted."[4] The poisoned drink which Braithwaite offers Redclyffe is, on the other hand, an undisguised loan from the novels of terror (8), and likewise the legend of the bloody footstep (12). Inserted in the story is also a mysterious tale of Ormskirk, a man in a lonely chamber, which is equipped with all the paraphernalia of Gothic Romance: "What is the furniture? An antique chair, — one chair, no more. A table, many-footed, of dark wood; it holds writing-materials, a book, too, on its face, with the dust gathered on its back. There is, moreover, a sort of antique box, or coffer, of some dark wood, that seems to have been wrought or carved with skill, wondrous skill, of some period when the art of carving wainscot arms and devices was much practised; so that on this coffer... you see faces in relief of knight and dame, lords, heraldic animals; some story, very likely, told, almost revelling in Gothic sculpture of wood, like what we have seen on the marble sarcophagus of the old Greeks. It has, too, a lock, elaborately ornamented and inlaid with silver.

[1] *Ibid.*, p. 214.
[2] Cp. p. 100 of the present work.
[3] *Works* XIII, p. 3.
[4] *Ibid.*, p. 5.

What else; only spider's webs spinning strangely over everything; over that light which comes into the room through the stone; over everything. And now we see, in a corner, a strange great spider curiously variegated. The ugly, terrible, seemingly poisonous thing makes us shudder.

What else: There are pistols; they lie on the coffer: There is a curiously shaped Italian dagger, of the kind which in a groove has poison that makes its wound mortal. On the old mantel-piece, over the fireplace, there is a vial in which are kept certain poisons."[1]

Here, Hawthorne has heaped more relics from the Gothic store-rooms of his mind than perhaps ever before. The accumulation may have been caused by the influence of the ancient buildings seen in England and the old traditions told him there. It may also have been the natural development of his own brooding fantasy, or a combination of both. We find the same tendency in the two later manuscripts.

Septimius Felton, which was written in 1861 and later on edited by Hawthorne's daughter Una in collaboration with Robert Browning, is subtitled "The Elixir of Life." Septimius Felton, a young student of theology with an Indian strain in him, is first introduced during a conversation with two of his friends, Rose Garfield and Robert Hagburn, in the course of which he expresses his opinion that human life is too short: "so much preparation to live, and then no life at all: a ponderous beginning and nothing more."[2] He wants an illimited space of time. Some time afterwards, the British soldiers of Boston go out to quench the revolutionary elements. Septimius takes up his gun and is challenged by a young British officer, whom he kills. Before dying, the officer, who belongs to a very old English family, the Nortons, gives him a miniature, pierced by a shot, his watch, a silver key and an old document. According to the wish of the deceased, Septimius buries him on the spot where he has died. The picture is sent to a specified address in England. Septimius occupies himself with the deciphering of the document, which is unintelligible to him. In a few months there arrives from England a pale girl, Sybil Dacy, who becomes a friend of Rose's and is often seen in the vicinity of the British soldier's unknown grave. Dr. Portsoaken, who has formerly been

---

[1] *Ibid.*, pp. 134—35.   [2] *Works* XI, p. 233.

a military doctor, tells Septimius of a lost recipe for an elixir of life. He also studies spiders — every thread of a spider's web is to him "more worth than a thread of gold" — and hints something about the interesting family history of the dead British officer. Dr. Portsoaken is also very interested in a recipe possessed by Septimius' old, hag-like, half-Indian Aunt Keziah, of which the story goes that "it was the very drink which used to be passed round at witch-meetings, being brewed from Devil's own recipe."[1] The description is really inherited from an old Indian sachem, and it lacks only one ingredient to become a veritable elixir of life. The doctor now tells Septimius that the very document in his possession is an old recipe of such an elixir, a concoction made by Friar Bacon, and upon closer examination, it turns out to be the very same description as Aunt Keziah's, containing one more ingredient, the wonderful herb Sanguinea sanguinissima. Sybil Dacy also tells of a man who needed for manufacturing this same drink the blood of an innocent maiden. Having slain her, he always left a bloody track behind him which remained for ever engraved on the steps in front of his family mansion.

Septimius, who has found out from the old document that the maker of the elixir must lead a completely passionless life — an opportunity for Hawthorne to criticize Emerson's theories of self-culture — renounces from his love, and Rose marries Hagburn. Portsoaken tells Septimius that a member of the Norton family emigrated to America many centuries ago and there married an Indian girl; their son was the sachem from whom Keziah has inherited her recipe, and Septimius is thus partly a descendant of the family of the man he has killed. Septimius decides to try to prepare the concoction and plucks a flower that grows on Norton's grave, believing it to be the Sanguinea sanguinissima. He wants to share his discovery with Sybil. She drinks the elixir, and then crushes the glass and dies. It is now explained that Sybil was formerly the fiancée of Norton. At first she had come to avenge herself on Septimius, but had instead fallen in love with him, and now she has saved his life. Septimius departs for England in quest of his ancestral home.

The fantastic story outlined here includes, as we have seen, a

---

[1] *Ibid.*, p. 307.

fairly complete set of Gothic paraphernalia. The central feature, the Elixir of life (8), we have already met with in the short stories of Hawthorne.[1] An old document plays a very important part (1), and the family castle (2) is there, though only in the distance. The flower on a grave belongs under (7) of our list. We may recall that Chillingworth looked for the ingredients of his concoctions among the graves, and that the English flowers on the churchyard outside Dr. Grimshawe's house were supposed to grow out of a young maiden's heart. Old Aunt Keziah, who is described as "as strange a mixture of an Indian squaw and herb doctress, with the crabbed old maid, and a mingling of the witch-aspect running through all, as could well be imagined,"[1] comes under (8). Dr. Portsoaken has also something of an old wizard in him, and the spiders, which we recently met in Dr. Grimshawe's study, are familiar to us as belonging to the equipment of Hawthorne's sorcerers. The bloody footstep (12), finally, is to be traced throughout the family story of the Nortons. The legend of Friar Bacon's drink, in which the heart's blood of a pure girl was the chief ingredient (12), is also of a sufficiently sinister character to be termed Gothic.

Once more, Hawthorne tried to use the theme of the elixir of life. *The Dolliver Romance* is only a short fragment of three scenes. The first of them describes the life of the old apothecary, Mr. Dolliver, and his little great-grandchild Pansie. The Doctor is bent and silverhaired, but keeps in good vigour thanks to a medicine concocted by his late grandson. The second scene depicts how the work on the composition of this medicine, that was to have been a veritable elixir of life, ended in the death of the man who undertook it. One morning, when Dr. Dolliver is working in the garden with little Pansie, she finds a herb which is afterwards thrown into a grave, soon filled. Dr. Dolliver remembers how his wife during the summer previous to her death used to wear this kind of flowers "day after day, through the whole season of their bloom, in her bosom, where they glowed like a gem, and deepened her somewhat pallid beauty with a richness never before seen in it."[3] The third fragment shows an old colonel, who has noticed that the apothecary is getting younger instead of older, coming to visit Mr. Dolliver.

---

[1] Cp. p. 100 of the present work.
[2] *Works* XI, pp. 304—5.   [3] *Ibid.*, p. 44.

He talks about a Bloody Footstep, "bearing its track through his race," and about a mysterious stranger, who has once given the apothecary a "musty bit of parchment, on which were written some words, hardly legible, in an antique hand."[1] The apothecary had tried to concoct the medicine described, and the stranger had finally returned and mixed a powder into the drink, whereupon he disappeared. This potation is, according to the colonel, his hereditary property, and he now demands it back. The apothecary tries to dissuade him on account of the danger of drinking more than one drop a day. But the colonel gives him a purse full of gold and finally points his revolver at him. When he gets the flask, he quaffs great draughts, and the effect is terrifying: "The Colonel sat a moment in his chair, panting for breath; then started to his feet with a prompt vigor that contrasted widely with the infirm and rheumatic movements that had heretofore characterized him. He struck his forehead violently with one hand, and smote his chest with the other: he stamped his foot thunderously on the ground; then he leaped up to the ceiling, and came down with an elastic bound. Then he laughed, a wild, exulting haha with a strange triumphant roar that filled the house and reechoed through it; a sound full of fierce, animal rapture — enjoyment of sensual life mixed up with a sort of horror."[2] Soon he falls down dead. His countenance is in the first instant a young man's, and in the next moment it is grown "ashen, withered, shrunken, more aged than in life."

In this fragment we encounter again several of the themes cherished by Hawthorne from the years when he wrote his short stories. There is the elixir (8) from *Dr. Heidegger's Experiment* and *Septimius Felton*, the recipe of which is written on a scroll of parchment (1). There is the mysterious exotic flower, which we first met in the story of *Rappacini's Daughter* (8), and the bloody footstep (12) that stalks through all Hawthorne's later works. There is little indication as to which was the central idea in this last work of Hawthorne's. But the short scenes we possess of this romance show him at his best as a stylist. The description of the life of Mr. Dolliver and little Pansie is a delightful idyll, and the painting of Mr. Dolliver's vigil is a good psychological study of an ageing man's reactions: "And thus it happened with poor Grandsir Dol-

[1] *Ibid.*, p. 61.   [2] *Ibid.*, p. 65.

liver, who often awoke from an old man's fitful sleep with a sense that his senile predicament was but a dream of the past night; and hobbling hastily across the cold floor to the looking-glass, he would be grievously disappointed at beholding his white hair, the wrinkles and furrows, the ashen visage and bent form, the melancholy mask of age, in which, as he now remembered, some strange and sad enchantment had involved him for years gone by."[1] As in the story of *Dr. Heidegger's Experiment*, the powerlessness of man against decay and death is here put before us. The end of the experiment is not so tragic in the short story, where Hawthorne makes the four enchanted persons revert to the customary tenor of old age. But Sybil Dacy (in *Septimius Felton*) has to forfeit her life for trying the powerful potation, and so has the colonel of the present fragment. The tools of the Gothic romancers have here, as elsewhere in Hawthorne's works, been put to an allegorical use.

*

Here our investigation of the influence of Gothic Romance on Nathaniel Hawthorne's work has come to an end. It is to be hoped that the facts adduced justify the view that Gothic Romance formed an important substratum of Hawthorne's productions — perhaps not always consciously used, but ever present and often employed for definite purposes. It would be unjust to stamp him as a surviving Goth. His artistic ambition places him on a much higher level than the European authors that are generally referred to as "Gothic." He belongs to the same generation and class of literary artists as Edgar Allan Poe or E. T. A. Hoffmann. But in him, the properties that are usually comprised under the term Puritan formed a strange and strong counterweight to his bent for the fantastical, and it is in the mingling and interaction of such influences from many quarters, but chiefly of these two currents, that Hawthorne's genius is to be sought and found. The amalgamation was made with great conscious artistry and followed carefully prepared lines. As we have seen, Hawthorne's use of the Gothic elements was comparatively profuse in his first short stories; it waned during the middle period of his productions, to be revived in his latest works.

---

[1] *Ibid.*, p. 31.

HAWTHORNE AND MME DE STAËL

Mme Germaine de Staël-Holstein, née Necker, daughter of a French minister and wife of a Swedish ambassador, a lady living in the centre of political and intellectual European activity, and frequently entangled in political and amorous intrigues, would seem to have little in common with the shy, dignified, erudite and provincial New England author of the first great American romance.

But Mme de Staël was not only a politician and a passionate woman. She was also an important literary personality. The influence she exercised on America through her book, *De l'Allemagne*, has already been mentioned. This phase of her work must have impressed itself on Hawthorne through many channels; it had coloured the Transcendentalist view of Europe, and it may with great probability be assumed that women as well-read as Elizabeth and Sophia Peabody were familiar with the writings of Mme de Staël. There is no direct evidence of Hawthorne's having read *De l'Allemagne*, but we know that he was familiar with *Corinne*, which he mentions several times in his notebooks, and in *The Marble Faun*.[1] In actual fact, in her capacity of novel writer, Mme de Staël has exercised no small influence on Nathaniel Hawthorne.

She belonged to an earlier generation than Hawthorne. She was born in 1766, and died in 1817. Regarded as a representative of the tradition of the French novel, she occupies, nevertheless, a position somewhat similar to that of Nathaniel Hawthorne in America.

In the earlier French literary tradition, the novel was not considered to be the highest form of literary art. In the early decades of the 18th century, Le Sage had initiated the social novel with his picaresque *Gil Blas*, but his followers had not succeeded in refining the novel to anything like the form and quality attained in France

---

[1] *Works* VI, p. 174.

by drama, comedy, essay or lyrics. When first-rate authors availed
themselves of the novel for literary purposes, they used it for satire,
like Voltaire when writing *Candide*. Rousseau's *Nouvelle Héloïse*
marked the invasion of sentiment in the domain of the French
novel, but Rousseau was not primarily a novelist. The great writers
who created the European novel were Englishmen, and one of the
most characteristic features of the new genre was its advocating of
social and democratic reform, and of the emancipation of women.
This trend was taken up by Mme de Staël. She had democratic
ideas and she was a pioneer for women's independence. Moreover,
she was a *femme du monde*, the counterpart of that "man of society"
that appeared in Nathaniel Hawthorne's self-portrait. The psychology of the figures in her novels bore the stamp not only of sentiment
allied to the gospel of reform, as in the case of *Pamela* or *Clarissa*,
but also of the cultured lady, the woman who had read and absorbed
the great thinkers of Antiquity, and still more thoroughly those
of France: Montaigne, La Bruyère, and La Rochefoucauld. Her
heroines were more or less idealized portraits of herself, they were —
as she expressed it — "une sorte de confession, dérobée à ceux qui
ont vécu comme à ceux qui vivront."[1] Above all, Corinne is the
ideal type of which she dreamed and which she attempted to
personify: the independent woman and genial poetess, unhampered
by convention, free to develop her talents and personality.

Mme de Staël has formulated many literary definitions, not all
of a general application. In her preface to *Delphine*, we find some
frequently quoted words on the art of novel-writing which afford
an expression and an explanation of her own aims:

"Observer le coeur humain, c'est montrer à chaque pas l'influence de la morale sur la destinée: il n'y a qu'un secret dans la vie,
c'est le bien ou le mal qu'on a fait; il se cache, ce secret, sous mille
formes trompeuses: vous souffrez longtemps par des moyens con-
damnables; mais tout à coup votre sort se décide, le mot de votre
énigme se révèle, et ce mot, la conscience l'avait dit bien avant que
le destin l'eût répété. C'est ainsi que l'histoire de l'homme doit
être représentée dans les romans; c'est ainsi que les fictions doivent
nous expliquer, par nos vertus et nos sentiments, les mystères de
notre sort."

---

[1] *Œuvres complètes de Mme la Baronne de Staël-Holstein*, Paris 1844, Tome
I, p. 335.

152

To these words, Nathaniel Hawthorne might have subscribed, in a measure. He would not, however, have endorsed the phrase "une sorte de confession." Hawthorne had little sympathy with the Romantic author's taste for opening his own soul to the world. He pronounced decided judgment on this method in his preface to the *Mosses from an Old Manse*:

"How little have I told: and of that little, how almost nothing is even tinctured with any quality that makes it exclusively my own. Has the reader gone wandering hand in hand with me, through the inner passages of my being? and have we groped together into all its chambers and examined their treasures or their rubbish? Not so. We have been standing on the greensward, but just within the cavern's mouth, where the common sunshine is free to penetrate, and where every footstep is therefore free to come. I have appealed to no sentiment or sensibilities save such as are diffused among us all. So far as I am a man of really individual attributes I veil my face; nor am I, nor have I ever been, one of those supremely hospitable people, who serve up their own hearts, delicately fried, with brain sauce, as a tidbit for their beloved public."[1]

If Hawthorne, for reasons of personal reserve and, perhaps, of principle, did not wish to appear before the public in his works, he nevertheless could appreciate other authors doing so — if they were men. In women, he resented it deeply. He might appreciate literary talent in a female writer, but as a man he disapproved of too great frankness in a woman. There are many instances of this attitude; in one of his intimate letters to George Ticknor, we find this eloquent expression of his opinion:

"In my last, I recollect, I bestowed some vituperation on female authors. I have since been reading 'Ruth Hall'; and I must say I enjoyed it a good deal. The woman writes as if the Devil was in her; and that is the only condition under which a woman ever writes anything worth reading. Generally women write like emasculated men, and are only to be distinguished from male authors by greater feebleness and folly; but when they throw off the restraints of decency, and come before the public stark naked, as it were — then their books are sure to possess character and value. Can you tell me anything about this Fanny Fern? If you

[1] *Works* II, pp. 43—44.

meet her, I wish you would let her know how much I admire her."[1]

As to the other thesis of Mme de Staël's, concerning the aim of the novel: to show "l'influence de la morale sur la destinée," Hawthorne shared this view. But he did not do so unconditionally. He did not believe in too ostensible a moral, and expressed his views as follows in the preface to *The House of the Seven Gables*:

"When romances do really teach anything, or produce any effective operation, it is usually through a far more subtle process than the ostensible one. The author has considered it hardly worth his while, therefore, relentlessly to impale the story with its moral as with an iron rod — or, rather, as by sticking a pin through a butterfly — thus at once depriving it of life, and causing it to stiffen in an ungainly attitude. A high truth, indeed, fairly, finely, and skilfully wrought out, brightening at every step, and crowning the final development of a work of fiction, may add an artistic glory, but is never any truer, and seldom any more evident, at the last page than at the first."[2]

The "subtile process" was greatly dependent for its success on the understanding always expected by Hawthorne of his intelligent reader, the interpreting of the intentions of the author through the haze of allegory that enveloped them. When Mme de Staël wrote a novel about a woman artist in Rome, she produced, besides a classic description of Rome, Italy, and Italian customs, the life story of a woman of this type in contemporary society, and a plea for her right to love and independence. When Hawthorne wrote a romance using the same type of woman as the main figure, it became, as well as the expression of a New Englander's view of Rome, Italy, and Italian life, a variation on the theme of the origin of sin. To the reader of both novels, there are few doubts that Miriam has inherited traits from Corinne. But Miriam was not the first child of Nathaniel Hawthorne's brain to originate from the reading of Mme de Staël's great Roman novel.

Mr. Randall Stewart, in the Introduction to his excellent edition of Hawthorne's *American Notebooks*, classifies Hawthorne's heroines

---

[1] Letter to George Ticknor, February, 1855. Cited from a copy in the Yale University Collection.

[2] *Works* III, p. 14.

according to three general types: the wholesome New England girl, the frail, sylph-like creature, and the woman with an exotic richness in her nature. The author counts among the last-named group Beatrice in *Rappaccini's Daughter*, Hester in *The Scarlet Letter*, Zenobia in *The Blithedale Romance*, and Miriam in *The Marble Faun*.

In the present connection, Beatrice will be left aside. She is still a young girl, living in seclusion with her father, and lacking the experience and the mature self-assurance that characterizes the three other women.

Of these three, Hester, Zenobia, and Miriam, Hester remains the one endowed with most real life. She is a lonely woman, forsaken by society because of her secret that is regarded by her environment, but not by herself, as a sin. "What we did had a consecration of its own,"[1] is the view she herself takes of her relation to Dimmesdale. And in the concluding chapter it is said that the scarlet letter became "a type of something to be sorrowed over, and looked upon with awe, yet with reverence too."[2] To the women afflicted by love sorrows and other conflicts who sought her counsel, Hester expressed her "firm belief, that, at some brighter period, when the world would have grown ripe for it in Heaven's own time, a new truth would be revealed, in order to establish the whole relation between man and woman on a surer ground of mutual happiness."[3] This sounds more like an echo of the gospel of Godwin and Mary Wollstonecraft than of *Delphine*, or *Corinne*, and we may be sure that the American interpreter of the Godwinian teachings about women's rights, Margaret Fuller, had not failed to impress her written and spoken word on Hawthorne. She may have lent some traits to Hester Prynne. But, of the three heroines treated here, Hester is the one most free from discernible literary or factual influences. Such are, on the other hand, to be found in the second of the figures under consideration.

Margaret Fuller was a frequent guest at Brook Farm, and even if Hawthorne repudiated all hints of his having used any definite patterns from the phalanstery in his *Blithedale Romance*[4], it can hardly be denied that the colouring of Zenobia has many shades in

---

[1] *Works* V, p. 234.   [2] *Ibid.*, p. 310.
[3] *Ibid.*, p. 311.   [4] *Works* V, p. 323.

common with her. Zenobia, however, was a greatly idealized Margaret. The latter evidently possessed no great personal attraction for Nathaniel Hawthorne.[1] Zenobia, on the other hand, is represented to us as endowed with intense womanly charm:

"It did one good to see a fine intellect (as hers really was, although its natural tendency lay in another direction than towards literature) so fitly cased. She was, indeed, an admirable figure of a woman, just on the hither verge of her richest maturity, with a combination of features which it is safe to call remarkably beautiful, even if some fastidious persons might pronounce them a little deficient in softness and delicacy ... There was another peculiarity about her. We seldom meet with women nowadays, and in this country, who impress us as being women at all — their sex fades away, and goes for nothing, in ordinary intercourse. Not so with Zenobia. One felt an influence breathing out of her such as we might suppose to come from Eve, when she was just made, and her Creator brought her to Adam, saying: 'Behold! here is a woman!'"[2]

Here, a suspicion may seem justified that Hawthorne had found the model for this portrait of a beautiful, intelligent, and sensuous woman, not in his immediate environment, but in another clime. When adding the evidence to be extracted from *The Marble Faun*, we feel in a position to regard Zenobia as partly endowed with the charms of Mme de Staël's Corinne. The same spirit of independence and selfassurance characterizes both women. Corinne was a poetess, and an *improvisatrice*. Zenobia "had the gift of telling a fanciful story, off-hand, in a way that made it greatly more effective than it was usually found to be when she afterwards elaborated the same production with her pen." As a matter of fact, Zenobia's plain legend, ennobled by "the emphasis of her inimitable voice, and the pictorial illustration of her mobile face"[3] can be compared with Corinne's famous improvisation on the Capitol. But Zenobia's tale is only to be regarded as a translation of the Roman eloquence into terms suited to a New England afternoon entertainment among

---

[1] "I was invited to dine at Mr. Bancroft's yesterday, with Miss Margaret Fuller; but Providence had given me some business to do, for which I was very thankful!" Letter to Sophia, dated Dec. 5th, 1839. Cited from the manuscript in the Huntington Library.

[2] *Works* V, pp. 338, 340.

[3] *Ibid.*, pp. 441—442.

intellectual would-be farmers. The Roman favourite is of unknown
origin:

"Son nom de famille était ignoré. Son premier ouvrage ...
portait seulement le nom de Corinne. Personne ne savait où elle
avait vécu, ni ce qu'elle avait été avant cette époque; elle avait
maintenant à peu près vingt-six ans."[1] The queen of Blithedale
has a past equally mysterious: "Zenobia ... is merely her public
name; a sort of mask in which she comes before the world, retaining
all the privileges of privacy ..."[2] Corinne is finally shown to be
the daughter of an English nobleman, and the half-sister of the
gentle, young English girl whom Lord Nelvil finally marries. In
the same way, Zenobia is actually the half-sister of the pale, ethereal
Priscilla, who is her rival for Hollingsworth's love, and who finally
marries him. Corinne dies from an illness caused by her sorrow.
Zenobia is driven, by her affliction, to drown herself. Even if
Miriam were not created later on as a definite proof of the deep
impression Hawthorne had taken from his reading of *Corinne*,
Zenobia has sufficient features in common with Mme de Staël's
heroine to warrant a hypothesis that she is a literary descendant
of hers.[3]

Passing further to *The Marble Faun*, the similarity, not to say
parallellism between this work and *Corinne* as regards setting and
construction, is obvious. Both may still be used as guides to Rome.
Mme de Staël is the more conscientious guide, and the better in-
formed. In her book, we get a picture of Italian literature and
Italian customs, of the Eternal City, its statues and pictures, its
popular festivals, etc. In *The Marble Faun*, which attempts to
give the same kind of information, we get an idea of contemporary
American appreciation of art rather than of Italy and Italian civili-
zation. The candid avowals of a surprising lack of insight into and
knowledge of art as well as of understanding for ancient tradition
that abound in Hawthorne's work, reveal the extent to which even
an American with real literary culture, not to say erudition, was
at this time unacquainted with the imitative arts. The great flow

---

[1] Mme de Staël, *Œuvres complètes*, p. 662.

[2] *Works* V, p. 328.

[3] The probability of an influence from Mme de Staël has been indicated by
H. Arlin Turner in an essay on *Hawthorne's Literary Borrowings*, PMLA,
June, 1936.

of sculpture and painting from the Old World to the New had not yet set in, and good pictures and statues were rare objects in the United States of 1850. Page upon page in Hawthorne's novel are filled with singularly naïve reflections on the subject of art and artists. Some of them are refreshingly frank, like the chapter on *The Emptiness of Picture Galleries*; others possess value only as illustrations of the contemporary stage of general culture in America.

The aim of Mme de Staël was to give, in her novel, two pictures — of Rome and of a superior woman. She never took great pains with the plot. Hawthorne was, as ever, first and foremost a story-teller. The idea of portraying Rome is, we think, part of a plan to depict Europe to his countrymen. His notebooks and later works, *Our Old Home* as well as the four posthumous fragments, show his wish to portray England. He intended to depict Italy in the same way, and in so doing he can hardly have escaped reminiscences of Mme de Staël's novel. Like the French writer, he takes his readers on walks all round Rome. But when it comes to delineating the plot of the story, he reverts to his constant idea, the origin of sin. The idea of the story is the development that takes place in the formation of the characters of two beings that have committed a murder together, and in the pattern of behaviour in the group to which they belong. Miriam who is, from the beginning, a person laden with heavy guilt, is freed by worldly justice. Donatello, who was, before the deed, unconscious of the existence of sin in this world, ends in a dungeon "as deep as those of the Castle of St. Angelo." Donatello has no connection whatsoever with the man of feeling who exerts such a devastating influence on the life of Corinne. Miriam, on the other hand, is related to her as also to Zenobia. She possesses artistic talent, but of another kind than that of the other two ladies, and of not quite such high quality as theirs. Her pictures had met, says the author, "with good acceptance among the patrons of modern art. Whatever technical merit they lacked, its absence was more than compensated for by a warmth and passion which she had the faculty of putting into her productions, and which all the world could feel."[1] She is depicted as being, like Corinne, of unknown origin, and, later on, reveals herself as "springing from European parentage, on the mother's side, but

---

[1] *Works* VI, p. 35.

158

with a vein, likewise, of Jewish blood; yet connected, through her father, with one of those few princely families of Southern Italy, which still retain great wealth and influence."¹ It will be remembered that Corinne, too, was revealed as the descendant of a noble English family. The scene of both romances is laid in Rome. Afterwards, both women repair to other cities. When Donatello goes to Florence, Miriam follows him, unseen and unknown. Corinne follows Lord Nelvil to England and Scotland, and is unsuccessful in her attempts to meet him there. Both fall ill. Corinne dies of sorrow and illness, and in her final letter to Lord Nelvil she evokes the happiness that he has scorned and the gifts that she would have had to offer him:

"Ah, trouverez-vous mieux que ma tendresse? Savez-vous que dans les déserts du nouveau monde j'aurais béni mon sort, si vous m'aviez permis de vous suivre? Savez-vous que je vous aurais servi comme une esclave? Savez-vous que je me serais prosternée devant vous comme devant un envoyé du ciel, si vous m'aviez fidèlement aimée? Eh bien, qu'avez-vous fait de tant d'amour? qu'avez-vous fait de cette affection unique en ce monde? un malheur unique comme elle."²

Corinne would have sacrificed her talents, her future, the adulation around her, for her love. Miriam, when separated from Donatello, also grows ill and pale, and explains herself to Kenyon as follows:

"There is none [disorder] that I know of save too much life and strength, without a purpose for one or the other. It is my too redundant energy that is slowly — or perhaps rapidly — wearing me away, because I can apply it to no use. The object which I am bound to consider my only one on earth, fails me utterly. The sacrifice which I yearn to make of myself, my hopes, my everything, is coldly put aside. Nothing is left for me but to brood, brood, all day, all night, in unprofitable longings and repinings."³

But Miriam's offer of love, and of help in atoning for their common sin, is accepted, and she takes up her life again. The hint given by the author in the appendix, added at the request of several readers, as to Miriam's past, has caused a critic to conjecture that

¹ *Ibid.*, p. 486.
² Mme de Staël, *Œuvres complètes*, p. 858.
³ *Works* VI, p. 323.

Hawthorne may have had the Praslin murder in mind in this connection.[1] Such a possibility does not exclude other influences.

The outward picture of Miriam is basically that of Hawthorne's "glamorous" women. Many traits are obviously borrowed from a beautiful Jewish lady whom Hawthorne had admired at a dinner in London at the Lord Mayor's house, in April 1856:

". . . My eyes were mostly drawn to a young lady, who sat nearly opposite me, across the table. She was, I suppose, dark, and yet not dark, but rather seemed to be of pure white marble, yet not white; but the purest and finest complexion, without a shade of color in it, yet anything but sallow or sickly. Her hair was a wonderful deep raven-black, black as night, black as death; not raven-black, for that has shiny gloss, and hers had not, but it was hair never to be painted or described — wonderful hair, Jewish hair. Her nose had a beautiful outline, though I could see that it was Jewish too; and that, and all her features, were so fine that sculpture seemed a despicable art beside her, and certainly my pen is good for nothing. If any likeness could be given, however, it must be by sculpture, not painting."[2]

In *The Marble Faun*, Hawthorne paints Miriam thus:

"She was very youthful, and had what was usually thought to be a Jewish aspect: a complexion in which there was no roseate bloom, yet neither was it pale; dark eyes, into which you might look as deeply as your glance would go, and still be conscious of a depth that you had not sounded, though it lay open to the day. She had black, abundant hair, with none of the vulgar glossiness of other women's sable locks; if she were really of Jewish blood, then this was Jewish hair, and a dark glory such as crowns no Christian maiden's head."[3]

That Hawthorne has here painted from a living model, is obvious. He also used the device of copying traits from old Italian masters' pictures. There is a strain of Gothicism in Hawthorne's use of this device. When speaking of Beatrice Cenci's ghost, Miriams' expression becomes "almost exactly that of the portrait"[4] of

[1] Wright, Natalia, *Hawthorne and the Praslin Murder, The New England Quarterly*, 1942.
[2] *Works* VIII, p. 238.
[3] *Works* VI, p. 65.
[4] *Ibid.*, p. 85.

that unhappy girl painted by Guido Reni and successfully copied by Hilda. This well-known picture of a dark young girl in a white turban has in common with Mme de Staël's description of Corinne on the Capitol that the poetess wore "un châle des Indes tourné autour de sa tête, et ses cheveux, du plus beau noir, entremêlés avec ce châle; sa robe était blanche . . ."[1] More important, however, than details in dress that correspond more or less in the two figures, is the idea of comparing the living women with famous pictures. Miriam evokes the image of Beatrice Cenci; Corinne that of the Sibyl of Dominichino. When visiting Bologna, together with his wife Lucile, Oswald for a long time contemplates the Sibyl, while his wife timidly asks him if that picture appeals more to his heart than the Madonna painted by Correggio which is, needless to say, strongly reminiscent of herself.

The devices that, in this work, Hawthorne has in common with Mme de Staël may not have been consciously borrowed. In the explanatory remarks attached to *The Marble Faun*, he says about his character drawing:

"He [the author] designed the story and the characters to bear, of course, a certain relation to human nature and human life, but still to be so artfully and airily removed from our mundane sphere, that some laws and proprieties of their own should be implicitly and insensibly acknowledged."[2]

In the opinion of the present writer, it is probable that Hawthorne had for years been familiar with the works of Mme de Staël, and especially *Corinne*, and that the heroine of that novel had impressed him and lent several features to Zenobia in *The Blithedale Romance*. When arriving in Rome, the scene of the French novel, vague recollections as to the plan, and also the character of Corinne, arose, and coloured the romance that was the outcome of Hawthorne's Roman experience.

*

Hawthorne's different types of women have intrigued more critics than Mr. Stewart; many of them have distinguished only between the dark and the fair ones; the Zenobia type, as we might

[1] Mme de Staël, *Œuvres complètes*, p. 663.
[2] *Works* VI, p. 522.

for brevity call it, and the Phoebe type. This latter name we chose
because it is related not only to the soft and gay heroine of *The
House of the Seven Gables*, but because Hawthorne gave that name,
in his letters, to the woman who more or less served as prototype
for all his heroines of that kind — his wife Sophia. This fair type
possesses, again to quote Mr. Stewart, "cheerfulness, prettiness, and
a simple-minded domesticity," to which is added, in the later
works, the artistic talents that were the pride of Mrs. Sophia Hawthorne. Another characteristic is that most of these heroines are
unmarried. They represent chastity, which, however, does not
prevent independence. Priscilla earns her own living as a seamstress. Hilda lives by herself as a free artist in Rome, which causes
the author to philosophize over this kind of life:

"This young American girl was an example of the freedom of
life which it is possible for a female artist to enjoy at Rome. She
dwelt in her tower, as free to descend into the corrupted atmosphere of the city beneath, as one of her companion doves to fly
downward into the street; — all alone, perfectly independent,
under her own sole guardianship, unless watched over by the
Virgin, whose shrine she tended; doing what she liked without a
suspicion or a shadow upon the snowy whiteness of her fame. The
customs of artist life bestow such liberty upon the sex, which is
elsewhere restricted within so much narrower limits; and it is
perhaps an indication that, whenever we admit women to a wider
scope of pursuits and professions, we must also remove the shackles
of our present conventional rules, which would then become an
insufferable restraint on either maid or wife."[1]

This is a picture of the way of life advocated by Mme de Staël.
Hilda leads the free existence that Corinne coveted for all women
of talent. But Hilda lacks the brilliance, the glamour of Corinne.
Of the two women in *The Marble Faun*, it is evidently Miriam,
not Hilda, who is moulded after the likeness of Corinne.

In the three women, Hester, Zenobia, and Miriam, in whom we
have found traces of Mme de Staël's heroine, there is, however,
also to be found a trait that does not belong to her. Corinne is
beautiful, she is intelligent, even learned, she advocates the rights
of her sex, and wants to be loved for her own sake, but she is not —

[1] *Works* VI, p. 71.

as she explicitly tells Lord Nelvil on their visit to Pantheon — a woman experienced in love. Her reputation is morally irreproachable:

"Je ne crois pas, dit-elle, qu'une femme sensible soit jamais arrivée jusqu'à vingt-six ans sans avoir connu l'illusion de l'amour; mais si n'avoir jamais été heureuse, si n'avoir jamais rencontré l'objet qui pouvait mériter toutes les affections de son coeur, est un titre à l'intérêt, j'ai droit au vôtre."[1]

This kind of declaration is never made by any of Hawthorne's heroines of the Zenobia type. From the beginning, Hester carries her stigma as an adulteress. She is a mother, and her love is referred to, in accordance with Puritan conceptions, as her sin, though the book is a tribute to the beauty of character and morality revealed by the noble courage with which she suffers the consequences of her act. Zenobia is an enigma. Possibly, the reception given to *The Scarlet Letter* by certain religious quarters[2] had prevented Hawthorne from referring directly to illicit love. Instead, he speaks of a previous marriage, and the reader is induced to suspect a relationship to the mysterious necromancer Westervelt. In that case Zenobia could not be a widow. She must either be divorced, or in danger of committing bigamy by marrying Hollingsworth. True to his methods, Hawthorne does not press the point. He only alludes to the fact that Zenobia is not likely to lack the experience of love:

"One subject, about which — very impertinently, moreover — I perplexed myself with a great many conjectures, was, whether Zenobia had ever been married. The idea, it must be understood, was unauthorized by any circumstance or suggestion that had made its way to my ears. So young as I beheld her, and the freshest and rosiest woman of a thousand, there was certainly no need of imputing to her a destiny already accomplished; the probability was far greater that her coming years had all life's richest gifts to bring. If the great event of a woman's existence had been consummated, the world knew nothing of it, although the world seemed to know Zenobia well ... Pertinaciously the thought, 'Zenobia is a wife; Zenobia has lived and loved. There is no folded petal, no latent

---

[1] Mme de Staël, *Œuvres complètes*, p. 678.
[2] Cp. above p. 57.

dew-drop, in this perfectly developed rose', irresistibly that thought
drove out all other conclusions, as often as my mind reverted to
the subject."[1]

Not even here does Hawthorne pronounce judgment on his
heroine's rebellion against convention. He suspends it, as he also
does in the case of Miriam, the mysterious woman painter in *The
Marble Faun*. Miriam is a sinner through her complicity in the
crime of Donatello. But, in addition, she has a sense of guilt
because of some dark secret in her past. Here a reminiscence of
the Cenci motive has no doubt played a decisive part in the composition of Miriam's character. Hawthorne seems to have viewed
the Cenci legend much in the same sense as Shelley in his preface
to the drama:

"The person who would treat such a subject must increase the
ideal, and diminish the actual horror of the events, so that the
pleasure which arises from the poetry which exists in these tempestuous sufferings and crimes may mitigate the pain of the con-
templation of the moral deformity from which they spring. There
must also be nothing attempted to make the exhibition subservient
to what is vulgarly termed a moral purpose . . ."

In fact, many things point to Hawthorne's intention of creating
a kind of sequel to the events depicted in *The Cenci*, an illustration
to Beatrice's words:

"... If there should be
No God, no Heaven, no Earth, in the void world!
If all things thus should be — my father's spirit,
His eyes, his voice, his touch surrounding me;
If sometimes, as a shape more like himself,
Even in the form which tortured me on earth
Maskt in gray hairs and wrinkles, he should come
And wind me in his hellish arms, and fix
His eyes on mine, and drag me down, down, down . . ."

But while these thoughts are only dark musings with Shelley's
Beatrice who feels herself destined to perform a just retribution,
they are fundamental in the secretive Miriam, who considers herself a doomed being. When leaving the Coliseum on their nightly

[1] *Works* V, pp. 372—73.

stroll, and finding the lazzarone dogging their steps, Miriam warns
Donatello:

"I tell you, there is a great evil hanging over me. I know it; I
see it in the sky; I feel it in the air. It will overwhelm me as utterly
as if this arch should crumble upon our heads. It will crush you,
too, if you stand at my side. Depart, then; and make the sign of the
cross, as your faith bids you, when an evil spirit is nigh. Cast me
off, or you are lost forever."[1]

And, regarding Hilda's copy of Guido's Beatrice whose expression bears such a striking likeness to herself, Miriam declares:

"If I can pretend to see at all into that dim region, whence she
gazes so strangely and sadly at us, Beatrice's own conscience does
not acquit her of something evil, and never to be forgiven." A
little later, she adds: "I would give my life to know whether she
thought herself innocent, or the great criminal since time began."[2]

Miriam's guilt may be of incestuous nature. It may also be of
the same character as the Praslin murders — an inference that
would not have seemed as far-fetched to contemporary readers as
to us. The question is of less interest for the present purpose.
Miriam stands for guilt: like Hester, like Zenobia, unlike Phoebe
and Hilda.

This fact has been noticed by Mr. Stewart. In addition to his
analysis, the present writer would like to make a further point.

When Hawthorne states his cases in his different studies of the
effect of sin and guilt on human nature, he does not attempt to
render his exhibition "subservient to what is vulgarly termed a
moral purpose." Still, he makes some distinctions. One of them
is a differentiation between the representatives of the two sexes.
The guilty men may be Europeans (Chillingworth, Donatello) or
Americans (Dimmesdale, Hollingsworth). But when guilt is
personified in a woman, she is a European with rich emotional
experience. She belongs to his glamorous type. We already find
this tendency in his short stories. Lady Eleanor, who carries a
gorgeous mantle[3] containing the germs of a deadly disease, and
with it a burden of personal pride, comes from the other side of
the Atlantic. Beatrice[4], whose beauty is a deathly menace, is an

---

[1] *Works* VI, p. 187.   [2] *Ibid.*, p. 84.
[3] *Works* I, p. 307.
[4] *Ibid.*, p. 107.

Italian. Hester, in Hawthorne's first great romance, is a European immigrant, and Zenobia, in the novel based on his Brook Farm experience, is a cosmopolitan. Miriam, finally, is of mixed European descent. All these daughters of the Old World are beautiful, intelligent, and passionate women with a past.

To "Puritan" New England of old, and even of Hawthorne's own time, passion was taboo. To the Romantic school, the celebration of passion was essential. As Brunetière has expressed it, speaking of George Sand's novels, "selon l'esthétique romantique, la passion même, la passion toute seule est à celles qui l'éprouvent un signe ou un témoignage de leur propre supériorité."[1] The heroines of Nathaniel Hawthorne mark a stage in the same development as the one that led, in France, from those of Mme de Staël to Indiana and Valentine. To introduce these beautiful, intelligent, and passionate women, conscious of their own superiority, into the American literature of the eighteen fifties, was an audacious enterprise and, when undertaking it, Hawthorne was careful not to represent them as deriving from true yankee stock. They were all depicted as recent immigrants from Europe, the old continent containing the faults, and the charms, of romance. The aura of sin that surrounded them was far from repulsive. It had the glamour of romance, of liberation from convention, and though, in accordance with Puritan conceptions and Hawthorne's own view of the psychology of crime, all these women had to pay high penalties for their trespassings, they never lost their integrity.

Features derived from women Hawthorne had met in real life served to diversify the picture of the dark, glamorous, intellectual and free woman of European descent who had early been born in Hawthorne's mind, and who was, basically, a representative of the Romantic heroine. The present writer is of the opinion that the facts stressed above permit the conclusion that this picture was to a considerable extent dependant on the figure of Corinne, the glamorous and idealized self-portrait of Mme Germaine de Staël-Holstein.

---

[1] F. Brunetière, *Etudes critiques sur l'historie de la littérature française*, Paris, 1904, 4me série, p. 376.

HAWTHORNE AND BALZAC

At about the same time as Nathaniel Hawthorne was preparing
for his future by studying, and by writing and rewriting his first
essays in the "lonely chamber" of his uncle's house in a provincial
New England town, another young man, nurturing similar hopes,
was preparing for the same kind of career, in an attic on the Rue de
Lesdiguières, in Paris. At twenty-one years of age, Honoré de
Balzac had, in 1820, completed his legal studies, and then declared
to his astonished family that he intended to prepare for a literary
career instead of an official one. Though his father was well off,
the allowance given to the prospective author was not a large one.
For nine years, Balzac led an obscure existence, certainly not the
life of a recluse, but rather that of a Paris bohemian, experiencing
different kinds of life and society, and experimenting in different
kinds of writing, trying his hand at journalism, drama, and fiction.

If the material conditions of the two authors present but few
points of similarity, their possibilities of esthetic and literary experience were even more divergent. In the early 19th century,
Paris was more than ever the capital of the world of artistic and
literary culture, as full of experimenting poets and painters, of
audacious new creation and *joie de vivre*, as provincial Salem in
New England was starved of all such amenities. Balzac needed
have no inhibitions in launching his first works into the literary
current; he had no feeling of responsibility for being a pioneer
author of his race, but possessed, on the contrary, the reassuring
knowledge of belonging to a nation that had fostered generations
of young writers who, after innumerable more or less successful
attempts, had acquired an acknowledged literary reputation.

Of the two, Balzac, who was by a few years the older, attained recognition first. But not till after his death did he acquire fame, and
fame of a wider and more universal kind than the young New
Englander would ever win. Balzac's struggle to accomplish the

literary task he had set himself was uninhibited and gigantic, very unlike the diffident strivings of his unknown New England contemporary. But despite all dissimilarities, there are between the works of both authors, between the literary physiognomies of Honoré de Balzac and Nathaniel Hawthorne, affinities and perhaps connections that have not passed unremarked either by contemporary readers or by later critics, and that justify a comparative study.

*

Balzac's definite success came with the publication of *Les Chouans*, in 1829. Before this novel — later on the first to be included in his *Comédie humaine* — he had written, alone or in collaboration with other authors, a series of plays and novels of uncertain value. When acknowledged, in the early thirties, Balzac immediately became known outside the boundaries of France, and, as we have already seen, was read also in America, where Hawthorne, according to contemporary evidence, had got to know those of his works written before 1836.[1] It is, however, unlikely that Hawthorne's works were read by Balzac. The latter died in 1850, the year in which Hawthorne wrote his *Scarlet Letter* and thereby achieved renown. The American author's volumes of short stories are hardly likely to have fallen into the hands of the French writer, though Balzac evidenced a lively interest in contemporary American literature and was a great reader of Cooper's works, of which traces are to be found all through Balzac's production.[2]

Hawthorne himself never makes any reference to Balzac, as little as to other contemporary authors. But surmises of the French author's influence have been expressed by readers and critics. The first reference of this kind that the present writer has found is given in a letter to Hawthorne from the English authoress Miss Nancy Mitford, who was a great friend and correspondent of many contemporary American intellectuals. After having thanked Hawthorne for sending her the *Blithedale Romance*, she continues:

"I forget, dear Mr. Hawthorne, whether I told you that, the writer of whose works you remind me, not by imitation, but by resemblance, is the great French novelist, Balzac. Do you know

---

[1] Cp. above, p. 46.

[2] See F. Baldensperger, *Orientations étrangères chez Honoré de Balzac*, Paris, 1927, pp. 68—73.

168

his books? He is untranslated and untranslatable, and it requires
the greatest familiarity with French literature to relish him
thoroughly ... I doubt if he be much known amongst you; at least
I have never seen him alluded to in American literature. He has,
of course, the low morality of a Frenchman, but, being what he is,
Mrs. Browning and I used to discuss his personages like living
people, and regarded his death as a great personal calamity to
both."[1]

Later students of Hawthorne have echoed Miss Mitford's
opinion[2], but none has given precised reasons for doing so. " 'Peter
Rugg, the Missing Man,' is Hawthornish; so is 'Peter Schlemihl,
the Man without a Shadow,' or Balzac's 'Peau de chagrin' or later
work, some of it manifestly inspired by Hawthorne ..." says
Henry A. Beers in his study. Evidently, these similarities emanate
from a common Romantic leaning. The works mentioned by
Beers have in common a certain dimness, a lack of substance; their
main figures exist in a borderland between fairy tale and reality.
That region is situated far from the Paris, or the rural France that
is the background of the *Scènes de la vie mondaine*, or the *Scènes de
la vie de campagne* of the *Comédie humaine*. *La Peau de chagrin*
forms part of the *Etudes philosophiques* that are without doubt the
section of Balzac's work most likely to have influenced a reader like
Nathaniel Hawthorne, even if the admirer of Anthony Trollope[3]
must have relished Balzac's realistic pictures of contemporary
French society and admired the gigantic plan of his work.

Balzac was an observer, a materialist, but also a visionary and a
romanticist. Taine classes *Louis Lambert* and *Séraphita*, two of the
Etudes philosophiques most concerned with mysticism and occultism,
as the climax of Balzac's work, the achievements that crown his
production "like the flower the plant."[4] To Taine, these fantastic

[1] G. P. Lathrop, *A Study of Hawthorne*, Cambridge, Mass., 1891, p. 230.
[2] Cp. Anton Schönbach, *Beiträge zur Charakteristik Nathaniel Hawthornes*,
Englische Studien, 1884.
Julian Hawthorne, *The Salem of Hawthorne*, *The Century*, May, 1884.
G. P. Lathrop, *A Study of Hawthorne*.
Henry A. Beers, *Fifty years of Hawthorne*, Yale University Press, 1919.
Walter Just, *Die romantische Bewegung in der amerikanischen Literatur:
Brown, Poe, Hawthorne*, Weimar, 1910.
[3] Cp. p. 73, n. 2 of the present work.
[4] H. Taine, *Nouveaux essais de critique et d'histoire*, 7me éd., Paris, 1901, p. 94.

tales are the most complete expression of Balzac's genius, the "cherries of the cherry-tree."

To the student undertaking a parallel evaluation of Balzac's and Hawthorne's work, this part of the former's production will prove to be of special interest. It is on the romantic, philosophical line, that the affinity between the two writers is to be found.

As we have seen, Hawthorne was somewhat well versed in French literature. He was less acquainted with the German Romanticists, who were quite familiar to Balzac. Both had taken strong impressions of very similar nature from English Romantic fiction. To both of them, the novels of Walter Scott had been of decisive importance. In Hawthorne, this feature is best discernible in his first novel *Fanshawe*, that he himself destroyed.[1] In Balzac, we find it fully developed in *Les Chouans*[2], the first novel he acknowledged by signing it with his own name. Features drawn from the works of the great Scotsman were to recur in the productions of both authors, though they sought, and found, interpretations of their own.

The second current in English fiction to exercise a strong influence on both Hawthorne and Balzac, was Gothicism. Both were from childhood eager readers of the literature generally stamped with the name of Mrs. Radcliffe[3], and both show clear traces of this predilection in their mature production. While the curve of Gothicism in Hawthorne's work declines during the middle years of his career, again to rise at the end, Balzac's development proceeds steadily withdrawing from the Gothic mode.

Influences like these that have strongly affected both Hawthorne and Balzac may, of course, be regarded as causing some of the similarities to be found in their respective works. Some of them may be mere coincidences. It is, for example, surprising to meet the phrase "blood to drink" in both authors. In Balzac, it occurs in *Les Chouans* where the beautiful secret agent Mlle de

---

[1] Cp. G. Harrison Orians, *Scott and Hawthorne's Fanshawe*, New England Quarterly, 1938.

[2] Cp. F. Baldensperger, *Orientations étrangères chez H. de Balzac*, Paris, 1927, pp. 59—68, and A. Prioult, *Balzac avant la comédie humaine*, Paris, 1936, pp. 85—86.

[3] Concerning Hawthorne, see Chapter IV of the present work. Concerning Balzac, see A. M. Killen, *Le roman terrifiant ou roman noir* Paris, 1924, pp. 80 ff. Also Baldensperger, p. 144, and Prioult pp. 81—85.

Verneuil uses it as a quotation of Danton's words about not being frightened by "une partie de plaisir où il y a du sang à boire."[1] In Hawthorne, it constitutes the expression of the hate born by the wronged Maule family against the Pyncheons of the house of the seven gables, and forms the malediction that underlies the action of the novel. Theoretically, it might be thought possible that Hawthorne should have taken the expression from Danton, via Balzac, as he had read *Les Chouans* long before writing the *House of the Seven Gables*, but a far more credible explanation of the origin of the phrase is given by Edward Dawson, who has found it in one of the American historic works read by Hawthorne.[2]

The influence reaching Hawthorne through his reading of Balzac's novels was certainly of a much more subtle kind than a borrowing such as the one referred to above. In gathering details of realistic or historical value, Hawthorne depended on his own research work in life and literature. His aim was to picture America in an American way, and he was very particular about his means of doing it.

Balzac's aims, and his position in regard to the Romantic school, have been the object of animated discussions. Zola[3] regards him as the father of the Naturalism born about 1870, that may be regarded as essentially a logical continuation of the Romantic novel. Balzac's great originality consists in his planning of the *Comédie humaine*, this unique attempt to "read the universe, as hard and as loud as he could, into the France of his time," as Henry James has once expressed it.[4] And the France of this time was, to continue quoting James, "a great garden, cultivated for centuries past, with a rich and manysided social and cultural life."

Hawthorne's task was of a different nature: the immense country that surrounded him was unexplored and partly still unlimited, yet too undifferentiated and rough to form an entirety, much less fit to mirror anything outside itself.

This juxtaposition recalls the discussion already touched upon[5],

---

[1] H. de Balzac, *Œuvres complètes*, Paris 1870, Vol. 13, p. 63.

[2] Edward Dawson, *Hawthorne's Knowledge and Use of New England History*, (Vanderbilt University), Nashville, *Tenn.*, 1939.

[3] E. Zola, *Œuvres complètes*, Vol. 44, Paris, 1928, pp. 63—64.

[4] Henry James, *Notes on Novelists*, London, 1914, p. 88.

[5] Cp. pp. 73—74 of the present work.

concerning the difficulties of the American writer. The question is an old and often debated one, and opinions have constantly differed. One side may well be represented by Henry James, deploring in his Hawthorne biography the scarcity of fictional material in his mother country in contrast to the riches of the European continent, and echoing in these regrets Hawthorne himself.[1] The other side has representatives in all the Romantic authors who eagerly left their highly differentiated and developed native societies, to seek in far away countries, among forests or deserts, the experiences and environments their hearts were longing for, or who deserted the life of big cities and their society to depict the joys of the humble, the provincial and small town life. Flaubert has summed up their attitude in the sentence "Yvetot vaut Constantinople." Herbert Read has expressed the same idea in commenting on Hawthorne's environment and its influence on his work.[2]

The manner in which both authors set about their work is also widely different. Balzac is sure of himself and of his vocation; he definitely abandons other careers than the literary one, though he is forced by financial difficulties to enter an unsuccessful publishing venture. He seeks sentimental experiences as eagerly as he hunts for concrete details for his novels, and then shuts himself up to work frenetically. He draws a gigantic ground plan and follows it, but gives little care to chiselling out the language. His style is turgid, and sometimes hard to read.

Hawthorne's life contains no extravagances. He loves one woman and marries her, begets a family to provide for, and is for many of the best years of his life only able to devote stray hours to his writing. The far-reaching plans that he had once cherished have to be restrained. To begin with, he keeps to short stories, and later on to his "romances," the vehicle he found most apt to express the results of his psychological observations and experiences.[3] He once termed the romance a "neutral territory." What could be more

---

[1] Henry James, *Hawthorne*, London, 1902, p. 43.

[2] Cp. above, p. 74, n. 2.

[3] Amy Louise Reed, in her study of *Selfportraiture in the Work of Nathaniel Hawthorne* (Studies in Philology, Vol. 23, 1926), shows how Hawthorne had, at the time of writing his Custom House sketch in *The Scarlet Letter*, accepted a certain amount of defeat and "deliberately determined not to deal with life as a whole, not to attempt a 'serious task' as he calls it, of novel writing, but rather to confine his efforts to what he considered the lesser art of the romance."

remote from Balzac's intense endeavours to fathom the whole of humanity, to include as many types and strata of society as possible in the wide canvas he was painting with colours of all shades, from the dark and mysterious hues of the terror novels, appearing for example in l'*Histoire des Treize*, to the mild and luminous tones that he uses in depicting women such as Ursule Mirouet or Mme Graslin.

Hawthorne's lonely childhood and youth had restricted his horizon and subdued his colours. The deeply serious attitude to moral problems that he had in a measure inherited from his Puritan ancestors, even if he had abandoned their opinions, made what he called sin his major theme, and also gave him his strength and originality as a psychological writer.

Balzac's attitude to moral questions had not the severity that Hawthorne possessed. To Hawthorne, the developments of the soul were of primary importance. To Balzac, society was the great subject. Mr. Ernest Seillière, in his study of Balzac's relation to what he calls "la morale romantique," quotes some lines from *Autre étude de femme*: "L'individualisme est la maladie de l'époque. La religion en est le seul remède."[1] To Balzac, morality and religion as codified and administered by the church, were a necessity to the welfare of society and therefore to be defended. He did not possess the ingrained individualism of the American writer. As Mr. Seillière acutely remarks, his idea of the rôle of individualism was psychologically and morally unripe, not comprehending that a sound individualism is the very root of personality, while the "maladie de l'époque" consisted in an irrational and exaggeratedly mystical kind of individualism.[2] Balzac's greatness lies on another plane than Hawthorne's greatness. The former looks at his universe, created within the limits of France, from the outside, from the social point of view. His attitude to the pageant he proffers is eloquently expressed in the title he has given to it: *La Comédie humaine* is written with a social rather than a moral purpose. As one of Hawthorne's critics has remarked, the New England author would probably, had he attempted a task similar to that of Balzac, have called his cycle not a human comedy, but a tragedy.[3] He

---

[1] E. Seillière, *Balzac et la morale romantique*, Paris, 1922, p. 85. The quotation is taken from Balzac, *Œuvres complètes*, Paris, 1870, Vol. II, p. 447.

[2] Cp. S. B. Liljegren, *Essence and Attitude in English Romanticism*, Upsala, 1945, p. 35 ff.

[3] W. C. Brownell, *American Prose Masters*, New York, 1923, p. 80.

was not less objective and rather more sceptical than his French contemporary, but the whole cast of his personality was of a far more sombre and pessimistic kind, and whereas Balzac's Catholicism was rationalistic, Hawthorne's religious inheritance had a stronger connection with moral sentiment.

There are no proofs, as far as the present author has been able to verify, that the early works of Balzac — written under various pseudonyms — ever reached America. They have an interest chiefly as forming the background of his later work, showing his reading and his power of observation, but they possess little of the width and the depth characteristic of his later production. In only one of these novels, *La dernière fée*, are to be found features that have anything in common with the works of Nathaniel Hawthorne. The introduction to this story consists of a description of one of these scientists or magicians that abound in Romantic literature, and of his workshop or laboratory. The setting of the story is very similar to that of Hawthorne's *The Birthmark*. In both stories, a scientist is living in seclusion with his young and beautiful wife, working in his laboratory together with an assistant whose character is indicated by the name he bears in Balzac's story, Caliban. Both scientists have abandoned the grosser interest in chemistry. Balzac tells us that

"cette perfection de science ne regardait pas seulement le corps, elle s'appliquait à l'âme, et il [le chimiste] discernait la cause de nos peines et de nos plaisirs, de nos passions et de nos vertus avec une telle supériorité que d'abord ils avaient atteint, lui et sa femme, la perfection du bonheur . . ."[1]

Hawthorne introduces the scientist Aylmer who has left his laboratory to the care of his assistant, and in marrying the beautiful Georgiana, has "made experience of a spiritual affinity more attractive than any chemical one."[2]

The conception of the scientist, a figure borrowed from the Gothic novels, is very similar in both stories. The later developments, however, differ. Balzac tells a kind of humourous fairy tale in a tone of banter, inserting remarks on the author's part, like the sigh of the author of serials that ends the first chapter:

"La chaumière dans laquelle vivaient . . . Que vois-je? Quinze

---

[1] H. de Balzac, *La dernière fée*, Ed. du centenaire, Paris, n. d:, p. 9.
[2] *Works* II, p. 47.

pages, grand Dieu! les temps sont si durs que jamais on ne pourrait lire un chapitre plus long."

"The last fairy" that appears in the story to Abel, the young son of the chemist and his wife, finally shows herself to be a rich woman of the world. Abel's real name proves to be a noble one, and the couple for some time lead a gay society life together. After endless complications, Abel returns to his humble village, marries his first love, and finds happiness in a simple life.

Hawthorne, on the other hand, makes of his story — as we have seen in a previous chapter[1] — a fantastic tale with a serious moral. Using the same background as Balzac, he creates a kind of parable with a message.

One more example of early parallelisms between the two authors is found in Hawthorne's *The Gentle Boy*, and Balzac's *L'Enfant maudit*.

The Gentle Boy is one of Hawthorne's early masterpieces, illustrating the intransigency between the rivalling sects of early New England. The gentle boy, Ilbrahim, is the son of Quaker parents, who have had to flee from the persecutions of the Puritans. A kind couple takes care of the angelically mild and patient child who becomes the object of hatred and persecutions from his playfellows, as well as from the adult Puritans around him. Finally he dies the death of a saint, forgiving his enemies and transmitting to his hard and intolerant mother something of his own spirit of love and forbearance.

Balzac's story of the accursed child is enacted in the France of civil war and religious strife following St. Bartholomew's Eve. Etienne d'Hérouville is prematurely born, and from the beginning an object of his father's hatred. He is forced to live by himself in a hut on the seashore below the castle, and is never permitted to enter his father's presence. Count d'Hérouville begets another son, who is more to his liking, but he as well as the Countess dies. In order to prevent his family dying out, the Count acknowledges Etienne, but when the latter is forced to abandon the lady of his heart, a young and simple girl, in favour of a haughty damsel chosen by his father, he and his beloved both die.

In these stories, similarities appear not only in the general subject — the gentle and weak, but spiritually highly developed

---

[1] Cp. above, p. 107.

child encountering adversities and hatred, and finally dying from unloving treatment — but also in details of description. Ilbrahim is first introduced sitting alone on a grave late at night. He turns his face to the man who has discovered him:

"It was a pale, bright-eyed countenance, certainly not more than six years old, but sorrow, fear, and want had destroyed much of its infantile expression."[1]

A little further on, we are told how

"The pale, spiritual face, the eyes that seemed to mingle with the moonlight, the sweet, airy voice, and the outlandish name, almost made the Puritan believe that the boy was in truth a being which had sprung up out of the grave on which he sat."[2]

Etienne, the hated son of the French nobleman, though described at another age, that of sixteen, is of very similar appearance:

"Sa peau, transparente et satinée comme celle d'une petite fille, laissait voir le plus léger rameau de ses veines bleues. Sa blancheur était celle de la porcelaine. Ses yeux, d'un bleu clair empreints d'une douceur ineffable, imploraient la protection des hommes et des femmes; les entraînantes suavités de la prière s'échappaient de son regard et séduisaient avant que les mélodies de sa voix n'achevassent le charme."[3]

Ilbrahim, left in peace, develops his beautiful character thus:

"In his general state, Ilbrahim would derive enjoyment from the most trifling events, and from every object around him; he seemed to discover rich treasures of happiness, by a faculty analogous to that of the witch hazel, which points to hidden gold, where all is barren to the eye. His airy gayety, coming to him from a thousand sources, was like a domesticated sunbeam... Of the malice, which generally accompanies a superfluity of sensitiveness, Ilbrahim was altogether destitute: when trodden upon, he would not turn; when wounded, he could but die. His mind was wanting in the stamina for self-support; it was a plant that would twine beautifully round something stronger than itself, but if repulsed, or torn away, it had no choice but to wither on the ground."[4]

Etienne, again,

[1] *Works* I, p. 89.   [2] *Ibid.*
[3] Balzac, *Œuvres complètes*, Vol. 15, p. 165—66.
[4] *Works* I, p. 108—109.

"demeurait pendant de longues journées couché sur le sable, heureux, poète à son insu. L'irruption soudaine d'un insecte doré, les reflects du soleil dans l'Océan, les tremblements du vaste et limpide miroir des eaux, un coquillage, une araignée de mer, tout devenait événement et plaisir pour cette âme ingénue. Voir venir sa mère, entendre de loin le frôlement de sa robe, l'attendre, la baiser, lui parler, l'écouter, lui causaient des sensations si vives que souvent un retard ou la plus légère crainte lui causaient une fièvre dévorante. Il n'y avait qu'une âme en lui, et pour que le corps faible et toujours débile ne fût pas détruit par les vives émotions de cette âme, il fallait à Etienne le silence, des caresses, la paix dans le paysage, et l'amour d'une femme."[1]

The outward appearances of Ilbrahim and Etienne have much in common (the pallor, the musical voice), and their characters also show strong similarities. Both demand little of life, but are at the same time oversensitive to unkindness and hard treatment. Balzac's tale shows far more influence of Romantic mannerisms than that of Hawthorne; Etienne's existence is really of a somewhat improbable kind, and the whole story reminds one of old folk-tales like *Havelock* or *Horn*. Hawthorne keeps to more plausible developments. His evoking of the Puritan past bears the stamp of realism in practical detail as well as in the depicting of human behaviour. The background of *l'Enfant maudit* is colourful, and the sentiments highly romantic. The love between Etienne and his mother and his relationship to the girl he wants to marry as well as his father's jealousy of his mother and hatred towards his first-born son are passionate. In comparison, Hawthorne's story with its severity, its lack of passion, may seem bleak. But the bleakness is suited to the subject, and the story of *The Gentle Boy* leaves a persistent impression. The two stories of these gentle and accursed boys, so like in appearance and temperament show a similarity in perception that may be explained by the similarity in the literary interests of their authors. They also show the wide dissimilarities in their native historical material and in their personal temperament. The respective laboratories of the chemists in *La dernière fée* and *The Birthmark*, as well as the title personages in the two later stories and the similarities found in them, may serve

---

[1] Balzac, *Œuvres complètes*, Vol. 15, p. 167.

as a caution for interpreting as influence what amounts in reality to an independent parallellism. If we exclude the slender probability of Hawthorne's acquaintance with the work of Balzac before 1831, and proceed to look for the traces his reading of the French author's subsequent work may have left in his own production, the first novel to attract attention is *La Peau de chagrin* of 1830—31.

In *La Peau de chagrin*, the reader meets for the first time, in Balzac, the visionary mode of expression which is one of the outstanding components of his later technique, and has been partly attributed to his reading of De Quincey's works.[1] This dreamlike quality, though more of a phantasmagorical kind, is what Miss Mitford and other readers must have felt as a trait related to Hawthorne. All Hawthorne's essays in the cataloguing manner, such as *Earth's Holocaust*[2], *P's Correspondence*[3], and, most of all, *A Virtuoso's Collection*[4], are brought to mind when the reader encounters the description of the strange establishment on the Quai Voltaire visited by Raphaël.

Raphaël first enters the ground floor of the shop, where he finds a conglomeration of objects of the most various kinds — "les ossements de vingt mondes."[5] Among the objects enumerated are things like a Sèvres vase bearing the picture of Napoleon painted by Madame de Jacotot, standing beside a sphinx dedicated to Sesostris, not far from a portrait of Madame Dubarry. The spectator likens the whole to "a philosophic refuse-heap." Inspired by the items of the collection on the second floor, Raphaël first evokes the historical epochs and far-away countries, symbolized by Japanese idols or a golden salt-cellar from the workshop of Benvenuto Cellini. He is induced, by admiring works of great artists, to muse over the different worlds represented in their pictures, from the Flemish scenes depicted by Teniers to the Madonnas of Raphael and Correggio.

The Virtuoso's collection, in comparison to the multiplicity and picturesque confusion of the one where the *peau de chagrin* is found, is better classified and less perplexing. In reading the two de-

---

[1] Randolph Hughes, *Vers la contrée du rêve*, Mercure de France, August 1st, 1939.
[2] *Works* II, p. 430.   [3] *Ibid.*, p. 407.   [4] *Ibid.*, p. 537.
[5] Balzac, *Œuvres complètes*, Vol. 14, p. 12.

scriptions and comparing them, one is, however, struck by the similarity in the manner of presenting the various objects and describing their provenance. The actual objects are not the same — Hawthorne was never guilty of plagiarism. But when we find, among the collection of animals which is the first to be explored by the Virtuoso's guest, Byron's tame bear, Cerberus, Bucephalus and Rosinante, the enumeration recalls that which symbolized the "twenty worlds" of Balzac.

Both authors mention Cuvier in connection with the accumulation of objects that brings to mind the observations made by this great geologist. Balzac devotes a couple of pages to an enthusiastic eulogy of "le plus grand poète de notre siècle," comparing Cuvier's reconstructions in the world of science to Byron's poetical structures. Hawthorne gives the French naturalist a passing thought in saying that some of the animals shown "might have deserved the notice of Cuvier himself,"[1] but reverts to his own fantastic evocations of Peter Bell's donkey and Ulysses' dog Argus, that can have nothing to do with any geological finds. His mere mentioning of Cuvier, however, may be a reminiscence from Balzac's novel.

Some characteristic differences between the two collections should also be signalled. In the Paris establishment, all objects — in spite of their fantastic nature — are things that may be imagined as existing or having existed in the real, tangible world. In the Virtuoso's collection, a large percentage belongs to the fantastic realm where Hawthorne loved to dwell, and from which he so often drew his symbols. Items like the heart of the Bloody Mary, "with the word 'Calais' worn into its diseased substance, preserved in a bottle of spirits" or "the golden thigh of Pythagoras" or "a vial of the tears into which Niobe was dissolved" are typical examples of Hawthorne's predilection for symbolism of a sometimes exaggerated nature. Hawthorne uses the occasion to exhibit, not without a certain coquetry, the wide extent of his reading. His collection contains objects only known to the specialist on ancient myths and antique history, as for example two pictures by the

---

[1] "Cuvier, Georges, *The Animal Kingdom*, London, 1824, New York, 1831" is found among the books listed by Arlin Turner as "drawn or mentioned in Hawthorne's six issues of *The American Magazine of Useful and Entertaining Knowledge*." *Hawthorne as Editor*, Selections by Arlin Turner, Louisiana State University Press, 1941.

legendary painter Zeuxis and three by Apelles, but no works by Flemish or French artists.

Not only the collections, but also their owners show features of a related kind. Hawthorne identifies his virtuoso, whom he regards with "pity and horror," with the wandering Jew. At the same time, he makes him a symbol of the sin, he regards as unpardonable: the intellectual pride that was one of the recurring themes in his stories. Outwardly, the virtuoso is of no extraordinary appearance:

"There was no mark about him of profession, individual habits, or scarcely of country; although his dark complexion and high features made me conjecture that he was a native of some southern clime of Europe."[1]

His wisdom consists in despising all things:

". . . the virtuoso was evidently a man of high cultivation, yet he seemed to lack sympathy with the spiritual, the sublime, and the tender. Apart from the whim that had led him to devote so much time, pains, and expense to the collection of this museum, he impressed me as one of the hardest and coldest men of the world whom I had ever met . . ."[2]

and also

". . . one cut off from natural sympathies and blasted with a doom that had been inflicted on no other human being, and by the results of which he had ceased to be human. Yet, withal, it seemed one of the most terrible consequences of that doom that the victim no longer regarded it as a calamity, but had finally accepted it as the greatest good that could have befallen him."[3]

The owner of the curiosity shop on the Quai Voltaire is far more picturesque in appearance:

". . . figurez-vous un petit vieillard sec et maigre, vêtu d'une robe en velours noir, serrée autour de ses reins par un gros cordon de soie. Sur sa tête, une calotte en velours également noir laissait passer, de chaque côté de la figure, les longues mèches de ses cheveux blancs et s'appliquait sur le crâne de manière à rigidement encadrer le front . . . Une barbe grise et taillé en pointe cachait le menton de cet être bizarre, et lui donnait l'apparence de ces têtes

---

[1] *Works* II, p. 538.

[2] *Ibid.*, p. 547.

[3] *Ibid.*, p. 558.

judaïques qui servent de types aux artistes quand ils veulent représenter Moïse."[1]

Even if the age attributed to this personage — two hundred years — seems to contradict his identity with the Wandering Jew, it may confidently be said that he would never have appeared in the imagination of Balzac in this guise if Balzac had not, from many stories of that illustrious personage, been familiar with the picture of an immensely old, wise and unfeeling Jew.

The lack of feeling which is, also in Balzac, an inherent feature of the old man's wisdom, finds its expression when the shopkeeper defines the philosophy symbolized in the *peau de chagrin*: the annihilation of sentiment and desire in man to the advantage of knowledge:

". . . en deux mots, j'ai placé ma vie, non dans le cœur qui se brise, non dans les sens qui s'émoussent; mais dans le cerveau qui ne s'use pas et qui survit à tout."

In the long speech on the philosophy of the bicentenarian, the very same view of life is expressed as that so often condemned by Hawthorne and personified in figures such as Ethan Brand, Rappaccini, Aylmer or Chillingworth.[2] In *La Peau de chagrin*, he found a parable, illustrating not so much a moral problem as one of the major dilemmas of the artist: should he live an intense life in order to gather experiences to be given shape in art, or should he lead a temperate existence, be a mere onlooker and student without any passions of his own? The question was closely related to Hawthorne's own constant personal preoccupation, and he cannot have remained indifferent to Balzac's treatment of it.

In view of the fact that Hawthorne was acquainted with the work of Balzac written before 1836, when he wrote the *Virtuoso's Collection* in 1841, the possibility that he was subjected to influence from *La Peau de chagrin* cannot, in the opinion of the present writer, be excluded. Another early novel of the French author may have contributed to the formation of the type of cold and selfish intellectual man that so often confronts us in Hawthorne's work, as, perhaps, also of some features in the setting of one of his great

---

[1] Balzac, *Œuvres complètes*, Vol. 14, p. 20.

[2] Cp. Randall Stewart's characterization of Hawthorne's villaneous types in the *American Notebooks*, New York & London, 1932, p. XLIX.

romances. We refer to *La Recherche de l'Absolu*, and its chief personage, Balthazar Claës.

La Recherche de l'Absolu, dated 1834, is the story of an old Flemish merchant family residing in an ancient ancestral house at Douai. Balthazar Claës has married Joséphine de Teminck, a descendant of a noble Spanish family, harbouring a valiant soul in a crippled body. His love for his wife and their children is, in Balthazar Claës, gradually superceded by his passion for chemical research, having for its ultimate goal the making of gold. By his experiments, he ruins the finances of his family. His wife dies, and the home and existence of the family are saved only by the eldest daughter, Marguerite. She marries Emmanuel de Solis, a modest and studious young man who finally attains a high position and also inherits a Spanish title. After having given his life to fruitless research, Balthazar Claës dies, with the exclamation *Eureka* — I have found it — on his lips.

In painting the background of this story Balzac, as usual, describes with the utmost care the immediate surroundings of the characters. His realistic method may in itself have influenced Hawthorne, whose work was, in accuracy — not to say meticulousness — of portraiture comparable to that of Balzac. Added to the careful description of the house of the Claës family at Douai — that has many counterparts in Balzac's work[1] — we also find here the expression of what might be called a philosophy of environment, revealing an attitude kindred to the one that Hawthorne, as we have already seen[2], later on evinced in *The House of the Seven Gables*. The happenings of human life, says Balzac, are intimately connected with the art of their time and surroundings and especially with architecture:

"Les évènements de la vie humaine, soit publique, soit privée, sont si intimement liés à l'architecture, que la plupart des observateurs peuvent reconstruire les nations ou les individus dans toute la vérité de leurs habitudes, d'après les restes de leurs monuments publics ou par l'examen de leurs reliques domestiques."[3]

---

[1] Cp. *e.g.* the introductory pages of *La Maison du chat-qui-pelote*, or the description of *Le Cabinet des antiques*.

[2] Cp. p. 120 of the present work.

[3] Balzac, *Œuvres complètes*, Vol. 1, p. 308.

Architecture is not mentioned in the early tales of Hawthorne, but it is evident that his interest in the art of building, and in its products, was awakened some time in the middle of the eighteen thirties — the period when he got acquainted with Balzac's work — and then waxed stronger and stronger. During his years in England, he gives a large space in his notebooks, and later on in *Our Old Home*, to descriptions of various buildings, and both his Italian note-book and *The Marble Faun* abound in passages concerning architecture.

The first tales of Hawthorne in which this interest is evinced are those told in and about the Province House (1838). Here we find something of the theory of Balzac, but tinged with Hawthorne's special nuance. To the New England author, age in architecture did not stand only for tradition, but also for prejudice. The influence which the Province House, a three-storied brick building bearing the date 1679, exerts on the Romantic loiterer, is only a beneficient, "pensive" one[1], but Sir William Howe, speaking of old Esther Dudley living her solitary life in the old edifice, exclaims:

"She is the very moral of old-fashioned prejudice, and could exist nowhere but in this musty edifice."[2]

This idea is the germ of the theory that sustains the story of *The House of the Seven Gables*, where the old house represents the symbol of the oppressive influence of the past. Hawthorne goes further than Balzac in finding connection between the houses and the people who live in them, between architecture and "les évène-ments de la vie humaine." As a counterpart to the quotation from *La Recherche de l'Absolu* given above, we cite the following from the opening page of *The House of the Seven Gables*:

"The aspect of the venerable mansion has always affected me like a human countenance, bearing the traces not merely of outward storm and sunshine, but expressive, also, of the long lapse of mortal life, and accompanying vicissitudes that have passed within. Were these to be worthily recounted, they would form a narrative of no small interest and instruction, and possessing, moreover, a certain remarkable unity, which might almost seem the result of artistic arrangement."

[1] *Works* I, p. 329.   [2] *Ibid.*, p. 332.

We can come to no definite conclusion as to whether an influence from Balzac has determined the direction of Hawthorne's
interest in architecture. Nor can we be sure that the tragic
figure of Balthazar Claës, in whom all human feeling is killed by
his cold passion for science, is in any way directly connected with
Hawthorne's coldhearted scientists: Aylmer, Rappaccini or Chillingworth. Spiritually, he is related to them and, like them, he
brings unhappiness and death to beings dependent on him. His
laboratory is, as Baldensperger remarks[1], another version of those
abounding in Romantic literature and appearing also in Hawthorne's
work.

The similarities existing between — on the one hand — Balzac's
owner of the curiosity shop in *La Peau de chagrin*, Balthazar Claës,
and, perhaps, also other creations of ruthless and gifted men,
and — on the other hand — Hawthorne's cold-hearted geniuses,
may result from un actual influence, or be due to a common basis
of reading. We can, however, observe in this respect, a definite
difference between Hawthorne's interpretation of the character of
genius and that of Balzac.

Balzac's conception of genius is that of the Romantic school,
strongly influenced by Byronism. His heroes go beyond the
boundaries of common morality, with the assurance of being
supermen and thus entitled to their extravagances. In *L'Elixir de
longue vie* (1830), Balzac has stated his view on this kind of hero, in
which he also reveals his strong dependence on the Gothic authors.
Speaking of Don Juan Belvidero, he says:

"Il fut en effet le type de Don Juan de Molière, du Faust de
Goethe, du Manfred de Byron, et du Melmoth de Maturin. Grandes images tracées par les plus grands génies de l'Europe, et aux-
quelles les accords de Mozart ne manqueront pas plus que la lyre
de Rossini peut-être. Images terribles que le principe du mal,
existant chez l'homme, éternise, et dont quelques copies se retrou-
vent de siècle en siècle . . ."[2]

Don Juan's claims to greatness are based on his complete and
detached knowledge of human nature and human society, and his
criminal arrogance is finally punished. Don Juan represents the

---

[1] F. Baldensperger, *Orientations étrangères chez Honoré de Balzac*, Paris,
1927, p. 115.

[2] Balzac, *Œuvres complètes*, Vol. 2, p. 403.

184

evil kind of genius of Romanticism. But Balzac shows us also other specimens of Romantic geniuses, whose ultimate aims justify their misdoings. The dying Balthazar Claës' cry of *Eureka* atones for his previous treatment of his family and friends. The painter Théodore in *La Maison du chat-qui-pelote* puts his art before the happiness of his bride, without getting any retribution. Hawthorne strongly revolted against this attitude. His background and up-bringing as well as his personal modesty, rose against this self-idolization of the artist. His own temptation to adopt the Romantic ideal of genius when, conscious of his vocation, he struggled through lonely years for recognition, had been a strong one, and the struggle left traces that stamped for ever his personality and his work. If other American authors revolted more consciously against Romanticism[1], none of them did so with a deeper conviction and perseverance than Hawthorne. Throughout his production we find the theory of the "unpardonable sin" which is, on nearer view, nothing but the condemnation of the Romantic ideal of genius. To Balzac, the misdoings of his gifted heroes, the painter Théodore neglecting his wife, or Balthazar Claës ruining his family, were justified by their position as geniuses. To Hawthorne, the coldness of heart engendered by putting the demands of art or science before those of sensibility was the retribution for the one human sin for which no forgiveness is possible. If Mark Twain consciously ridiculed the terror novel, and thus repudiated the feature of the Romantic novel most conspicuous to the great public, Hawthorne, in his thoughtful, well-balanced way, no less definitely repudiated another of its most salient features — the Byronic genius. He dreamed of a "master genius" of his day[2] and admired the great men of the past, but the self-idolization, the *hypertrophie du moi*[3] typical of European Romanticism, found no resonance in the first American writer of romances of the heart. In looking closer at Hawthorne's cold-hearted geniuses, we find that, if not born in Europe, they have generally spent a long time in that part of the world. In creating these figures, Hawthorne may have had in

[1] Cp. S. B. Liljegren, *The Revolt against Romanticism in American Literature as Evidenced in the Works of S. L. Clemens*, Upsala, 1945.

[2] Cp. p. 28 of the present work.

[3] Cp. S. B. Liljegren, *Essence and Attitude in English Romanticism*, Upsala, 1945.

mind reminiscences of the talented artists and scientists of Balzac, figures so very like those he himself was evoking, though considered from a different angle. Hawthorne stood in clear opposition to a point of view such as that of Balzac and Romanticism in general in this respect, but his opposition was hardly consciously directed against their literary principles. Hawthorne's repudiation of the Romantic ideal of the Byronic genius was based on reasons of moral and psychology rather than deliberate literary criticism.

Without pressing the point too much, a similarity between Hawthorne and Balzac in their choice of subjects can be noted in several works. The first part of *Jésus-Christ en Flandre*, that has much of the character of a Biblical parable, telling of a company being ferried from the island Cadzant to Walcheren in stormy weather, and how the simple worker, free of worldly cares and misdoings, walks on the water while others drown — the miser pressed down by his gold, the young girl drawn down by her beloved, and so on — brings to mind Hawthorne's manner of telling similar tales. We may mention *The Great Carbuncle*, where the innocent young couple survives the sight that kills the Seeker. Similarly, La Fosseuse in *Le Médecin de Campagne* (1832—33) has much in common with Priscilla in *The Blithedale Romance*. Both are shy beings, half belonging to a dreamworld of their own and with a career of hard work behind them.[1]

In addition to these superficial similitudes, we note, in one more of Balzac's works, a definite idea that, like the character sketch of the keeper of the curiosity shop in *La Peau de chagrin*, is used by Hawthorne in an entirely congenial spirit. We refer to *Séraphita* (1833—35), one of the *Etudes philosophiques*. In this instance the similarity applies to a theory of art, as in the case of *La recherche de l'Absolu* and *The House of the Seven Gables*, but this time it concerns not architecture but sculpture.

[1] Comparisons may be drawn with works by Balzac of a later date than 1836, such as *Pierrette*, that tells, like *The House of the Seven Gables*, the story of a country girl who comes to live with a couple of elderly, unmarried cousins. But while Phoebe is destined for happiness, the fate of Pierrette is a tragedy. A certain resemblance exists in the subjects of Balzac's *Le Curé de village* (1837—45) and *The Scarlet Letter*. Both novels are stories of secret guilt, for which no good deeds can atone. Madame Graslin is not forced to confession like Hester Prynne. Her crime and penitence are more like those of Dimmesdale, and, like him, she carries a hair-shirt and is forced by her conscience to a final confession.

Séraphita is one of the androgyns frequently met with in Romantic literature. She (or he) lives in Norway, nurtured on the teachings of Swedenborg and surrounded by the Nordic nature resplendent with icy alptops and immense snowy plains. Séraphita, who is at times called Séraphitus, is loved by a man, Wilfrid, and a woman, Minna, and finally adopts the state of an angel leaving them to live on together. The intrigue of the story is of less interest here, where we shall only stress a passage in which Minna questions Séraphitus about the real character of Wilfrid. Séraphitus answers that he knows everything about him, having the gift of "Speciality," and continues:

"La Spécialité constitue une espèce de vue intérieure qui pénètre tout, et tu n'en comprendras la portée que par une comparaison. Dans les grandes villes de l'Europe d'où sortent des oeuvres où la main humaine cherche à représenter les effets de la nature morale aussi bien que ceux de la nature physique, il est des hommes sublimes qui expriment les idées avec du marbre. Le statuaire agit sur le marbre, il le façonne, il y met un monde de pensées. Il existe des marbres que la main de l'homme a doués de la faculté de représenter tout un côté sublime ou tout un côté mauvais de l'humanité; la plupart des hommes y voient une figure humaine et rien de plus, quelques autres un peu plus haut placés sur l'échelle des êtres y aperçoivent une partie des pensées traduites par le sculpteur, ils y admirent la forme; mais les initiés aux secrets de l'art sont tous d'intelligence avec le statuaire: en voyant son marbre, ils y reconnaissent le monde entier de ses pensées. Ceux-là sont les princes de l'art, ils portent en eux-mêmes un miroir où vient se réfléchir la nature avec ses plus légers accidents."

The kind of relationship between a sculptor and his work, chosen by Balzac to explain a superhuman faculty of character-reading, constitutes the theory of art on which the romance of *The Marble Faun* is founded. Donatello is the offspring of a special kind of human being — "tout un côté de l'humanité" — embodied and interpreted in the statue by Praxiteles.

Hawthorne did not, from the beginning, take a great interest in art, nor did he know much about it, till he came to Europe. In London, he visited the British Museum for educational purposes. Having seen its sculpture galleries, he writes:

"In short, I do really believe that there was an excellence in ancient sculpture, which has yet a potency to educate and refine the minds of those who look at it even so carelessly and casually as I do."[1]

When his fantasy is captured, later on, in Rome, by Praxiteles' work, the idea of using the faun as the starting-point of a romance begins to take form in his mind:

"It seems to me that a story with all sorts of fun and pathos in it, might be contrived on the idea of their species having become intermingled with the human race; a family with the faun blood in them having prolonged itself from the classic era till our own days. The tail might have disappeared, by dint of constant inter-marriages with ordinary mortals; but the pretty hairy ears should occasionally reappear in members of the family; and the moral instincts and intellectual characteristics of the faun might be most picturesquely brought out, without detriment to the human interest of the story. Fancy this combination in the person of a young lady."[2]

The final outcome of his musings was not, however, a young lady, nor an androgyn, like Séraphita-Séraphitus. It was a young man, Donatello, bearing traits not only of the Faun of Praxiteles. There may, as has been suggested, be something of Thoreau, the gentle solitary of Walden pond, in him[3]; possibly, also features taken from Milton's Adam[4]. As a Romantic, fantastic creation he is, as far as the present writer is aware, unique in drawing the major part of his ancestry from Antiquity. The device of giving life to a work of art, a picture or a statue, was dear to the authors of the Gothic school. But Hawthorne did not allow Praxiteles' statue to assume life. He tried to penetrate the message given by the sculptor, to recreate the idea that had inspired him. There may have entered into this process of absorbing the ancient sculptor's idea a reminiscence of the theories expounded by Séraphita. The conception of a descendant of the fauns, living among ordinary mortals and experiencing in a vicarious crime the fall of Adam, may have been the outcome not only of the impact of pagan art in Old World

---

[1] *The English Notebooks*, Dec. 4th, 1857.

[2] *The Italian Notebooks*, April 22nd, 1858.

[3] L. Dhaleine, *N. Hawthorne, sa vie et son œuvre*, Paris, 1905, p. 67.

[4] M. D. Conway, *The Life of Nathaniel Hawthorne*, London, 1890, p. 172.

surroundings on a New England mind, but also of a conscience in Hawthorne of possessing the "Speciality" of which Balzac wrote.

*

The attempts made here to trace some parallels between Balzac and Hawthorne, and possible channels of direct influence from the former author to the latter, make no claim to be regarded as assertions. The examination of the two authors' works has been undertaken with a view to verify whether the placing of their names together that recurs in the works of several critics and biographers has been justified or not. As a result, the present writer finds that the affinities in Balzac and Hawthorne as to conception and treatment of similar subjects are in many cases so great as to have caused, by themselves alone, the juxtaposition of their names. On the other hand, Hawthorne's acquaintance with Balzac's work may have influenced his view of Old World art, that he had scanty means of studying in his own country. His conception of architecture may have received impulses from the reading of works such as *La Recherche de l'Absolu* and *Le Cabinet des antiques*, and his view of the relation between sculptor, work, and beholder, may have been influenced by the ideas expressed in *Séraphita*. Furthermore, the figures of the antiquarian in *La Peau de chagrin*, and Balthazar Claës in *La Recherche de l'Absolu* possess sufficiently many traits in common with Hawthorne's men guilty of coldhearted pride in their own intellect, to warrant a surmise that they have contributed to the American writer's constant preoccupation with the type. Finally, Balzac's definite elevation of the Romantic genius may have accentuated Hawthorne's reaction against Romanticism in this respect, and sharpened the examination of conscience in himself and others that led to the ultimate formation of one of his major themes, that of the "unpardonable sin."

CONCLUSION

For a long time, Nathaniel Hawthorne was considered by most biographers and by his countrymen in general, not only as the first great romancer of his nation, but also as the isolated New England genius, free from outside influences. This view was based on various circumstances: his Puritan background, his choice of New England subjects, his aloofness from international society in America. Compared to travelled Boston men like Ticknor, to Emerson who early in life visited England and France and entertained a wide correspondence with foreign friends, or to Long-fellow, who extended his journeys even to Scandinavia, Hawthorne, the recluse, appeared as an exponent of pure indigeneous culture.

Of late, a revaluation has taken place. Hawthorne's European experiences, though occurring late in life, have been shown to have exerted a profound influence on his mind and writing. This influence appears most conspicuously not in Hawthorne's fiction, but in his note-books that have recently been re-edited according to the original manuscript. As their distinguished editor, Professor Randall Stewart, remarks, no other American man of letters has studied the respective characteristics of England and America so painstakingly.[1] Interesting results may be expected from the further study of this source as well as from the future, complete edition of Hawthorne's French and Italian Note-books.

Hawthorne's familiarity with the English classics, and also with Latin and Greek authors has always been acknowledged as belonging to the equipment of a well-read New England youth of the early 19th century. Less has been said of his wide reading of French classics, and of his acquaintance with contemporary European literature, that was read by him in translation, when it was German, and in the original language, when it was French.

---

[1] *The English Notebooks* by Nathaniel Hawthorne, edited by Randall Stewart, New York & London, 1941, p. v.

Nathaniel Hawthorne had in some respects more in common with
his European contemporaries than with his American literary
colleagues. His philosophical views were tinged with scepticism,
from the beginning temperamental, but enhanced by his reading
of Montaigne and Voltaire. It made him stand aloof from the
extreme form of American transcendentalism, and contributed to
give him a unique position in American literature. He had absorbed
the essentials of Romanticism, though more in their English and
French form than in their German guise. Unlike Poe, who merged
into the international trend of mysticism and terror, Hawthorne
proceeded along his own, original line, mingling the habit of severe,
psychological examination of conscience, inherited from his
American forefathers, with lessons from English classics and with
methods and devices taken over from various European Romanticists.
Among the latter, the Gothic romancers, who had already earlier
found followers in America, exerted a decisive influence on his
art. In addition to various English models, of which Walter Scott
was the most conspicuous one, some French novelists of his own
time also contributed to the formation of certain types and personages in Hawthorne's work. Madame de Staël's *Corinne* suggested to him the type of mysterious women evoked in Zenobia
and Miriam; a type that was essentially Romantic but could not
be reconciled with the prevailing view of the American girl, and
therefore had to be stamped as European. Balzac's descriptions of
geniuses, immolating the happiness of others to the exigencies
of their own self-realization may have contributed to the shaping
of Hawthorne's bearers of "the unpardonable sin", who had, also,
generally some kind of connection with the Old World. To Balzac,
Hawthorne may also owe something of the interest in art that
awakened in him late in life on contact with the products of art
in Europe. A comparison between both authors shows a parallelism in their work, originating in great similarities in the cultural
and literary foundations on which their respective productions
were built rather than in personal or temperamental kinship.

The roots of Nathaniel Hawthorne's philosophy and work are
of a less exclusively American character than most critics have
asserted. Strong links of cultural and literary tradition, not only
of a classical but also of a contemporary character, connect him
with the general international development of literary Romanticism.

BIBLIOGRAPHY

I. TEXTS

A. MANUSCRIPTS

a. In the Huntington Library,
Hawthorne, Nathaniel, Letters to Sophia.
——, Diary, June 1858.
——, Letters.

b. In the Pierpont Morgan Library,
Hawthorne, Sophia and *Nathaniel,* Journal 1842—54.
Hawthorne, Nathaniel, Diaries, Jan.—Dec., 1856, Jan.—June, 1858, July 1858—Dec., 1862.

c. In the Yale University Library,
The Yale Collection of Hawthorne Letters.

d. In the New York Public Library, Berg Collection,
Nathaniel Hawthorne, Letters.

B. PRINTED SOURCES

a. Works by Nathaniel Hawthorne
The Complete Works of Nathaniel Hawthorne, with introductory notes, by George Parsons Lathrop, Riverside Edition, 12 vols, Boston, 1883.
Dr. Grimshawe's Secret, Ed., with preface and notes, by Julian Hawthorne, Boston, 1883.
Hawthorne's First Diary, Ed. by T. Pickard, Boston, 1897.
Letters of Hawthorne to William D. Ticknor, 1851—1864, 2 vols, Newark, 1910.
The American Notebooks, Ed., with introduction and notes, by Randall Stewart, New Haven, 1932.
The English Notebooks, Ed., with introduction and notes, by Randall Stewart, New York and London, 1941.
The Heart of Hawthorne's Journals, Ed. by Newton Arvin, Boston and New York, 1929.
Nathaniel Hawthorne, Representative Selections, with introduction, bibliography, and notes, by Austin Warren, New York, 1934.
Hawthorne's Spectator, Ed. by L. Chandler, *New England Quarterly,* 1938.
Hawthorne as Editor, Selections from his Writings in The American Magazine of Useful and Entertaining Knowledge, by Arlin Turner, Louisiana State University Press, 1941.

b. Works by Other Authors
Austin, W., *Peter Rugg, the Missing Man,* with an introduction by Thomas Wentworth Higginson, Boston, 1908.

192

Balzac, H. de, *Œuvres complètes*, Paris, Alexandre Houssiaux, 1870.
——, *La dernière fée*, Paris, Calmann-Lévy, n. d.
Beckford, William, *The History of the Caliph Vathek*, London, Sampson, Low, Marston, Searle, and Rivington, Ltd, 1888.
Brown, Charles Brockden, *Wieland, or The Transformation*, Philadelphia, n. d.
——, *Edgar Huntly*, Philadelphia, n. d.
Carlyle, Thomas, *Works*, London, Chapman and Hall, 1897.
Chamisso, Adalbert von, *Peter Schlemihl*, Leipzig, Verlag des bibliographischen Instituts, n. d.
Emerson, Ralph Waldo, *Complete Works*, Riverside Edition, n. d.
Godwin, William, *Caleb Williams*, London, George Newnes, 1904.
Hoffmann, E. T. A., *Sämtliche Werke*, Leipzig, Max Hesse, 1900.
Hugo, Victor, *Œuvres complètes*, Paris, Hetzel-Quentin, n. d.
Irving, Washington, *Collected Works*, New York and London, Putnam, 1865.
Lewis, Matthew Gregory, *The Monk*, Dublin, J. Charles, 1808.
Mathurin, Rev., *Melmoth, the Wanderer*, London, Bentley and Son, 1892.
Poe, Edgar Allan, *Works*, New York, Virginia Edition, 1902.
Radcliffe, Anne, *The Mysteries of Udolpho*, London, George Routledge & Sons, n. d.
Reeve, Clara, *The Old English Baron*, London, Cassel and Co., 1888.
Scott, Sir Walter, *Waverley Novels*, Edinburgh, 1901.
Staël-Holstein, Germaine de, *Œuvres complètes*, Paris, Firmin Didot Frères, 1844.
Tieck, Ludwig, *Gesammelte Novellen*, Berlin, Georg Reimer, 1852.
Upham, Thomas C., *American Sketches*, New York, 1819.
Walpole, Horace, *The Castle of Otranto*, London, Joseph Thomas, 1840.

II. HISTORY, BIOGRAPHY, AND CRITICISM

A. BOOKS

Adams, James Truslow, *The Epic of America*, New York, 1931.
Alcott, A. Bronson, *Concord Days*, Boston, 1872.
American Writers on American Literature, Ed. John Macy, New York, 1931.
Arvin, Newton, *Hawthorne*, Boston, 1929.
Baldensperger, Fernand, *Orientations étrangères chez Honoré de Balzac*, Paris, 1927.
Beers, Henry, *Four Americans*, New Haven, 1919.
Blankenship, Russel, *American Literature as an Expression of the National Mind*, London, 1931.
Böhmer, Lina, *Brook Farm and Hawthorne's "Blithedale Romance,"* Berlin, 1936.
Bridge, Horatio, *Personal Recollections of Nathaniel Hawthorne*, New York, 1893.
Brooks, Van Wyck, *The Flowering of New England*, New York, 1936.
——, *The World of Washington Irving*, New York, 1944.
Brownell, W. C., *American Prose Masters*, New York, 1923.
Brunetière, Ferdinand, *Etudes critiques sur l'histoire de la littérature française*, Sér. IV & VII, Paris, 1905.
Calverton, V. F., *The Liberation of American Literature*, New York, 1932.
Cambridge History of American Literature, Cambridge, 1933 ff.
Cambridge History of English Literature, Cambridge, 1908 ff.
Canby, H. Seidel, *Classic Americans*, New York, 1931.
Chandler, Elizabeth L., *A Study of the Sources of the Tales and Romances, Written by Nathaniel Hawthorne before 1853, Smith College Studies in Modern Languages*, 1926.
Cheyney, John V., *The Golden Guess*, Boston, 1842.
Chrétien, Louis E., *La pensée morale de Hawthorne, symboliste néopuritain*, Paris, 1932.

Collver, Robert, *Clear Grit*, Boston, 1913.
Conway, Moncure D., *The Life of Nathaniel Hawthorne*, London, 1890.
Cooke, Alice Lovelace, *Some Evidences of Hawthorne's Indebtedness to Swift*, University of Texas Publications, Studies in English, 1938.
Cross, Wilbur L., *The Development of the English Novel*, London, 1905.
Curl, Vega, *Pasteboard Masks, Radcliffe Honors Theses in English*, Cambridge, Mass., 1931.
Curti, Merle, *The Growth of American Thought*, New York & London, 1943.
Curtis, George W., *Homes of American Authors*, New York, 1853.
Dawson, Edward, *Hawthorne's Knowledge and Use of New England History; A Study of Sources*, Nashville, Tenn., 1939.
Dhaleine, L., *Nathaniel Hawthorne, sa vie et son œuvre*, Paris, 1905.
Drinkwater, John, *The Outline of Literature*, Vol. 21, London, 1923—24.
Elovson, Harald, *Amerika i svensk litteratur 1750—1820*, Lund, 1930.
Faust, Bertha, *Hawthorne's Contemporaneous Reputation*, Philadelphia, 1939.
Faxon, Frederick W., *Boston Book Company's List of American and English Periodicals*, Boston, 1899.
Faÿ, Bernard, *Civilisation américaine*, Paris, 1939.
Fields, Annie, *Hawthorne*, Boston, 1899.
Fields, James T., *Yesterdays with Authors*, Boston, 1901.
Frye, Prosser Hall, *Literary Reviews and Criticisms*, New York, 1908.
Gates, Lewis E., *Studies and Appreciations*, New York, 1900.
Goodrich, Samuel G., *Recollections of a Literary Life*, New York, 1856.
Gordon, George Stuart, *Anglo-American Literary Relations*, Oxford, 1942.
Gorman, Herbert, *Hawthorne: A Study in Solitude*, New York, 1927.
Green, Julien, *Un puritain homme de lettres: Nathaniel Hawthorne*, Toulouse, 1928.
Griffiths, Thomas Morgan, *Maine Sources in The House of the Seven Gables*, Waterville, Maine, 1945.
Hall, Lawrence Sargent, *Hawthorne, Critic of Society*, New Haven, 1944.
Hall, Thomas Cuming, *The Religious Background of American Culture*, Boston, 1930.
Hansen, Marcus Lee, *The Immigrant in American History*, Cambridge, Mass., 1942.
Harvard et la France, Recueil d'études, Paris, 1936.
Hawthorne, Julian, *Nathaniel Hawthorne and his Wife*, Boston, 1886.
——, *Hawthorne Reading*, Cleveland, 1902.
——, *Hawthorne and his Circle*, New York, 1903.
——, *Memoirs*, New York, 1938.
Hicks, Granville, *The Great Tradition*, New York, 1935.
Horne, Charles F., *The Technique of the Novel*, New York, 1908.
Ingersoll, C. J., *A Discourse concerning the Influence of America on the Mind*, Philadelphia, 1823.
James, Henry, *Hawthorne*, London, 1902.
Jessup, A., and Canby, H. S., *The Book of the Short Story*, New York, 1912.
Johanson, Klara, *Det speglade livet*, Stockholm, 1928.
Jones, H. Mumford, *America and French Culture*, University of North Carolina Press, 1927.
Just, Walter, *Die romantische Bewegung in der amerikanischen Literatur: Brown, Poe, Hawthorne*, Weimar, 1910.
Killen, Alice M., *Le roman terrifiant ou noir de Walpole à Anne Radcliffe*, Paris, 1924.
Lathrop, George Parsons, *A Study of Hawthorne*, Cambridge, Mass., 1891.
Lawrence, D. H., *Studies in Classic American Literature*, London, 1924.
Lewisohn, Ludwig, *Expression in America*, New York, 1932.
Liljegren, S. B., *The Revolt against Romanticism in American Literature as Evidenced in the Works of S. L. Clemens*, Upsala, 1945.
——, *Essence and Attitude in English Romanticism*, Upsala, 1945.

Loring, George B., *Papyrus Leaves*, Boston, 1880.
Mabie, Hamilton Wright, *Backgrounds of Literature*, New York and London, 1912.
Macy, John, *The Spirit of American Literature*, New York, 1913.
Mather, Edward, *Nathaniel Hawthorne, A Modest Man*, New York, 1940.
Matthiessen, F. O., *American Renaissance*, New York, 1941.
Mencken, H. L., *A Book of Prefaces*, New York and London, 1922.
Michaud, Régis, *The American Novel*, Boston, 1928.
More, Paul Elmer, *Shelburne Essays*, 1st and 2nd Series, New York, 1907.
Morris, Lloyd, *The Rebellious Puritan: Portrait of Mr. Hawthorne*, New York, 1927.
Mumford, Lewis, *The Golden Day*, Chicago, 1926.
Page, H. A. (Pseud. for Japp, Alexander), *Memoir of Nathaniel Hawthorne*, London, 1872.
Parrington, Vernon L., *Main Currents in American Thought*, New York, 1930.
Pattee, Fred Lewis, *The Development of the American Short Story*, New York, 1923.
Perry, Bliss, *Park Street Papers*, New York, 1908.
Peyre, Henri, *Writers and their Critics*, New York, 1945.
Phelps, William L., *Some Makers of American Literature*, Francestown, 1923.
Poe, Edgar Allan, *Works*, New York, Virginia Edition, 1902.
Prioult, A., *Balzac avant la comédie humaine (1818—1829)*, Paris, 1936.
Read, Herbert, *The Sense of Glory*, Cambridge, 1929.
Reinterpretation of American Literature, The, Ed. N. Foerster, New York, 1928.
Réti, Elizabeth, *Hawthornes Verhältnis zur Neu-Englandtradition*, Göttingen, 1935.
Richter, Helene, *Geschichte der englischen Romantik*, Halle, 1911.
Romanticism in America, Ed. George Boas, Baltimore, 1940.
Rourke, Constance, *American Humor*, New York, 1931.
——, *The Roots of American Culture*, New York, 1942.
Schneider, Herbert W., *The Puritan Mind*, New York, 1930.
Schubert, Leland, *Hawthorne, the Artist*, University of North Carolina Press, 1944.
Seillière, Ernest, *Balzac et la morale romantique*, Paris, 1922.
Sherman, Stuart P., *Americans*, New York, 1922.
Shock of Recognition, The, Ed. Edmund Wilson, New York, 1943.
Smith, Bernard, *Forces in American Criticism*, New York, 1939.
Stearns, Frank P., *The Life and Genius of Nathaniel Hawthorne*, Philadelphia, 1906.
——, *Sketches from Concord and Appledore*, New York, 1895.
Stephen, Leslie, *Hours in a Library*, London, 1874.
Taine, H., *Nouveaux essais de critique et d'histoire*, 7me éd., Paris, 1901.
Ticknor, Caroline, *Hawthorne and his Publisher*, Boston & New York, 1913.
Trollope, Mrs., *Domestic Manners of the Americans*, London, 1831.
Van Doren, Carl, *American Literature*, New York, 1934.
——, *The American Novel*, New York, 1945.
Veen, Wilhelm, *Die Erzählungstechnik in den Kurzerzählungen Nathaniel Hawthornes*, Münster, 1938.
Whipple, Edwin P., *Character and Characteristic Men*, Boston, 1884.
Williams, Stanley T., *The American Spirit in Letters*, New Haven, 1926.
——, *The Life of Washington Irving*, London and New York, 1935.
Winters, Yvor, *Maule's Curse*, Norfolk, Conn., 1938.
Woodberry, Edward, *Nathaniel Hawthorne*, Boston, 1902.
——, *Hawthorne, How to Know him*, Indianapolis, 1918.
Woodbridge, Benjamin M., *The Supernatural in Hawthorne and Poe*, Colorado College Publications, Language Series, Vol. II, No. 26.
Young, Charles Lowell, *Emerson's Montaigne*, New York, 1941.
Zola, Emile, *Les romanciers naturalistes, Œuvres complètes*, Vol. 44, Paris, 1928.

B. NEWSPAPERS AND PERIODICALS.[1]

Astrov, Vladimir, *Hawthorne and Dostoevski as Explorers of the Human Con-science*, New England Quarterly, 1942.

Belden, Henry Marvin, *Poe's Criticism of Hawthorne*, Anglia, Oct., 1900.

Bradfield, Thomas, *The Romances of Nathaniel Hawthorne*, Westminster Review, CXLII, 1894.

Bryant, W. C., *Brown's Essay on American Poetry*, North American Review, 1818.

——, *Review of "Redwood,"* North American Review, April, 1825.

Cargill, Oscar, *Nemesis in Nathaniel Hawthorne*, Publications of the Modern Language Association of America, Sept., 1937.

Cherry, Fannye N., *The Sources of Hawthorne's Young Goodman Brown*, American Literature, Jan., 1934.

Chorley, H. F., *Review of Twice-Told Tales*, Athenaeum, Aug., 1840.

Coad, Oral Sumner, *The Gothic Element in American Literature Before 1835*, Journal of English and American Philology, Jan., 1925.

Coleridge, M. E., *The Questionable Shapes of Nathaniel Hawthorne*, Living Age, 1904, Reprint from The Monthly Review.

Curtis, George William, *The Works of Nathaniel Hawthorne*, North American Review, Oct., 1864.

Dicey, Edward, *Nathaniel Hawthorne*, Macmillan's Magazine, July, 1864.

Doubleday, Neal Frank, *Hawthorne's Hester and Feminism*, Publications of the Modern Language Association of America, Sept., 1939.

——, *Hawthorne and Literary Nationalism*, American Literature, Jan., 1941.

Duyckinck, E. A., *Nathaniel Hawthorne*, Arcturus, May, 1841.

——, *Nathaniel Hawthorne*, Democratic Review, April, 1845.

——, *Review of "The Scarlet Letter,"* Literary World, April, 1851.

Eliot, T. S., *Henry James: The Hawthorne Aspect*, The Little Review, Aug., 1918. Reprinted in the Shock of Recognition, 1943.

Essex Institute Historical Collections, Jan., 1932. *Books Read by Nathaniel Haw-thorne.*

Forgues, E. D., *Nathaniel Hawthorne*, Revue des deux mondes, April 15th, 1852.

Hannigan, D. F., *Nathaniel Hawthorne's Place in Literature*, Living Age, 1901. Reprint from Literature.

Hawthorne, Julian, *A Look into Hawthorne's Workshop*, Century Magazine, Jan., 1883.

——, *The Salem of Hawthorne*, Century Magazine, May, 1884.

——, *Scenes of Hawthorne's Romances*, Century Magazine, May, 1884.

——, *Problems of the Scarlet Letter*, Atlantic Monthly, Vol. 57, 1886.

——, *Nathaniel Hawthorne's Blue Cloak*, Bookman, Sept., 1932.

Hawthorne, Manning, *Hawthorne Prepares for College*, New England Quarterly, 1938.

——, *Hawthorne's Early Years*, Essex Institute Historical Collections, Vol. LXXIV, 1938.

Hillard, Katherine, *Hawthorne as an Interpreter of New England*, New England Magazine, XII.

Howells, W. Dean, *The Personality of Hawthorne*, North American Review, Vol. 177, 1903.

Hughes, Randolph, *Vers la contrée du rêve*, Mercure de France, Aug., 1939.

Kern, Alfred A., *The Sources of Hawthorne's Feathertop*, Publications of the Modern Language Association of America, Dec., 1931.

Kouwenhoven, John A., *Hawthorne's Notebooks and Doctor Grimshawe's Secret*, American Literature, Jan., 1934.

Lathrop, Rose Hawthorne, *The Hawthornes in Lenox*, Century Magazine, Vol. XLIX, 1894.

---

[1] Periodicals are generally referred to by month and year of issue. When this has been impossible, volume numbers are given.

196

Longfellow, Henry W., *Hawthorne's Twice-Told Tales*, North American Review, July, 1837.
Lowell, James Russell, *Review of "The Marble Faun,"* Atlantic Monthly, April, 1860.
McCloskey, John C., *The Campaign of Periodicals after the War of 1812 for National American Literature*, Publications of the Modern Language Association of America, March, 1935.
Melville, Herman, *Hawthorne and his Mosses*. Two articles in The Literary World, Aug., 1850. Reprinted in *The Shock of Recognition*, 1943.
Montégut, Emile, *Un roman socialiste en Amérique*, Revue des deux mondes, Dec. 1st, 1852.
——, *Le roman populaire et le rôle du romanesque en Amérique*, Revue des deux mondes, July 1st, 1856.
——, *Un romancier pessimiste en Amérique*, Revue des deux mondes, Aug. 1st, 1860.
Orians, G. Harrison, *New English Witchcraft in Fiction*, American Literature, March, 1930.
——, *The Angel of Hadley in Fiction*, American Literature, Nov., 1932.
——, *Scott and Hawthorne's Fanshawe*, New England Quarterly, 1938.
——, *Hawthorne and the Maypole of Merry Mount*, Modern Language Notes, March, 1938.
Peabody, Elizabeth, *The Genius of Hawthorne*, Atlantic Monthly, Sept., 1868.
Quinn, A. C., *Some Phases of the Supernatural in American Literature*, Publications of the Modern Language Association of America, March, 1910.
Reed, Amy Louise, *Self-Portraiture in the Work of Nathaniel Hawthorne*, Studies in Philology, Jan., 1926.
Rémusat, Charles de, *Horace Walpole*, Revue des deux mondes, April 15th, 1852.
Schönbach, Anton E., *Beiträge zur Charakteristik Nathaniel Hawthornes*, Englische Studien, 1884.
Schuyler, Sidney, *The Italy of Hawthorne*, Nation, Vol. XL.
Smith, Sidney, *Review of The Statistical Annals of the U.S.A.*, The Edinburgh Review, Jan., 1820.
Stewart, Randall, *Hawthorne's Politics*, New England Quarterly, 1932.
——, *Hawthorne's Contributions to the Salem Advertiser*, American Literature, Jan., 1934.
——, *Hawthorne in England*, New England Quarterly, 1935.
——, *Letters to Sophia*, Huntington Library Quarterly, Vol. 7, 1944.
——, *Editing Hawthorne's Notebooks*, More Books, Sept., 1945.
Thomas, Horace E., *Hawthorne, Poe, and a Literary Ghost*, New England Quarterly, 1934.
Trollope, Anthony, *The Genius of Hawthorne*, North American Review, Sept., 1879.
Turner, E. Arlin, *Hawthorne's Literary Borrowings*, Publications of the Modern Language Association of America, June, 1936.
——, *Hawthorne's Method of Using his Source Materials*, Studies for William A. Reed, Louisiana State University Press, 1941.
——, *Hawthorne and Reform*, New England Quarterly, 1942.
Warren, Austin, *Hawthorne's Reading*, New England Quarterly, 1935.
Wright, Louis B., *The Purposeful Reading of our Colonial Ancestors*, Journal of English Literary History, 1937.
Wright, Natalia, *Hawthorne and the Praslin Murder*, New England Quarterly, 1932.